PENGUIN BOOKS
TIGER, TIGER

Margaux Fragoso grew up in Union City, New Jersey. At seven years old, she loved the red gumballs that came from gumball machines but left behind the blues and greens; later, she loved Madonna and still loves Nirvana. She still loves dogs and Kurt Cobain. Margaux is happily married with one child and is currently writing full time. Tiger, Tiger is being published in twenty-two countries.

TIGER, TIGER

A Memoir

MARGAUX FRAGOSO

PENGUIN BOOKS

PENGUIN BOOKS

Published by the Penguin Group
Penguin Books Ltd, 80 Strand, London WC2R ORL, England
Penguin Group (USA) Inc., 375 Hudson Street, New York, New York 10014, USA
Penguin Group (Canada), 90 Eglinton Avenue East, Suite 700, Toronto, Ontario, Canada M4P 2Y3
(a division of Pearson Penguin Canada Inc.)
Penguin Ireland, 25 St Stephen's Green, Dublin 2, Ireland (a division of Penguin Books Ltd)
Penguin Group (Australia), 250 Camberwell Road, Camberwell, Victoria 3124, Australia
(a division of Pearson Australia Group Pty Ltd)
Penguin Books India Pvt Ltd, 11 Community Centre, Panchsheel Park, New Delhi – 110 017, India
Penguin Group (NZ), 67 Apollo Drive, Rosedale, Auckland 0632, New Zealand
(a division of Pearson New Zealand Ltd)
Penguin Books (South Africa) (Pty) Ltd, 24 Sturdee Avenue, Rosebank,
Johannesburg 2196, South Africa

Penguin Books Ltd, Registered Offices: 80 Strand, London WC2R ORL, England

www.penguin.com

First published in the United States of America by Farrar, Straus and Giroux 2011
First published in Great Britain in Penguin Books 2011

2

Copyright © Margaux Fragoso, 2011
All rights reserved

Printed in Great Britain by Clays Ltd, St Ives plc

978-0-241-95015-9

www.greenpenguin.co.uk

Penguin Books is committed to a sustainable
future for our business, our readers and our
planet. This book is made from paper certified
by the Forest Stewardship Council.

TO EDVIGE GIUNTA
FOR NURTURING THE SEED

TO JOHN VERNON
FOR PATIENTLY HARVESTING IT

Tiger, tiger, burning bright
In the forests of the night,
What immortal hand or eye
Dare frame thy fearful symmetry?
—William Blake, "The Tiger"

Tell me, Lord, how could you leave a lass so long
so lone that she could find her way to me?
—Toni Morrison, *The Bluest Eye*

Contents

TIGER, TIGER

PROLOGUE

I started writing this book the summer after the death of Peter
Curran, whom I met when I was seven and had a relationship with
for fifteen years, right up until he committed suicide at the age of
sixty-six.

Hoping to make sense of what happened, I began drafting my life
story. And even during times I haven't worked on it, when it sat on a
shelf in my closet, I felt its presence in the despair that comes precisely
at two in the afternoon, which was the time Peter would pick me up
and take me for rides; in the despair again at five p.m., when I would
read to him, head on his chest; at seven p.m., when he would hold me;
in the despair again at nine p.m., when we would go for our night ride,
starting at Boulevard East in Weehawken, to River Road, down to the
Royal Cliffs Diner, where I would buy a cup of coffee with precisely
seven sugars and a lot of cream, and a bread pudding with whipped
cream and raisins, or rice pudding if he wanted a change. When I came
back, he'd turn the car (Granada or Cimarron or Escort or black Mazda)
back to River Road, back to Boulevard East, and we'd head past the
expensive Queen Anne, Victorian, and Gothic Revival houses, gazing

beyond the Hudson River to the skyscrapers' lights ignited like a thousand mirrors, where we would sometimes park and watch thunderstorms.

In one of his suicide notes to me, Peter suggested that I write a memoir about our lives together, which was ironic. Our world had been permitted only by the secrecy surrounding it; had you taken away our lies and codes and looks and symbols and haunts, you would have taken everything; and had you done that when I was twenty or fifteen or twelve, I might have killed myself and then you wouldn't get to look into this tiny island that existed only through its lies and codes and looks and symbols and haunts. All these secret things together built a supreme master key, and if you ask a locksmith whether there is a master key in existence that will open any lock in the world, he will tell you no, but you can make a key that will open all the locks in one particular building. You can configure the locks beforehand to match the grooves of the key in question, but it is impossible to design a key that will open any preexisting lock. Peter knew this because he once created a master key for a whole hospital; he was a self-taught locksmith, learning the trade in libraries at night and on the job after bluffing his way in.

Picture a girl of seven or so, who loves red gumballs that come from gumball machines but leaves behind the blues and greens; a child whose sneakers are the kind with Velcro, not laces; a child whose legs grip metal ponies activated by a quarter at Pathmark Super Center; a child who is afraid of the jokers in a card deck and insists that they be taken out before a game; a child who fears her father and dislikes puzzles (boring!); a child who likes dogs and rabbits and iguanas and Italian ices; a child who likes riding on the back of a motorcycle because what other seven-year-old gets to ride on a motorcycle; a child who hates to go home (ever) because Peter's house is like a zoo, and most of all because Peter is fun, Peter is just like her, only bigger and can do things she can't.

Perhaps he knew that human cells regenerate every seven years, that after each of these cycles, a different person rises up from the old nest of atoms. Let's say over the next seven years, this man, Peter, reprogrammed this child's fizzing cells. That he cleverly memorized her pathways to joy and followed her easy trails of desire, her cravings for Creamsicles, going shirtless like a boy, loving the lap of a dog's sweet pink tongue on her face and the sight of a rabbit crunching something crisp and green. Later, he assiduously learned Madonna's lyrics and, still later, the names of twenty Nirvana songs.

Four months after Peter died, I interviewed a corrections officer while working as a feature writer for my college newspaper. At her apartment, a studio in the Journal Square area of downtown Jersey City, we drank chamomile tea and chatted. I mentioned that I was writing a book. She wanted to know what kind, and I said it was about a pedophile and that it was only a first draft—very rough so far. I asked her if she knew any pedophiles in her line of work.

"Pedophiles. Sure. They're the nicest inmates."

"Nice?"

"Sure. Nice, polite, don't cause any trouble. Always call you miss, always say no ma'am, yes ma'am."

Something in her calmness compelled me to talk. "I was reading that pedophiles rationalize what they do by thinking of it as consensual even if they use coercion." That particular fact, something I'd seen in my abnormal-psychology textbook, shocked me by how perfectly it fit Peter's thinking. My next insight, though, wasn't gleaned from a book, but I pretended it was: "I also read that spending time with a pedophile can be like a drug high. There was this girl who said it's as if the pedophile lives in a fantastic kind of reality, and that fantasticness infects everything. Kind of like they're children themselves, only full of the knowledge that children don't have. Their imaginations are stronger than kids' and they can build realities that small kids would never be able to dream up. They can make the child's world . . . ecstatic somehow. And when it's over, for people who've been through this, it's like coming off of heroin and, for years, they can't stop chasing the ghost of how it felt. One girl said that it's like the earth is scorched and the grass won't grow back. And the ground looks black and barren but inside it's still burning."

"How sad," said Olivia, and she looked like she meant it.

After an awkward pause, the conversation shifted to other types of inmates and the general experience of working in a prison. During our talk, I began to feel nauseated, as though my surroundings, the warm kitchen that had felt so inviting at first, had become menacing. My perceptions were always devastatingly acute, a side effect of years of very little social contact with the world outside of the one I'd shared with Peter.

In Olivia's kitchen that day, I felt as though something in me was at a high pitch, as if the world were turned up, and roaring at me.

Union City, New Jersey, where I grew up, is said to be the most densely populated city in the United States. You can't get a real feel for it just from descriptions of the stale-stiff buttered breakfast rolls and paper espresso containers the size of doll teacups, or the long doughy-sweet churros, just as you can't get a feel for Manhattan by simply mentioning the shish kebab stand by the Port Authority Bus Terminal or the Strand Bookstore with its eighteen miles of books or the skateboarders at Washington Square Park.

You might try to envision the pigeons and bars and night (spelled "nite") clubs, the young "hoods" in baggy pants displaying their boxer shorts, the cars parked bumper-to-bumper and the bizarre narrowness of some of the streets, where it's not unusual to get your side mirror cracked by a passing truck. There are the hissing sounds men of all ages make at any girl over twelve, the fruit stands selling cheap papaya, mango, and avocado (my father, an avocado lover, insisted they could make us live forever), the blackened pieces of gum packed tightly into cracked cement sidewalks. It's not unusual to hear the kids chant, "Step on a crack, break your mother's back!" and, I, superstitious like my father, would dutifully avoid them, which was difficult since they zigzag the concrete like the rivulets on a crumpled map when you open it. Just as carefully, I would avoid stepping on my shadow for fear I'd be trampling on my own soul.

If you visit, don't forget to hold your nose as defense against the foul smell while passing the Polleria Jorge live poultry market on Forty-second Street between New York Avenue and Bergenline. Crossing the street to where Panda Shoes has been as long as I can remember brings you to El Pollo Supremo. There, the kind smells of roasting chicken, simmering yucca, rice with black beans, and frying *tostones* greet you like the elixirs of the Atlantic Ocean. We used to go there to eat, Peter and I, and one wet Halloween during the two years my parents kept us apart, Peter sat in a lone booth and stared out the rain-splashed window for eight hours, hoping to catch a glimpse of me trick-or-treating with my mother.

I still have twelve spiral notebooks of dated daily letters, all beginning with "Dear Princess." Peter made Xs for the kisses and Os for the hugs. He wrote ITOYOALYA on each, an abbreviation for "I think of you often and love you always." I have seven videotapes, each dated, with titles such as *Margaux on Roller Skates*, *Margaux with Paws*, *Margaux Sitting on the Back of the Motorcycle, Waving*.

Peter would watch these every day toward the end of his life: Margaux scuffling in the dirt with Paws, Margaux playing Criminal on the couch, Margaux waving from atop a tree, Margaux blowing a kiss. Nobody watches Margaux now. Even Margaux herself is bored at the sight of Margaux in headbands, Margaux in cutoff jean shorts, Margaux with drenched hair, Margaux by the ailanthus tree where the white hammock used to hang.

I was Peter's religion. No one else would find the twenty photo albums of me alone, or with Paws, or with Karen, or with my mother, engrossing. The wooden box made in eighth-grade shop class contains loose pictures, and they are equally uninteresting. The two locks of hair, braided together, brown and gray, laminated so they would always last. An album of autumn leaves, the names of the trees that they came from listed underneath: sugar maple, blackjack oak, sweetgum. My glittery fairy wand, my tiny gray felt mice Peter threw out in a fight but later dug through the trash to retrieve, the cast-iron skeleton key we found by the boat docks; my silver bangles and huge faux-gold cross that I got from the West Village, the tight black leggings (my Madonna pants, he called them), my black choker with the silver heart, my red lace-fringed bodysuit and the vinyl biker-chick pants he got me; a book of Wicca spells, Nirvana, Hole, and Veruca Salt cassettes for our car rides, bootleg Nirvana videos, also from the West Village; cassettes with our four novels recorded on them (different voices for each character); a wooden amulet Peter gave me of a fairy looking into a crystal ball. All of this was stored in a black trunk with a broken latch that he used to keep by the foot of his bed.

Peter, you couldn't walk more than a few blocks toward the end of your life and you could no longer ride a motorcycle. You walked a little ways to the edge of a cliff at Palisades Park and there you jumped and fell 250 feet, or so the Parkway Police report stated. You left an envelope in my mailbox containing ten suicide notes and several statements on lined notebook paper signing your car over to me. You drew a map for me to find your black Mazda so I wouldn't be charged for towing and storage. You left me a copy key inside the envelope; the original key you left inside the Mazda's ignition. I was twenty-two and you were sixty-six.

PART ONE

1

"CAN I PLAY WITH YOU?"

Nineteen eighty-five. It was spring, and cherry blossoms fell when the wind blew hard. The gay feathers and asters were in bloom, and I smelled the sweet, dizzy scent of honeysuckle fumes, which rode on the shoulders of the wind, along with that dazzle of newly shorn pink and white cherry blossoms, and the white wisps of dandelion seed heads. It was the season of yellow jackets, those sluggish wasps that were always hanging around trashcans and soda bottles. A yellow jacket stung me on the tip of my nose when I was three, and my nose swelled to twice its size; ever since, my mother had fiercely hated them.

"Get out of here!" she yelled, waving her hand at the yellow jackets that had come, unannounced, to our picnic on the lawn at Liberty State Park with my parents' friends Maria and Pedro, and their son, Jeff.

Poppa collected a bit of Pepsi on the tip of his plastic straw and set the straw atop our green-and-red beach blanket. The wasps all rushed to the straw and Poppa grinned.

"You see, *I* solve problems with common sense. They like sugar, and as long as that soda is there, they will all stay by that straw. Right, Keesy?"

Poppa began to call me Kissy (with his Spanish pronunciation he said "Keesy") as a toddler, after he taught me to kiss his cheek good-night and, for a while, I went around kissing everything: all my dolls and stuffed animals, even my own reflection in the mirror. Only when Poppa was pleased with me did he call me Keesy and, occasionally, Baby Bow. Whenever he was angry he didn't call me anything; he spoke of me in the third person. Poppa rarely used my first name, Margaux (pronounced Margo), though he had named me himself, after a 1976 vintage French wine he once drank: Château Margaux. He *never* called my mother Cassie, and he never kissed or hugged her. I didn't think anyone else was different until I saw other parents kiss, like Jeff's, and to be honest, I thought they were the odd ones.

Maria was my mother's best friend and my occasional babysitter. Jeff was seven, a year older than I. At Jeff's house, if he agreed to play Stories, I'd agree to play G.I. Joes and Transformers. War got tiresome for me, and Jeff hated to play Ladybug and Lost Dog, because those stories didn't include toys; these deals made our friendship possible.

Mommy and Maria were talking about the usual things mothers talk about: the benefits of vitamin C, the child snatched from Orchard Beach, the boy recently killed on a roller coaster. "Such a shame," Mommy would say, and "God works in mysterious ways." Mommy kept a small spiral notebook, in which she recorded, among other things, every single disaster she heard about on the radio or TV. That way, she'd always have something important to talk about whenever she called or visited friends. She referred to the notebook as her Fact Book. Poppa hated the Fact Book. Whenever my mother got sick, she started talking about starving children and other horrible things in the world. At home, she'd constantly play her album *Sunshine*, a chronicle of a young woman with terminal bone cancer who made tape recordings of her final goodbyes to her husband and daughter. Mommy found it romantic.

I heard Maria say that I needed more chicken and yucca in my diet, and my mother scribbled this in the Fact Book. They couldn't decide what was more fattening: chicken or beef. Poppa, elbowing Pedro, said, "What do these women know? I know more than them. Don't give girls too much meat or the hormones from the cow get into them. Black beans and rice, fruit, spaghetti; that is the way to go. You do not want a too skinny child, because people assume you are starving your child. But you do not want a little girl looking older. So do not give girls too much steak or pork. Seafood—okay. Boys, on the other hand, need to get strong. Sons—you feed a lot of pork. Maybe you are feeding yours a little too much pork." Poppa smiled; he had a way of insulting people and still staying in their good graces. "Myself, I eat salad. I eat a lot of pistachio nuts and, occasionally, a papaya. Vitamin A. I am not saying your son is fat. I am saying he could afford to lose a few pounds; I hope you do not take me wrong. I tell my friends the truth. But he is a strong boy, a healthy boy, a good-looking son!"

Jeff leaned over and whispered in my ear, "Skinny-skinny chicken legs. Bock! Bock! Bock! Bock!"

"Shut up!"

"Bock! Bock!" He flailed his arms. "You run just like a chicken, too! Bock! Bock! Bock! Bock!"

Chicken legs didn't bother me much, but when he said I ran like a chicken I slapped his face. "Shut up, fatso! You can just die and go to hell!"

Everyone looked at me, and when Maria saw my eyes, she turned away.

Poppa broke out in a grin and said, "All boys, beware of my daughter!"

"Louie!" Mommy yelled. "Don't teach her to hit!"

A yellow jacket buzzed right by Mommy's face and Jeff, playing hero, tried to shoo it away with a stick. He smacked the wasp, and with a loud happy whoop he charged at the other yellow jackets, whacking at them. The wasps turned on him and he dropped the stick. All the adults started yelling, and the wasps, now maddened, began to go after everyone. Yellow jackets landed on my head, arms, hands, and chest. Poppa looked me in the eyes and said, "Stand still, Keesy, stand still, or they will sting." I felt their tiny black legs, their underbelly down. I obeyed. Poppa and I were the only ones not stung that day.

For the first seven years of my life, my parents and I lived in an orange brick building located on Thirty-second Street. Our tiny one-bedroom apartment was infested with roaches, which, despite arming himself with cans of Raid and Combat roach hotels, Poppa could not get rid of. "They come in from other people's apartments. They come through the space under the door. The people in this building are savages. All dirty savages at this end of town. In upper Union City, it is better. Here, the drug addicts, the lowlifes. I cannot wait to get away from here."

Poppa hated graffiti, fire escapes, the abandoned lots filled with trash, the whistling and hissing teenage boys, boom boxes, the way that people constantly littered. But he liked walking a few blocks to Bergenline Avenue to get his espresso and buttered roll (bits of it he'd hand-feed me, even allowing me to sip his espresso). He liked that most everyone spoke Spanish, because he found it extremely humiliating to mispronounce a single English word when ordering food. Back when they were dating, my mother once playfully teased him about the way he said "shoes" (choos) and he wouldn't speak to her for the rest of the day.

Poppa never encouraged my mother and me to learn Spanish, which she thought was intentional. He didn't want us to listen to his phone conversations. I begrudged him this. Not knowing Spanish meant you wouldn't be able to read most of the storefronts or order at local restaurants and bodegas. In Union City, people always assumed I was from Cuba or Spain because of my light complexion, not half Puerto Rican. My mother was a mix of Norwegian, Swedish, and Japanese. I had black eyes that I assumed were from my half-Japanese grandfather, a heart-shaped face, plumpish lips, and straight dark brown hair.

When I was very little, I would punch random women riding on the bus or walking down the street, which my mother said was because I had watched her being hit by my father. She said I witnessed him break a large picture frame over her back at three, but I was too young to remember. What I do recall is that my father used to turn the lights on and off to poke fun at my mother's mental illness. My mother, father, and I slept on a giant king bed because I had constant nightmares and was terrified of sleeping alone. To help him sleep, my father wore a piece of cloth cut from one of his old undershirts over his eyes, and I thought he looked like a bandit with his auburn beard and longish auburn hair. In the mornings, if feeling cheerful, he would tell me stories about a mischievous monkey, an evil frog, and a stoic white elephant set in Carolina, Puerto Rico, where he'd grown up. Or sometimes he'd tell me about his boyhood. He used to climb the tall coconut trees by wrapping his entire body around the tree's rough hide and hoisting himself up by the arms, inch by inch.

My father loved to tell stories. He liked to exaggerate and use his hands. He did all the cooking and cleaning in our household, saying my mother was only capable of taking our clothes to be laundered in the basement of our building, and grocery shopping at the nearby Met; she brought the food home in a little red cart because she didn't drive. But she always overbought and overspent, which Poppa would yell about.

Poppa was such a high-strung man that I never understood how he could tolerate a job that required him to sit still all day. He was a jeweler who specialized in design and manufacture. He also cut, set, and polished gemstones, in addition to repair work. In the eighties, jewelers didn't have ergonomically correct workbenches and they spent all day uncomfortably hunched over.

When Poppa came home, he was so excitable he'd act like a dog let loose from its leash. Sometimes, it was a happy excitement and he'd pound Heinekens as he whipped up dinner, singing as he removed the spices from drawers and cupboards, later offering me samples of his cooking to taste on a spoon, or handing me the rice pot so I could scrape out the slightly burnt, crunchy kernels stuck to the bottom, which Poppa called "popcorn rice." He'd touch my nose a lot, if he was feeling cheerful—his way of showing affection, since he rarely kissed me. My mother would be in the bedroom listening to her 45s of John Lennon, the *West Side Story* soundtrack, the *Sunshine* album, or Simon and Garfunkel. She wouldn't come out until dinner was ready. She knew that as soon as he saw her, his mood would sour. Once, my mother told me she was undressing by the window and Poppa said, shutting the drapes, "You're not a pretty baby, you're a fat cow, and no one wants to look at you."

Whenever Poppa came home in bad spirits, I'd scramble into the bedroom with Mommy and turn up the volume on her Gibson record player, surrounding us with pillows in a kind of mini-fort and throwing the quilt over our heads. Inside our makeshift tent, I would (even at five and six) suck on my plastic pacifier and hold close to my face a yellow stuffed dog whose gingham ear was ripped from my constant tugging. Poppa would yell about how his boss demeaned him, or about how bad the market was. Poppa was usually out of work at least once a year, since the jewelry business got slow after Christmas. After a while, his tirades would gather momentum and turn into uncontrollable rages that often lasted for hours at a time. When he was this way he was like a man possessed and we were terrified to go anywhere near him. He'd scream that we'd cursed him with a life of misery, and he would never be free again, that God couldn't send him to hell because he was already in it, and that he wondered what he'd done to deserve being cursed with two burdens: a sick woman for a wife and a wild beast for a daughter. Often, I wished he would yell in Spanish so we couldn't understand what he was saying.

We were still living on Thirty-second Street the summer I turned seven and had to walk several blocks to get to the Forty-fifth Street pool. It was heavily chlorinated, had dead bugs rafting on its surface, and was only about four feet deep. Older kids called it the Piss Pool. I'm ashamed to admit that I contributed to its name, nonchalantly drifting to the blue borders of the pool, casting glances to make sure no one was looking.

The pool water was a clear, light, wide-open blue that spread itself to take in my wet, bulleting body, my body with its closed fists and feet pressed together and legs arched like long fins; my mouth clenched so I could hold the air like a purse snapped shut; my mermaid self, my goldfish self, my dolphin self, myself without weight. When I rose, bursting my head up, to slurp the air, I felt my brain grow light with pleasure. After a few seconds, I would look to my mother, sitting with the big black purse strapped to her neck and shoulder. She never took it off for fear of thieves. What I did sometimes, when my private games got boring, was stand in the middle of the pool and gaze around me. When I stopped and looked about, it was as if all the people—kids in groups, mothers with tube babies, kids with plastic floaties around their arms to hold them up, boys diving by the NO DIVING sign—leaped out from nowhere. Sound came on, all of a sudden, the sounds of splashing, shouting, whistles blowing, the sounds of birds and cars from behind the green slatted fence.

On the day I met Peter I saw two boys and their father wrestling at the other end of the pool, splashing and laughing. One of the boys was very handsome. He was the smaller of the two, maybe about nine or ten, skinny, with longish brown bangs. He wasn't just handsome; he exuded happiness. There was brightness in his face and skin, supple quickness to his legs and arms and hands, and a gentle quality to his eyes and face that was rare for a boy. His older brother looked happy too, but not with that same vividness.

Their father had bowl-cut sandy-silver hair with sixties bangs like a Beatle. He had full lips, a long, pointy nose that might have looked unattractive on someone else, but not on him, and a strong, pert chin. When he looked in my direction, I saw that his eyes were vigorously aquamarine. He smiled at me, his face full of lines—on his forehead, by his eyes, and around his jaw. I knew he must be old, to have lines and graying hair and loose skin on his neck, but he had so much energy and brightness that he didn't seem old. He didn't even seem adult in the sense of that natural separateness adults have from children. Children understand the distance between themselves and adults the way dogs know themselves to be separate from people, and though adults may play children's games, there is always that sense of not being alike. I think he could have been lined up with a hundred men of

similar build and disposition and I could have pulled him out from
that line, and asked, "Can I play with you?"

I crossed the length of the pool and asked just that. He answered,
"Of course," and then immediately splashed my face, frolicking with
me as though I were his own child. I splashed the boys' faces and they
mine, for these boys didn't seem to mind playing with someone so
much younger and a girl to boot. At one point the handsome boy
gently dunked my head, and when I rose, I laughed so hard that for a
moment it seemed all I could hear was my own laughter. Then the
father lightly took me under the arms and whizzed me around, laughing like a big kid. When he stopped, the world was off balance and a
strange burst of white flooded his features, like a corona.

Later, when the lifeguards called everyone out of the pool for closing,
the father, whose name was Peter, introduced us to a sweet-looking
Hispanic woman named Inès, who had been wading by herself in the
shallowest part of the pool while we played. Peter teased her about her
need to be close to the pool's edges and joked to my mother and me
that Inès was nervous about things no one thought to worry about,
such as going on carousels or riding a bicycle. Inès had an awkwardly
pretty face, drowsy, sun-lined eyes, long curly hair that started out dark
but midway changed to a dyed apricot shade, and the mild, disoriented
look of a wild fawn. She had purple press-on nails; two had gone missing, and the rest had tiny black peace signs painted on them.

Peter told us everyone's names: the older boy, Miguel, looked
about twelve or thirteen and the younger boy, Ricky, only a couple
of years older than I was. By the end of the day I'd forgotten all the
names but I remembered the first letters of the parents' names: P and I.
I kept thinking of them, P and I, and their promise to invite my mother
and me to their house. A few days passed and nothing happened, so I
forgot them.

———

I might have permanently forgotten, except for some vague stamp of joy that the incident left on me. We were in Poppa's 1979 Chevy when Mommy said they had called her up, or, rather, Peter had called.

"We're invited to go to their house. Isn't that nice?" When Poppa said nothing, she continued. "Peter and Inès. And the boys, Ricky and Miguel. Miguel and Ricky. Such nice boys. Well-behaved boys, not rough at all. Such a nice family."

"Their house? It is around here?"

"Not far. On the phone, Peter said Weehawken, right where it meets Union City. I just wanted to run it by you. See what you think?"

"About what?"

"Going there. On Friday while you're at work."

"I don't care."

"Well, I thought I'd run it by you."

"I don't care. These people are not ax murderers, right?"

"They're a very nice family. Very nice people. A lovely family."

"Everything is so nice to you. Everyone is so nice. Everything is so lovely."

"So it's set, then," said Mommy. "For Friday at noon."

2

THE TWO-STORY HOUSE

I n front of the two-family house sat a two-tiered white fountain and three large resin statues—a pink bear, a black Lab with wings, and a mermaid. The bear was half sunk in ivy. The strange, dark, coiling ivy braceleted the mermaid's plump tail, and up the side of the house it crawled, swallowing the chipped purple shingles like a wild man's beard; sprouting out from the clotted ivy on the ground were tall red and pink roses. There was a ragged gold and red Spanish flag on a pole, and flowerpots on both sides of the welcome mat. The bell that my mother rang lolled out of the frame on its wires. When she didn't hear it, she resorted to a heavy gold-colored door knocker.

At first I didn't associate the slender, lithe man who led us up the stairs with the father from the pool. I clung to the mahogany banister in deference to my mother's command: she called the winding stairs "tricky." I almost slipped at one point because I was too busy watching a set of golden-key wall ornaments by the stairwell ascend with me, positioned so that each key seemed larger than the one beneath it.

"These stairs are a killer," the man said, holding his back. "I wish we lived in the first-floor apartment instead. But it's too small for all of us. Plus, it's not in the greatest shape. I can't even rent that floor out right now. I keep meaning to fix it up, but there's so much to do upstairs. You'll see."

At the top of the stairwell was a mirror that my mother asked about, and the man said, "It's an American girandole, with the federal eagle on the top. I spray it gold each year or so to keep it looking nice. I got it at a flea market. It's an antique." Then he laughed, and said, "So am I."

The man continued: "Everything in our house is an antique. Our stove is a Bengal gas-on-gas, installed in 1955. And we have an old clawfoot bathtub, too, the really deep kind of tub you never see anymore. And a deep double sink: one side is meant for washing dishes, and the other side for clothes."

I sensed he was stalling on opening the wooden door at the top for some reason; that like all adults, he enjoyed making children wait. I slunk my way between him and my mother and gave him my sternest yet most amicable pout and said, "Uh, what's your name again?"

"Peter, don't you remember?"

"Peter, can you open that door? Please?"

Swiftly, with a smile as sweet as a Cracker Jack, he placed his wide, kind hand over my eyes. "Now, don't peek. I'm going to take my hand off all at once, fast, and, when I do, you're going to see something amazing, okay. Promise you won't try to peek?"

"Promise."

I heard the door open and did attempt to look, but all I saw was the light fringing the cracks in his fingers. "Ready?"

"Ready!"

A square glass tank sat in the middle of the floor—about the size of a small living room sofa. Inside were large brown branches, and on the branches there were iguanas with spikes on their heads; a small dirty pond held a black, whiskered catfish. On perches by the windows, parakeets and finches fluttered; the floor was covered in newspapers to collect their droppings; the walls contained built-in bird feeders, and from the ceiling hung bird toys: bells and colored rocks strung together. A big furry dog, tongue hanging, came to me for petting, and

I plunged my hand into his long autumn-colored fur; he sank to the floor with pleasure, and rolled onto his back to get his soft white belly rubbed and scratched.

"This is Paws," Peter said. "He's the friendliest dog in the world, part golden retriever, part collie."

"Oh, those are nice breeds!" my mother said, and though she was allergic, she couldn't resist petting him.

Peter then led us into the kitchen, which contained a tank with a small box turtle swimming in it. The turtle ate worms, Peter said, and showed me the gray cubes, which were really worms, crushed and dried up. He took the wire netting off the top of the tank and I dropped the gray cube in and saw the flat, wrinkled head bob up to get it. The turtle's tank and the tank in the front room had a wild, rank smell that mixed with every other smell: bird droppings and feathers and old newspapers and Paws's fur, which had that warm, dirty, doggy smell. He followed us everywhere and kept looking at us with his moist eyes. The bird chatter merged with the ticking of dog claws on the kitchen linoleum, and the sound of that crazy, happy tail swiping everything he passed. Paws's entire bottom swished with it, nonstop. "It's like he's dancing," I said.

We went to the living room, which had red carpeting, a red velvet sofa and velvet-cushioned chairs, red drapes, and three huge bookcases jammed with books. On the floor was a small mesh cage with a stout brown-and-white hamster in it, and by the window, in a huge tank about half the size of the one in the front room, goldfish swam— orange, black, spotted. They drifted among aquarium plants, a stone cottage, a stone mermaid, and a stone toad, past a windmill churning bubbles. On the left of the tank was another, smaller tank, and with a grin, Peter led us to it, pointing inside to a small alligator.

"He's a caiman—part alligator, part crocodile," Peter explained, and I saw that in length he was half the size of my arm, maybe a bit wider. He had skin full of ripples, ancient unblinking eyes, and sat as still as the creatures made of stone.

"How can he be so tiny?" I asked.

"Well, if he was in the wild he'd grow bigger," Peter said. "But here, in captivity, he grows only to about the size the tank allows. His body knows, instinctively, that if he got bigger, he would outgrow his surroundings. He's happy there, see, with his little stream and log to sit on: he'll never really get bigger than he is. Unless I get a bigger tank."

"Will you?" I looked up to his smiling face. "Get a bigger tank?"

"Maybe someday. But I like him the size he is. Wanna see a trick, something really neat?"

"Yeah!"

Peter put his hand into the tank, which made Mommy and me gasp. But he kept right on smiling and nudged the little alligator over, and I moved closer to see the smooth, white, lined belly and plump, stubby legs raised in what seemed total submission; and that oddly shaped face with its mouth forming a sort of serene grin, exposing the tiniest triangles of teeth. Those teeth, though tiny, looked like they could hurt, and my heart beat in fear for Peter's hand. I thought about library books I'd read about tigers and other big cats, a subject of endless fascination for me. Supposedly, crocodiles, hiding under swamp water, could suddenly spring up and grab the neck of a drinking tiger, yank the big cat down with all those small mean teeth digging into thick orange fur while the tiger's back legs tried to keep a hold on the earth.

But Peter stroked its belly, and I watched the pale, clear reptilian eyes dilate. And soon, to the awe of Mommy and me, the caiman's eyes shut completely and Peter said, in a whisper, "He's sleeping." I whispered back to Peter, "I thought he was going to bite you. I was scared."

"All animals love to have their bellies rubbed. There are no exceptions."

"What's his name?"

"Warden."

"He sure looks like one," said Mommy. "Awake, that is. Peter, how do you find the time to take care of all these animals?"

Peter lit up a King 100. I knew my mother worried about me be-ing around secondhand smoke, but she kept quiet. "I'm on veteran's disability. My job is taking care of this house, because as you can see, something's always breaking, and I was trained as a carpenter so I know a lot about fixing things." He blew out some smoke rings and I stuck my finger in them, giggling as they dissolved.

"You see, I was working as a stateside carpenter during the Korean War and I was driving down a hill in the rain and a truck rear-ended me. I ended up having to get a spinal fusion. Sometimes I have to wear a back brace, but I don't let it get me down. I keep busy. Fixing this house and taking care of the animals. Without that, I'd be pretty bored. But a person can never run out of things to do in this place." He paused. "You know how old this house is?"

"How old?" Mommy asked. I started tracing circles on the sleep-ing caiman's tank.

"Over a hundred years. This house was built during the Civil War era; it's one of the oldest houses in Weehawken. Inès inherited it from her husband. He was killed in a car crash while her kids were still in diapers."

My mother's eyes widened. "Did you know over a hundred peo-ple a day die in car accidents? That's why I always tell Margaux to wear her seat belt. My husband won't." She shook her head. "That must have been devastating for her. I can't even imagine a thing like that."

Peter nodded. "It was traumatic for Inès, very much so. Anyway, Miguel and Ricky really needed a dad and Inès—I don't know if she could have managed it without someone to help her out with this place. Believe me, it's in an eternal state of . . . oh, what's the word? It's falling apart. She works at the *Pennysaver*; one of her jobs is typing up the personal ads and such. She decided to put in one for herself but there was some kind of mix-up and the ad wasn't even supposed to run that day. But *it did*. Some things are fate, I guess. Anyway, your name, Cassie, it comes from Cassandra, right?"

"Yes. Cassandra Jean. My father named me. He used to call me Sandy."

"Would you mind if I called you Sandy, then? I think it's important to stay close to our childhoods. Childhood is the most important time, really."

"Yes, I agree. Call me Sandy, then."

"There's a little poem I had to learn in school and I still remember it today. Funny what we remember. It goes like this: 'Blessings on thee, little man, / Barefoot boy with cheek of tan! / With thy turned-up pantaloons, / and thy merry whistled tunes; / With thy red lip, redder still / Kissed by strawberries on the hill; / With the sunshine on thy face, / Through thy torn brim's jaunty grace; / From my heart I give thee joy, / I was once a barefoot boy!' John Greenleaf Whittier."

"Bravo!" Mommy said. "You didn't miss a beat."

Peter cleared his throat. "For all I've lived, I still try to have that attitude. I don't want to lose my cheer. Did you ever feel, Sandy, for everything that's happened in your adult life, you've still kept the heart of a little girl? I can see that in you."

Mommy blushed and paused before speaking. She kept her voice low; I think she thought I was so caught up with the caiman that I wasn't listening. "Well, I might as well be a child, the way my husband treats me. He's always saying I can't do anything right. When I was a little girl, my father gave me responsibilities. I used to wash the dishes every night and my dad would give me a nickel." Her face glowing, she said, "I was the youngest child and my father's pet."

"I bet you looked just like Shirley Temple back then."

"This is the zoo and you're the zookeeper!" I blurted out.

"Well, I guess you could say that. You want to see some more animals?"

"Yeah!"

"There's a guinea pig in the attic I haven't shown you yet. The attic is Miguel and Ricky's room. And there's some rabbits outside, in hutches."

"Where are Miguel and Ricky today?" Mommy asked. "I was hoping Margaux might get to play with them."

"Out at Big Mouth Arcade, probably. Wasting this sunny day."

"With Inès?"

"No, Inès doesn't get home from work until around five thirty. Lately she's been putting in overtime. They don't pay her extra, but she'll never say anything." He rolled his eyes.

"I want to see the rabbits now!" I grabbed Peter's hand. "Please take me?"

"Let's go!"

As I skipped away, I heard Peter say, "I love that. When children skip. The most innocent, worry-free thing someone can do is skip."

When we got back to our apartment, I picked up the rotary-dial phone in our kitchen. "Let's call Peter; let's ask him when we can come back to his house."

"Well, I'll give you the number. You call him. I wouldn't want us to look overeager." On the phone, I said, "Peter, can we come over to your house again, it isn't polite to ask so soon, but I loved being there so much and you're so much fun, I had such a good time and I love Paws so much, I just love him, and Warden too, though he looks like he could be a bit moody, and the rabbits—they're so soft and I like their little bunny noses. I love Peaches and Porridge! I want to come to your house every day for the rest of my life!" I paused; my mother was always talking about the importance of routines. "I want you to make a schedule of days when we can visit your house."

I couldn't explain why I felt it was all right to be so bold with Peter; I just knew it was.

Peter laughed. "When you want something you get it, don't you? Put your mother on."

After what seemed like forever, I heard my mother laugh and say, "Okay, Mondays and Fridays, then. That's good for us. My husband likes to take us out on the weekends, so that works out." She paused. "You're very good with kids; Margaux took an incredible liking to you. Oh, you've had foster kids? Well, that's nice. I've always admired people who do good deeds; I wish I could do good deeds myself but my husband doesn't believe in giving money to charity or anything of the sort. Yes, do unto others . . ."

3

A BAD HABIT

After we'd gone to Peter's house for three straight Mondays and Fridays, arriving at ten and staying until about four thirty so we would be home before Poppa, I slipped up in front of Peter and began to play with my hair in the weird way Poppa hated— I would snatch up strands in my fingers to shake and twist them. Sometimes I had done this so frenziedly that I had actually contorted portions of hair into impossible snarls and knots, which Mommy had given up trying to comb out. We were in the yard, Mommy snug in a lawn chair, me standing by the birdbath. I'd just finished playing ball with Paws.

My mother quickly said, "Oh, my husband and I are trying to stop that. We've told Margaux time and time again. But I wish her father wouldn't be so critical of her. It's just a nervous habit like biting your nails."

"For God's sake, she's only seven. I think it's cute when she does that. She's feeling free and happy doing it. I can't understand why adults put so much pressure on children." Mommy shrugged, and Peter said, "Margaux, let me see you do it again. You're free, here in this yard, just let go, do what you want. Go on, feel free, play with your hair."

I didn't want to. Playing with my hair in front of Peter, as much as he said he would enjoy the sight, seemed to stir up even more feelings of shame than the times Poppa had scolded me for doing it. The only thing I didn't like about Peter was that he could be pushy. So I decided to distract him by flopping onto his lap, sideways, almost knocking him out of his lawn chair.

"Be careful!" said Mommy. "You know Peter has a bad back!"

Peter didn't get angry; he just started tickling me. At one point, Ricky came into the yard and Peter handed him the garden hose so he could spray me. He chased us both until Ricky got bored and left. As the hours flew by, the yard became engulfed in long shadows. My mother started to say after a while that we should probably get home for dinner. Peter said, "Why don't we have a little barbecue here? You said on Fridays Louie leaves leftovers?"

"Yes, every Friday after work it's off to the bar," said Mommy, and Peter shook his head.

As Peter cooked hot dogs on the grill, Inès wandered into the yard with a sandwich on a paper plate. "Want some dogs instead?" Peter asked her.

"Nah, I've got olive loaf on wheat," said Inès, and she lay on a flowered towel with a book, reading while she picked at her sandwich. "I made the guys some, too," she said. She always called her sons "the guys."

Later, Inès got up to make a call, leaving her barely eaten sandwich lying on the towel as we ate grilled hot dogs with an open can of cold pork and beans. On the walk home, my mother told me that when she walked by Inès, her sandwich had been covered with tiny, swirling brown ants; apparently, Inès had bitten into them without even noticing.

"She's a dreamer, like you," Mommy said.

———

Sometimes my mother liked to get Peter started up about how terrible Poppa was. Lately, I'd been joining in, too, and one Friday the three of us were making fun of Poppa as we ate lunch at the Blimpie on Bergenline Avenue. As Mommy ate her tuna on rye and Peter and I shared salami and provolone on Italian bread saturated with oil and vinegar, Mommy started talking about Poppa's obsession with one of the kitchen cabinets.

"He has everything in his cabinet so neatly arranged, each pen has to be in order, and he has this perfectly folded handkerchief, he said he got it from Madrid, and he has matchboxes from every country he ever visited while he was in the army in these precise little stacks. One time, Margaux, when she was three, little devil that she can be sometimes, climbed up on the countertop and got into that cabinet and moved everything, and when he came home—keep in mind, I wasn't aware of what she'd done—he took one look in there, and went to his closet for his belt. I knew how scared Margaux was of his belt so I tried to get in the way, and he ended up hitting me with it, but at least Margaux wasn't hurt. Anyway, Peter, get this, he has a pair of actual nunchakus—did you ever meet anyone who has a set of nunchakus in his house? He does tricks with them to be impressive; he's such a show-off."

Right in the middle of the Blimpie, I mocked all of Poppa's finest moves with the nunchakus in front of Peter and Mommy, getting them to howl with laughter. That night, when I saw Poppa, I felt a little guilty. I knew he only did these tricks for my entertainment, and to convince me that he could protect us in case an intruder broke in.

Poppa, Mommy, and I were sitting outdoors under a large bright umbrella at a Westchester restaurant. Poppa liked to stop here for a basket of steamers on our way to City Island; then, for dinner, we'd eat lobster or fried clams in white-and-red paper baskets at Tony's by the ocean. Tony's had video games, so I'd run to Poppa constantly for the quarters he kept in his pockets as he drank Heinekens, smoked cigars, and talked to Mommy. At home he didn't speak to her much, except to yell, but if we were eating at a restaurant he'd get into all kinds of subjects with her. Maybe he just didn't like the apartment or he was happy on the weekends when he didn't have to work. Whatever the case, when we went out, he could be very nice to my mother, buying her piña coladas without rum (she couldn't drink because of her medication) and her favorite thing to eat, fried shrimp dipped in tartar sauce with coleslaw. He still treated her like a baby, fastening a paper napkin around her neck as a bib and even wiping her face for her, which I noticed she seemed to like, though she often griped to Peter, "I can't stand it when he treats me as though I'm not even a wife, but a daughter."

Another thing she must have always enjoyed was showering Poppa with praise: "Oh, Louie, your cooking is like a five-star restaurant" or "Louie, can you show me that picture of you in San Juan again? You look just like Robert Redford in that one." The only reason I noticed it now was because the way she talked about Poppa to Peter was so different. Poppa loved compliments. At home, we had a game: "Tell me all about your Poppa-pa." Snuggling with him, I'd tell him everything a girl believes about her father—that he's the biggest man and the most handsome, the wisest and the best. But I often wasn't the best in Poppa's eyes.

As we were sitting at the eatery, I must have slipped up and started playing with my hair, because Poppa said, "Look at that. She makes herself a public spectacle. This child has no comprehension of anything. Not life, not me, not anything." He said the last without anger, but regret. He was quiet for a minute, almost thoughtful. Then he went on, "There is nothing worse than a bad habit. A bad habit," he repeated, looking at Mommy. "Is there anything that you can think of that will end this bad habit of hers? This habit that—"

Mommy quickly started talking with the hope of derailing the speech that was just starting to gather steam, because she knew—we both did—that once he got going, it would be a long while before he stopped. "I'm sure she'll outgrow it. Dr. Gurney always said some children are more nervous than others and we shouldn't worry about a silly little thing like Margaux playing with her hair. He actually said nail biting is worse and we should be glad she's not one of those types; that leads to hangnails and infections. And Puh—" Mommy said, and I knew that this was the start of Peter's name; she quickly swallowed the sound with a gulp of orange Hi-C. She knew Poppa got annoyed when Peter was mentioned, except in the context of his living conditions. Poppa had asked Mommy to describe what "that house" was like, and had smiled when Mommy told him about the toilet that didn't always flush or the ants on the windowsill, or the fact that Peter once said he had picked up most of his furniture from curbs on garbage night and bragged that there was nothing a little Krazy Glue or some wood filler couldn't fix. Poppa was delighted to hear of a sink that some days brimmed with dirty dishes—not even properly scraped. "The smell of those animals must be insufferable," Poppa had said.

Poppa narrowed his eyes at the "P" sound, but he didn't say anything.

"Anyway," Mommy said, looking away. "Like Dr. Gurney said: it's not permanent. He said these exact words, 'Children outgrow things.' And Margaux *will* outgrow playing with her hair."

"Outgrow," Poppa said, not too loudly, but with a severity that indicated that if he were in charge of the English language, he would omit this particular verb from every dictionary. Then, as though granting the offending word a chance to redeem itself, he tried pronouncing it slightly differently, in a gentler tone, while hooking a steamer in his thumb and forefinger.

The storm of Poppa's nerves seemed to have quieted.

He cleared his throat and said, "Keesy, I am going to tell you the story of a young girl in Puerto Rico who had bad habits; they were different habits than yours, but equally destructive. The mother and father worried because the children at school thought the girl was crazy. But this child was not aware of how the others had made her a laughingstock, nor the pain and humiliation she had inflicted upon her poor parents." He sipped his beer. "Anyway, she was always inside a dream and never looked where she was going. One day, at least as the story goes, the girl took a long walk and as she walked, she sang and hummed. She came to some train tracks and laid her legs across the tracks, singing and looking at the sky. Too busy in her dream, she did not hear the train. The train driver honked, but the girl would not look up, and trains cannot be stopped once they are in motion. The train ran right over her legs and cut them both off right to about here." He indicated his hip. "Yes, Keesy, do not look so shocked. Her legs were severed and left in the middle of the tracks for the buzzards. And the poor child—to the great sorrow of her mother and father— was left with two bloody stumps."

"Louie, that's a terrible story!" Mommy said. "You don't tell stories like that to a child!"

"What happened to her after that, Poppa? What happened?"

"Your mother is right; it is a difficult story. If I were to tell you more, you might have nightmares."

The waiter came and took the empty bottles of Heineken and gave my father a fresh beer. I couldn't stop thinking of those two bloody stumps left on the track. "Poppa, please! You can't tell a story without telling the ending!"

"You have a good imagination. You make the ending for yourself, Keesy."

"You're drunk, Louie! You are just drunk and it's ninety degrees! It is ninety degrees! You could have a sunstroke!" my mother said in a whisper-yell; she was aware of how angry he would get if he was publicly humiliated. "There's a pay phone in there. I'm calling Dr. Gurney. I'm telling him what you do to frighten Margaux!"

"You do that! I will give you the quarter myself!" He reached into his pocket. "Here is some change; call him! Maybe I can have a break then! I can sit here and enjoy the shade! Go!"

When my mother left the table, I put my hands gently around the metal pole holding the large sun umbrella in place over our heads. I felt safer holding it.

"That woman is comical. The heat gets to her. What does she think? That it is wrong to have some cold beer on a hot day? That woman is crazy. On a hot day, I don't like to fight. I like to sit in the shade and enjoy a cold beer under a big umbrella. She acts as though

I like hot weather. I despise the heat and humidity! That is why I left Puerto Rico! I came here to escape. But then I found that woman."

"Poppa, tell the rest."

"Well," he said, and I stared at his auburn beard and thought of a beetle I had squashed recently, to see what color its blood was. The blood had been orange and had smelled bad; I'd been surprised that its blood wasn't red. He went on: "No one really knows. There are two versions. One version is that she stayed with her mother and father caring for her in bed until she grew old and died. The second version is that one night she prayed to the devil to get her legs back. She had been praying to God and he never responded. So, legend goes, her mother opened the door to her bedroom one day, and she was missing, never to be seen again. But sometimes the mother thought she heard on the roof a strange tapping sound that wasn't rain or branches hitting the tar paper, it sounded like feet. And some have said, though you can never be sure, for children tell lies, but some of the children of my great-grandfather's time have said that at night, they have seen the girl with a great horned beast on top of the roof that they assumed must be the devil himself. They were dancing together!" He paused to drink some beer, and continued. "Now, I myself do not know what to believe. The first version is a little more plausible. But the second version could also be true."

I looked miserably into my napkin confetti; I'd been shredding napkin after napkin without even noticing. My father reached across the table, touched the tip of my nose, and caressed my cheek.

"I am telling you this, Keesy, for your own good. One must live in reality and not always with her head in the clouds. I want my daughter to be strong like me and firm in the world."

Despite Poppa's cautionary tale, I only got dreamier as the summer soared by, and story upon story started to take shape in my head. Peter not only asked me to talk about my stories, he helped me build a story that was just ours. The story was called "Danger Tiger": it was about a winged tiger that went around rescuing people. I don't remember much about it, just that Peter played different characters, some of them villains, while I played only one character, Danger Tiger himself. Danger Tiger was a *he*; I insisted on this, otherwise he would be called Danger *Tigress*. I didn't know why, but I enjoyed playing male characters when I talked about stories with Peter; Peter, in response, often took on the roles of female characters, with a silly high-pitched voice, which was good for laughs. I was glad that my mother was too busy writing in her Fact Book or just lazing in her lawn chair, watching us, never joining in our stories. I was also glad that Inès worked full-time and that the boys were often off skateboarding, visiting the arcade, or watching TV in the attic. Peter once mentioned to my mother that it was a good thing I'd come along, because Ricky and Miguel were getting older and they didn't want to spend that much time with him: he even joked that getting everyone together as a family on the weekends, even if it was just to go to the Forty-fifth Street pool, was like getting a group of monkeys to sit down for tea. I played ball with Paws as they sat in lawn chairs, talking. Peter said, "The boys are in that stage where they're obsessed with their friends. Ricky is going into fifth grade and Miguel into eighth, so I guess it's normal. I used to get lonely before you and Margaux started coming over. You two have brought a lot of joy into my life."

Mommy looked up from the Fact Book and swatted at a summer fly. "Thank you, Peter. You've been an absolute godsend yourself."

Peter smiled, but then looked unhappy. "It'll be sad when she starts school in September." He lit a cigarette.

"We can still come," Mommy said, casually waving her hand. "We'll be here by three, the latest. And we can stay as late as we want. Louie'd be glad to have another night off from cooking. More time for the bar." She paused, and then said, "But it will be stressful, with school starting. It's so hard . . . what with getting Margaux's uniforms, you have to go to a special store, and then for the shoes, a different store. And then the textbooks! Peter, every year you have to cover the textbooks with contact paper, and Louie gets mad if I ask him to do it, and it's not easy! You have to cut it a certain way, and I'm not that good with crafts, not anymore."

"I can help you with Margaux's schoolbooks," said Peter. "When the time comes, bring me the textbook covers; I'll show you a simple way of doing it."

"Oh, I wouldn't want to bother you . . ."

"It's no problem, really, Sandy."

Mommy said Peter's yard was the most relaxing place on earth, more tranquil than even his living room. Her favorite thing to do was to pet Paws; I don't think anyone petted him more than my mother. "No rest for the weary," she joked, and when Paws finally drifted away to see Peter or me, she would resume scribbling in the Fact Book. The little spiral notebook was now completely full, so she had resorted to writing in the margins and on the back and front. Eventually, Peter gave her a new notebook, persuading her that two separate books would not be too much to keep track of. So she began anew her recordings of local news and worldwide catastrophes, shopping lists and children's songs, her reminders of things to do or people to call. Occasionally, she would ask Peter if it was all right if she used his phone, and she would go upstairs to begin calling numbers from her address book—people she'd met in psychiatric wards, Dr. Gurney, or friends from college whom she complained avoided her calls. At home, she was always talking about "blacklisting" her unresponsive friends, but as far as I knew, she never crossed out anyone's number. Once Mommy got through her entire address book, she would call 1-800 suicide hotlines, or the Pathmark Super Center to ask a question about the price of this and that, or St. Mary's Hospital to request that they send her a packet on cancer or some other dire disease she was afraid she or I would get.

In addition to "Danger Tiger," Peter and I also played a lot of games that he made up. One was an enhanced version of "Itsy Bitsy Spider." Peter would claw his fingers inward and wiggle them frenetically to form the legs of two friendly tarantulas that would then climb all over my body, tickling me. Two other games were Mad Scientist and Mad

Gardener, the latter played in the yard. Peter would chase me with the garden hose, spraying me full blast whenever I was cornered. Mad Scientist was another game that involved tickling and, when caught, I'd be held down and subjected to what we called Tickle Torture Time. Peter would start at what he referred to as the third degree, which was mild— he wouldn't tickle my belly, armpits, or the soles of my feet, but he'd later upgrade to those (what he called the first degree) if I didn't surrender. Peter said he'd never met anyone before me who'd gotten all the way to the first degree without begging for mercy. I was proud at first when he said that, but then I was a little put off and jealous: I'd thought Mad Scientist was our own special thing and I couldn't help but wonder who else he'd played the game with.

4

SAVAGES

Apparently, Poppa had put a down payment on a house, yet there was no anticipation of the move, just a September day replete with sealed UPS boxes and a big white truck. We donated my old toys to the Emanuel Methodist Church across from the Thirty-second Street playground. The previous day, Poppa and I had taken a short drive through our end of town, so he could point out all the ugly things we were escaping by moving nine blocks. Poppa had offered to take Mommy on the drive with us, but she said she'd rather stay home and listen to the radio. The bedroom was depressing now, with all our stuff packed and just my mother and the radio flat on the white sheet. Mommy hadn't gotten dressed and wore a long checkered garment with snaps down the front that she had gotten from one of her hospital stays. The bare living room was a worse sight—now that all my toys were packed up, the only whisper of my presence left was the marker scribbles on the wall, from the many times Poppa had gotten angry at the landlord and granted me artistic liberty.

"Always dragging your feet!" Poppa said, and briskly pulled me along. On our way down the hallway stairs, which smelled like urine and beer, he said, "Keesy, when I take you driving today, take a good look around at the things and places you have enjoyed. That woman is lazy and I am sure she will not take the trouble to walk to this end of town once we have moved, and, to be honest, I am not sure I want you in this area anymore."

When we got to Thirtieth Street, Poppa parked the car to buy cigars from Havana Cigars one last time. In the Chevy, I had nothing to do but stare forlornly at Beeline Arcade, where I would always go to play Galaga and Ms. Pac-Man. I thought of the roller rink a block away from our apartment with a giant red-wheeled skate painted upon its white brick wall; my mother had never allowed me to skate there, for fear I'd fall and break my neck.

Just when I thought I'd start crying, Poppa came back with two kinds of cigars, Ninfas and Senadores.

"You know something," Poppa said, gripping the wheel even though he hadn't started driving yet, "I was talking to the man in there and he said we got out of here just in time. There are more drug addicts than ever and gangs and lowlifes creeping up from the twenties and teens. They creep in, like roaches, and they cannot be stopped. I heard there are even prostitutes sleeping in the Toys R Us parking lot now, can you believe this?"

As he pulled out into traffic, Poppa looked around. "This is a bad section of town, Keesy. Look at that man spitting in the street. I would not spit in the street even if I were choking to death! This is why I carry a handkerchief at all times; I never spit, and I never curse on the street like a lowlife savage, and I do not throw trash on the ground. Look over there, Keesy, at those two pigeons pecking at cigarette butts; they think it is food! It is a depressing sight. This whole place is so depressing to me. I thought one day I would simply get in my car and drive away from here and live anywhere, anywhere but this place. But I am a responsible man; I am not a deserter. Who else would put up with a woman like your mother? I am going to tell you something, Keesy. Enjoy being young. Because you don't know how your life is going to turn out."

He sighed and continued: "You cannot have what you want in life. But you can be yourself, the kind of person who has done brave things, that has overcome fears, and you can look back on your youth with pride. This is why I joined the army when I was eighteen. My father had been in the army and my brothers were in the army and I knew that it was my turn. Do you think I enjoyed sitting in a tank that got up to a hundred and thirty degrees in Germany? But now I am glad to have been that young man almost dead from the heat in that tank, because if that young man had not withstood the test, I would not be the man I am today. The most important thing, Keesy, is self-respect. Other people can hate me, I may be hated by co-workers, despised by my boss, disliked by these savages on the street, but I know that I have sat in that tank and that I have made my bed every day to perfection when I was in the army and that my clothes were always correct. I look at myself, and know that I have kept to the contract of life. Life is a contract, Keesy."

Poppa pulled the car over briefly, reached into the six-pack he kept on the car floor in the back, stuck the empty bottle into a Met shopping bag, and put a fresh beer inside the crumpled paper bag. He offered me a sip, and I refused, saying that I liked my beer cold. He laughed and patted me on the leg.

"When I married your mother, I didn't know I was getting stuck with a sick, helpless woman. Her sister is a bitch, but I still should have listened to her. That bitch in Connecticut gave me a warning, but I did not pay attention. Do you know what she told me, Keesy? She said she noticed that when she and your mother would go to the beach, your mother would always wear headphones. Most people would want to listen to the sounds of the surf, the breeze blowing through the sand, the cries of the gulls. But your mother always needed music playing. I should have known something was wrong then. But the young are foolish. I don't know why I wanted a wife. I would have been happier living alone, a hermit. But I wanted to have children, I wanted to pass my genes down to another generation; I had the basic drive of life, which is to reproduce. Your instincts—

remember that they are almost always wrong. What's right is what your friends and family tell you to do, they always know better; even a stranger on the street who doesn't know the first thing about you: tell that person your situation and you'll get better advice than if you sit down and think about it yourself."

Poppa had driven dreamily through the usual congestion of Bergenline Avenue up to where it turned into Kennedy Boulevard. We had passed Pastore Music, the Burger Pit, and the Four Star Diner; we had gone all the way up to Sears and back again. Poppa was right, there was something sad and wasted about these city blocks. Maybe it was because Bergenline Avenue became desolate around Twenty-ninth Street and it just kept going downhill from there: fewer stores, fewer people, more teenagers sitting on the hoods of parked cars, more older men slumped on steps with bottles of hard liquor wrapped in paper bags.

"I tell you, Keesy, I would rather die than be seen like that in the street, drinking cheap whiskey!" Poppa snorted. "But at least these bums here in Union City have respect, they do not beg for money. They sit quietly and meditate on what has gone wrong in their lives, and you pass by, and they do not ask anything of you, or make themselves a pity case." He took another sip of beer. "Yet I have to carry a gun, or they might rob me. I have fine jewelry and people are jealous. I like to look my best and the underdogs despise me, wishing they, too, could have fine things. Often, Keesy, I think that without beauty to admire, what do we have? Even any of these bums, a good-looking girl turns and smiles at them and they feel their lives restored. A beautiful woman's face and a fine horse, well groomed and ready to run on the track: these sights do not last. The face of Elizabeth Taylor. And Brooke Shields. Some of my friends say you look like her. But I think you are more beautiful. I do not like her eyebrows. Keesy, let's stop here for a moment." We pulled up by Los Precious Supermarket on Twenty-ninth Street, across from the NJ Transit Bus Station. "Do you want some chips?"

Inside the store, Poppa bought himself some Donita pork rinds, a bag of La Dominica plantain chips, and some cassava chips. For me, he bought vanilla sugar wafers and a Tampico Citrus Punch. Before we got back into the Chevy, Poppa lifted my chin and said, "I feel sad for the day you become a woman. The men around here have no respect. They howl and hoot like a bunch of baboons at anything that passes by; I do not know what kind of families they come from. Even though we are moving, there are still going to be animals around. There are savages all over this city. I wish we could move to the suburbs."

The mood turned dreamy as we listened to the Beatles' *Rubber Soul*. When the song "Run for Your Life" came on, Poppa sang and drummed his hands against the steering wheel. The song, Poppa explained to me, when the tape ended, was about a jealous man who suspected his girlfriend was cheating on him; he was warning her that if he ever caught her and her lover together, he would kill her.

"Why does he have to kill her, Poppa? Can't he just get a new girlfriend?"

"It is not that simple, Keesy. It is about honor. But I don't think a man should punish his girlfriend for indiscretion. Women are frivolous; they love easily and they cannot help that they are creatures of passion. They are not rational like men. To be mad at a cheating girlfriend is like yelling at the clouds for raining. I have a girlfriend, Keesy, that your mother knows nothing about." He paused. I felt pleased for a second, understanding that he trusted me not to tell Mommy. A lot of times it was him and me sneaking around behind Mommy's back. For instance, when I was with him, he would let me sit up front and not wear a seat belt, but when Mommy was there, I had to be strapped in, sitting in the back. And every time he brought me with him to get the car inspected, he would buy me four chocolate-frosted doughnuts for lunch, saying, "Don't tell your mother." But I was sad, too. I knew his having a girlfriend had something to do with him never hugging or kissing Mommy, and never saying "I love you."

He continued: "For all I know my girlfriend is with ten other men, but what can I do about it? I cannot worry about everything. Daughters, sisters, mothers—they are sacred because they are of your blood, and if a man does something to them, that man is wronging you directly. Through my years of experience and watching the experiences of my friends, I have found that men will wrong your sister, your mother, your daughter, and all to get at you, to try to destroy another man's honor, because it makes them feel powerful. I know there are two sons in this family your mother takes you to see: beware of the sons—play with them in front of company, but do not go off alone with them. It is just practical advice, from someone who knows." I didn't dare tell Poppa I rarely saw either of the boys; that I was with Peter most of the time, both alone and with my mother.

As we neared the apartment, Poppa pointed to a patch of graffiti on the side of a building and said excitedly, "Look, it is that macho man, Bones, that vandal they can never catch, messing up our city! Well, today, Keesy, good riddance to our old friend Bones, we never have to look at his name again!"

At our new house, Poppa said we had to take short showers, not the leisurely ones we were used to at the apartment, where we didn't pay for water. Our furniture was new and encased in plastic wrapping, which Poppa would not remove for fear of ruining it. The plastic was uncomfortable, and as a result no one sat on it, not even Poppa himself. As I saw from watching the mustached moving men, the couch was terribly heavy. It had oak claw feet and was long enough for Poppa to stretch his entire body across. The new TV Poppa bought was huge and had ornate mahogany curls but Poppa would rarely sit in the living room and watch it; he preferred going to his bedroom to watch his tiny TV from the old apartment. We had gotten rid of our rotary-dial phone and got a new touch-tone that lit up when I pressed the buttons, and I couldn't help but miss the sound the rotary wheel made when I'd turn it. It had sounded like blades on a fresh rink, and would remind me of the times Poppa would take me to Rockefeller Center, where we would watch the ice-skaters.

One day, I overheard Mommy say on the phone that she had thought we would all be happier living in our cozy one-family, side-gabled colonial house than we were in that cramped, roach-ridden apartment, but we weren't and she didn't know why. This was true: it seemed that ever since we got the house Poppa went into three-hour screaming tirades even more often, and having a whole house to roam didn't stop Mommy from lying in one room with her radio or Gibson record player. There was even more for Poppa to clean, and now a greater responsibility for caring about the way things looked. If even a small amount of water spilled on the bathroom floor, Poppa yelled that the tiles were going to rise up. This was such a great fear of Poppa's that he insisted we mop after bathing, and then he mopped again himself, the entire time yelling about how expensive it would be if the entire floor needed to be retiled. Poppa had a rule that no one could take baths during the day, when he couldn't oversee the tiles.

Around this time, Poppa was having more difficulty at work than usual and his especially foul mood caused him to rage about my mother's sister Vera more often. She was the one he called "the bitch in Connecticut." My mother had two sisters: Vera, who was three years older, and my beloved aunt Bonnie, Mommy's twin, who lived in Ohio.

One rainy day, while sitting in Peter's living room after watching *Old Yeller*, which had made both him and me cry, my mother managed to cheer us up by getting me to do an impression of Poppa's rant one weekend when he came home from the bar and started on the subject of Aunt Vera. "Watch this, Peter!" Mommy said. "Margaux is better than a stand-up comic!"

So I stood up. "Okay, okay, but don't laugh, either of you, or I'll start laughing too, and that'll ruin it. Okay, here goes . . . That old witch in Connecticut—she looks down on us because she lives in luxury in that rich place, and I invited her here once and she wouldn't come! She made an excuse, some stupid, far-out reason, but I knew she did not want to set one foot into Union City! Well, I hope she dies of a terminal illness! I hope she dies in bed, screaming! She looks down on me! She thinks she is too good for my cooking! And what is more—I know about this kind of woman; she studied French not for love of the language but to meet that rich banker husband! There they are in that house—the bitch and the banker in that cold house— I swear she turned the heat down when we came to discourage us from visiting! I cannot understand such a person! I learned French and

German out of my love for the language and the culture and the food! I respect European culture! I love the French! She pretended to play that flute, too, to attract the banker, but not because the music was in her blood. I cannot stand a fake person! I studied the Spanish poets because of my appreciation for them; I listen to music for the love of it! I will tell you people something. Even if I go to hell and burn it will be worth it, just to see that bitch down in the flames with me! Because she will be there, I guarantee it! I guarantee it!" I flopped down on the carpet, laughing.

"Margaux should be an actress," Peter said, his face lit by awe.

"She sure has talent when it comes to impersonations," said Mommy. "You know something, for all my husband's complaining about Vera, the truth is she did help us in a time of need. She took care of Margaux for the first two months when I was in the hospital. That's the first time I got sick and they realized I needed to be on medication for the rest of my life. I couldn't even hold her. I was terrified of dropping her. I felt like such a failure. I wanted to be with the baby, but I knew I wasn't well, I was crying all the time, and I knew there was no way I could possibly take care of a baby."

"Can we watch another movie?" I asked, and Peter put in one of his videotape recordings of *Punky Brewster*. I think Peter liked the show just as much as I did; he said the relationship between Punky's adopted father, Henry, and Punky reminded him of the two of us.

Mommy continued: "And I feel guilty because I create so many bills. Every time I go to the hospital, it costs Louie about a thousand dollars."

"So who's the one who makes you sick?" Peter said, sitting straighter in his chair. "It's him. Him with all his physical and mental abuse! He brainwashes you, Sandy, into thinking you're no good when it's really him! There's something wrong with him! Sandy, I'm going to ask you a question. Why don't you leave that man, once and for all? Leave him and get an apartment for you and Margaux. You're an attractive woman. You can meet somebody else."

"Oh, Peter, thank you, you're so kind, but the truth is I'm over-weight and no man would want me. I don't know how to manage money and I don't know a thing about housekeeping: when I was growing up in Westport, we had a maid. And I have all those hospital bills, which he pays . . ."

"Out of your and Margaux's Social Security checks!" My mother received an SSI check for me in addition to her own, since her mental illness qualified her as disabled.

"Yes, yes, out of our checks, but still, still he keeps track of the medication and he cooks the dinners and . . . and I'm sick." She looked into the fish tank as she said this. "I'm not functional; I go to hospitals. I mean, the court would take one look at my record, my being in and out of psych wards, and they would grant him custody. They would take her from me, Peter."

"Not if you could prove in court that he's violent with you and Margaux, Sandy," Peter said, gently placing his hand on her arm.

5

HIGHER, HIGHER

When the weather started to get really cold and we were forced to spend more time indoors, it was up to Peter to invent new games. No more outdoor barbecues with hot dogs and burnt marshmallows harpooned on sticks, no more pool or chases with the garden hose, no more tree climbing. The winter air made my mother languid; she would get tired out from the walk to Peter's house, so she spent more time in the living room listening to her headphones while watching the swirling fish (Peter encouraged her to stare at them, saying this would lower her blood pressure), writing letters to Aunt Bonnie, or working on her Fact Book. Poppa had given her a terrible haircut and some of her hair had fallen out due to all the medications she was on. Her face, despite its floridness, nevertheless appeared sunken. Only at Peter's house did she seem slightly more alive, as if she was vaguely hopeful about something.

Inès wasn't fond of my mother's presence in the living room when she came home around six to reheat a plate of food that Peter had cooked and then head off to read under the gold-bronze lamp whose red fringe hung in wavy tendrils. Peter confided in me that after a tiring workday, Inès didn't like to be pushed into chitchat, but my mother was the type who couldn't take a hint. Often, Inès read anyway while my mother talked. Peter said she was lucky to have a rare ability to tune out her surroundings. "I can't," he said once. "People have mistaken me for a cop before; that's how alert and aware I am of everything that's going on around me."

Peter was determined to keep me active and happy even though we were confined to the house most of the time: with movies, board games, even chess, which he managed to teach me slowly so I wouldn't get frustrated, and, of course, helping him feed and care for the animals. He even started letting me handle the iguanas when once he'd feared they could scratch me in the face. But now he said I was nearly eight, and getting responsible and mature. He could tell I was ready. He had me wear thick black mitts that looked like boxing gloves before he handed me one of the wise old lizards, who sat very still as I gently caressed him. There is a picture of me taken at that time, my head bent and black bangs falling into my eyes; the lizard's spiky head lifted and claw curled affectionately on my pant leg—an ancient infant whose keen skin sensed my soft fingertips even through the heavy gloves.

We also had a thousand-piece jigsaw puzzle we worked on. He'd give me a swift kiss on the lips each time one of us found a piece, after making sure no one was looking. Sometimes Miguel or Ricky could wander into the kitchen for food, but thankfully they were always loud, and so was my mother; she shuffled her feet when she walked. Peter said it was important that no one see us kiss, because people were so weird nowadays—in this day and age, any show of affection was suspect; back in the days when he was a kid, fathers kissed their daughters on the lips all the time.

One Friday in January that was as cold as an open grave, I threw my first tantrum in front of Peter.

"I can't take being inside anymore! I'm sick of it! I hate the winter!" I looked out the living room window at Miguel and Ricky, who were skateboarding outside and, what was more, weren't even wearing heavy coats. "Look at those stupid boys, they get to be out all year round and they don't get frostbite. I think frostbite is a rumor, an ugly, false rumor invented to keep girls cooped up! I just wish I could go to the park! I just wish I could go on the swing! I just wish! I just wish! I just wish!" I stamped my feet.

My mother looked to Peter without saying anything.

Peter said, "Margaux, I have a great idea. Come!"

I followed him down the twisty hall stairs, touching each golden key as I passed them, which is something I did every time I went up or down those stairs. I felt excited when we walked into the narrow hallway by the door to the downstairs apartment. We came to an unpainted wooden door, which Peter unlocked with a small silver key. He reached up to pull a long string, and when a naked bulb came on, he beckoned for me to follow him.

"Hold the banister," he cautioned, but it didn't even begin until halfway down the little staircase. The steps felt like they were made out of old soft wood and were a little wobbly, so I thought of pirate ships and walking the plank. When Peter reached the bottom he pulled on another string, activating another naked bulb.

"Let there be light! So what do you think? A big old mess, wouldn't you say? Inès is a pack rat; she doesn't like to throw anything away. She couldn't part with her husband's old clothes. She still has the moccasins he wore when they went to Woodstock."

I looked around: two motorcycles, some rusty bikes, skis, a few umbrellas, a refrigerator, beach chairs, and some wide-open tool-boxes containing nails, screwdrivers, bolts. Piled in stacks on the floor were dusty books; there were boxes, crates, and trunks, which made me curious. But before doing anything else, I leaped onto the leather seat of one of the motorcycles, grabbed both handles, and went, "Vroom, vroom, vroom."

"I have to get that motorcycle up and running this summer, so we can go for rides. Will you go for rides with me?"

"If my mother lets me. Vroom, vroom, vroom."

"I have a feeling she will. Your mother is overprotective, but I think I might be able to talk her into it."

The basement was cold, so I was glad for the cable-knit sweater my mother had made me wear. I'd never been in a basement before. It smelled damp and musty and something reminded me of the air in a cave, or at least what I imagined a cave would be like. The floor looked as though it was made of metal and the ceiling was a collection of long wooden beams so low that Peter had to stay stooped over.

"You look funny all hunched over like that," I said.

"Well, people in the old days used to be smaller. Each generation gets a little bigger than the one before it. Pretty soon we'll be a race of giants." He paused. "You're a tall girl, Margaux, you're shooting up like a stalk. You've grown a couple of inches, it seems, in just a few months. Or maybe it's my imagination. The time has flown by so fast. Sometimes don't you wish you could put a hold on it? I sure do."

I got off the motorcycle and walked to an oak Victorian wardrobe, similar to the one that Poppa had in his bedroom. I opened it, without asking, and waited to see if Peter would say anything, but he didn't. That was one of the things I liked most about Peter—he had hardly any rules. Whatever rules he did enforce were ones my mother made up, and I think he just did that to keep her happy, not because he believed in them. Sometimes I fantasized that my mother would just vanish and Peter and I could be alone, all the time, and there would be no more rules.

Inside the wardrobe were dresses, hats, and feather boas. There was also a kind of crown, which Peter said was a tiara. "Try it on," he said, and though I'd rather have tried on the dusty black fedora, the flamenco hat, or the floppy velvet one, I put it on anyway.

"You look so beautiful," Peter said, very softly. "Just like a princess."

"I'm not a princess, though," I said, "I'm the Queen of Hearts! Off with their heads! Off with their heads!" I made a chopping motion with my hands.

Peter frowned. "Wouldn't you rather be a princess than some crabby old queen?"

I dropped the tiara onto the floor. "This thing is ugly anyway. I don't like these dresses; they're too old and dingy looking. Why does she keep this stuff anyway?" And I didn't know why, but I tore the dresses off their hangers and scattered them all over the floor. I looked at him and smiled.

He looked horrified. "Pick those up! That's her past! Most of her family is in Spain and she never gets to see them! That dress you just threw on the floor was her dead mother's wedding gown!"

Humbly, I picked them up and put them back on the hangers. We were silent.

"Anyway," Peter said, "the reason I brought you down here was not to show you Inès's things. I came here to get some plywood and a little bit of rope and some sandpaper to sand the wood down and my drill so I can drill some holes in the wood. And, oh, some paint, I need some paint. What's your favorite color?"

"Purple."

"Well, I don't know if I have purple. Is pink okay?" He smiled.

"Are you making something for me?"

"Maybe." He smiled again. I rushed over and hugged him.

"Everything you do is for me. You make me so happy." I paused. "Is it a skateboard? Are you making me a skateboard? Tell me: am I warm or cold?"

"Chilly as the Arctic. Now come on, we have to go and get started on this. But first you have to give me a kiss, for strength. My back is starting to hurt from bending over. I don't know if I'll make it back up the stairs."

I went over to give him a peck on the cheek, but he turned his head so my kiss would meet his mouth.

Peter fastened the pink handmade swing to the attic ceiling, where it would hang for the next year and a half on large knotty ropes. I would often sit on this swing on the days when it was too cold out-side, and Peter would push me. "Higher, higher!" I would yell, kick-ing my legs up to the slanted ceiling's wooden beams. Through the windows, light made buttery patches on the hardwood floor; and I would look to the boys' bunk beds, where blankets were tousled and sheets unhinged (no one kept after them about cleaning the room) and I could see egg-shaped indentations in the pillows from the boys' heads. Here, upstairs, lived Blackhead the guinea pig; I was responsible for changing his water bottle and giving him food pellets, which was a job Ricky once had. But the boys, at thirteen and ten, were more interested in skateboarding and playing arcade games than caring for animals, Peter had said. For two days a week, I not only relieved the boys of their usual duties concerning the animals, but I started to take over the dishwashing whenever Peter cooked. Peter was fond of saying that I would make a perfect wife.

6

"EIGHT IS THE MOST BEAUTIFUL AGE FOR A GIRL"

In Peter's basement, it was easy to forget the outside world. We couldn't hear much, Peter and I, from within those concrete walls. Not the bumping of cars as someone struggled to parallel park, not teenagers whistling through their fingers, nor two pigeons fighting over a bread crust. In the basement, I couldn't hear someone wheeling laundry or groceries home in a shopping cart purloined from the Pathmark parking lot, and I couldn't hear the wheels of bustling baby carriages, or the mothers affectionately calling their little daughters "Mami."

Some stray cats had learned they'd get food and milk if they managed to slip into the basement; there was one pretty tabby that had carried a sagging belly for weeks before the afternoon when she wearily lay down in the tightest corner of that basement; the next time we saw her, she had a nest of suckling kittens. Peter said he had named her Little Mama; she'd given birth twice already in this basement. The kittens were so much fun to play with. I had found a small bag of marbles and would roll them across the floor; then I'd watch the frisky kittens try their best to still the quick, slippery balls in their paws, a feat they could never quite manage. "You're very maternal," Peter would say as I played with the kittens. "I bet you dream of having a big fat belly someday. I like that little girls have potbellies. It makes them look like they're pregnant. Isn't that what every girl dreams about? A baby of her very own to love?"

I hadn't thought of it before, but Peter brought it up so often when we were alone that I began to fantasize more and more about having a family just like Little Mama.

The first few times we went to the basement, Peter would insist on hugging and kissing me mouth to mouth for long periods of time. The first time we kissed like grown-ups, I thought too much about the largeness of his face and the feeling of his skin close up. That I couldn't breathe well bothered me, so I dropped to the floor, pretending to be Sleeping Beauty. While I was positioned on what I imagined to be a bed covered with tulips, I felt like I was really sleeping or in a trance as he continued to kiss me. These games went much deeper than regular playing. As I sat playing with the kittens, Peter would begin to stroke my back, face, buttocks, neck, and between my legs. He always found ways to make me accept more touching when I was past my threshold. For instance, when I sank to the cement floor to show him I'd had enough, he'd caressingly remove my pelt, as big-game hunters do to tigers. Convinced I really was dead, I no longer felt the overwhelming sensations.

As the weather got warmer, Peter suggested I undress, and he'd play hide-and-go-seek with me in my underpants. Peter would count to ten and I'd try to figure out where to go, since there were so many hiding places in the huge basement. A few times, I hid in the oak wardrobe, or climbed into a trunk; occasionally, I crouched behind the motorcycles. It was strange and freeing to run about in just my underpants. Then came a day when Peter dared me to take off the underpants, saying real animals in the jungle didn't wear clothes. After that first time, I had no problem getting naked; it made me feel less like myself and more like a tiger or a rabbit, or whatever I pretended to be. Often, while naked, I would growl under my breath or lick the

Suzuki's handlebars. Another time I wouldn't open my eyes or stand up until Peter shone a flashlight in my face. Afterward, he remarked, "Boy, you get so wrapped up in your games it's like you disappear. It's a little scary."

Down in the basement, I sometimes climbed atop the Suzuki nude: seizing the big handles, I pretended to drive. One time Peter slipped the motorcycle key into the ignition, turning it on; I felt a roaring, searing feeling rise from somewhere inside the engine and radiate out, through the cracked leather seat, spreading all through me like the strands of one of the arching cobwebs in the crevice of a wooden beam, and I gripped the handles, barely able to take it, my eyes tearing; I said something weird, that I felt like Little Mama having her kittens; and then this melting, searing, crazed feeling burst like a sac containing millions of dazzling pearl-sized eggs, like pollen swirling through the air, like the white wisps of exploding seed heads. I got off the motorcycle, drowsy, almost falling over, wondering what had just happened to me.

By spring, I was getting naughtier than ever, throwing more tantrums, and bossing Peter around so often that he started to call me Sergeant Ma'am. My mother often said that he was giving in to me way too much lately, and that if he wasn't careful I'd be spoiled rotten. I was even starting to do mean things just for the thrill of it, like letting go of Peter's hand when we went to the playground and running across the street by myself. I also started to deceive Peter by breaking something and then concealing the damaged object, or hiding his cigarettes and lighter and then insisting I didn't know where they were.

"I don't like deception," Peter said. "We have a really strong bond now. Every lie you tell, whether large or small, is making a crack in our bond. It's just the tiniest crack, you can't see it, but this lying stuff—it only gets worse and worse. Let's make a pact right now, never to lie to each other and never to break any promises."

We made the pact and, for some reason, I took it very seriously, so I stopped lying. But I still had a habit of being naughty, which didn't upset Peter as much as the lying had, and he even tolerated downright nastiness from me—cruel practical jokes such as spilling his coffee down the sink when he was in the bathroom, or the times I mocked his false teeth or ugly ingrown toenails.

Mommy told Peter that I had many reasons for "acting out" and they were all linked to Poppa in some way. Recently laid off from work, he now started drinking early in the morning and continued to drink all day. He'd taken to spending the night in my room while I slept in the master bedroom with my mother. Whenever I went into my old room to get clothes, Poppa would scream at me to shut the door behind me because any light hurt his head. If he was really hungover he'd hurry me to the point where I came out with the wrong clothes, such as two shirts instead of a pair of pants and a shirt. According to Mommy, Poppa burned through his unemployment checks drinking and gambling, and he said if he wasn't allowed to do either he'd go into such a fit of despair he wouldn't even be able to get dressed in the morning.

I didn't know if I was acting out the day of my eighth-birthday party when I let the guinea pig loose. Peter had told me to go upstairs and feed Blackhead and put fresh water in his bottle. He also said to play with him for a while because Blackhead was looking a little lonely lately. I was thrilled to be given the responsibility. Peter had never sent me up to the attic alone before. Maybe since we'd made the pact not to lie he trusted me more. I raced up the attic stairs, nearly tripping on Ricky's skateboard, which clattered down the steps, blue twisty steps that wove and wound all around the wall. Inside the attic, the walls were dark blue. I hadn't known the room was blue until I saw it without Peter. Now that he wasn't with me, I noticed how messy it really was. Boy clothes, paper plates, paper cups, and cards were strewn all over the floor. I picked up a card and saw that it was a Garbage Pail Kid card with a picture of a tubby doll-like child lying on a bed of nails. I didn't know Miguel and Ricky collected those things, and it considerably lowered my opinion of them; I knew that boys liked gross things, but this was too much!

I sat cross-legged on the floor and began to look at the cards, hating their grossness but feeling unable to resist examining them. Kids at my school had taken to collecting these cards, and some of the girls had started to sing a hand-clapping song that was just as bad:

Say, say, my enemy, come out and fight with me,
We'll bring our B.B. guns; we'll have us lots of fun.
I'll gouge your eyes out and make you bleed to death.
When I was younger, I used to fight with girls,
But now I'm older I fight with B.O.Y.S.
Boys, boys, boys, boys, boys, boys!
Crisscross applesauce.

That day, I thought of the nurse's office at school, which was the most comforting place in the world. I'd been getting a lot of stomachaches lately. Sister Mary, the school nurse, had a very small room in her office with a white ceiling and white walls and stiff white bedsheets and a white fluffy pillow and a small brown cross with Jesus crucified yet looking serene with his arms outspread, his feet nailed safely down, his head bent to expose his crown of thorns. The ritual Sister Mary and I shared was the same each time: she would take my hand, lead me to the white bed, and then tell me to lie very flat and very still and look to the figure of Jesus on the cross for comfort and support.

On the white bed, ankles together, arms at my sides, I would wait for prickles to shoot up my legs, for the blood to thicken in my feet. Slowly, I would spread my arms out to the very upper corners of the bed: right arm, palm up; left arm, palm up. Legs straight, knees slightly lifted, and feet stilled by the nails that I imagined kept them safely pinioned. Chest cavity, elbow, belly, ankle, eyelash, all accounted for. Hair, fingernails, hip bones, shins, eyes, all accounted for. Be still, I would tell them like the conductor of some grand orchestra, you are all under my power now, my brain is in charge of you all. I could feel the tiny hairs in my nostrils and the down on my forearms and thighs and calves listen and obey. I could hear the gate to some tremulous heaven open and summon, palms, freckles, chest, ribs, hips, jaw, private parts. Like Noah leading the animals in pairs to the wide cedarwood ark, I hurried my heart and eardrums and navel into the wide white peace. When every part of me was packed up in the ark and sent down the rolling waves, the peace would come, drowsy as the sun, warming the wood of the cross that Jesus lay upon, warming the thorns that pierced his forehead, winking off the nails in his feet and palms.

Now, alone in the attic, I saw the pink wood swing hanging by brown braided ropes, looking shabbier than usual. I sat on it and started to push with my feet, but soon realized I couldn't get myself high enough.

I went to Blackhead's tank and saw him huddled in a corner. "Wake up!" I said, banging on the glass. "Wake up!"

When I saw his furry head rise, I lifted the chicken wire that was his ceiling. I pictured seeing the wire above, with all the round holes in it, suddenly lifting, and the hand surging down, and taking my body into it. I was rising, rising with the hand that was holding me just so snugly, and yet I was afraid. Blackhead was afraid. Poor Blackhead! I kissed his fur. I put his body to my face and breathed in his hot rodent smell. Poor, poor baby to be lifted from his nice small warm tank! But it was nicer outside; there was more space. I whispered this into his pink ear, but still the little heart beat too fast inside my hand.

My eyes turned back to the glass tank. Inside was a plastic yellow bowl that contained brown food pellets and a water bottle with a long metal tip. The wood shavings he slept on smelled sweet and dusky.

I set Blackhead on the floor. "Go, Blackhead! Run! Run!" I yelled, clapping my hands. But he wouldn't run; he just turned about in circles and sniffed at the floor. I knew I should put him back, but instead I headed for the stairs.

Downstairs, everyone erupted from hiding places, yelling, "Surprise!" There was a cake on the kitchen table, with candles. Peter lit one; then he touched that newly lit candle to all the others, until they, too, were burning. I looked to the faces around me, all lit. Flames were in the eyes of Ricky, Miguel, and Inès, in the eyes of my mother.

"Make a wish," Peter said, and I had to think of what my wish should be.

I blew hard and the flames turned to blackened wicks. All had extinguished but two, which Peter gently blew out for me.

"What was your wish?" he whispered, leaning over so I could whisper in his ear.

Normally, I wouldn't have told, for fear of destroying the wish's power, but at this moment, I felt giddy enough to get away with anything. "A tiger's tail," I told him.

"Eight is the most beautiful age for a girl," said Peter, after I opened my presents. "Though it makes me sad to see you growing up."

I was a little sad about it, too. When I was four or five, people would tell me that I would grow up, but I wouldn't believe them. I would not believe that my abilities as a child would end—fitting my body under tables, squeezing it under chairs and into tight corners. How I treasured this animal freedom, the joy of being able to tuck my legs and arms under, to slip through a hole in a fence or in the space between a giant tree trunk and a brick wall; this was my glory. Like a mouse living in an opening where the wall has cracked, or the brown recluse who builds her web in a wood beam in the ceiling and can see everything, or the ant that has a whole city of intersecting tunnels in the dirt, it's the glory of Blackhead . . .

Blackhead! I started to cry, and covered my face with my hands.

"What's wrong, honey?" Peter knelt on the cracked kitchen linoleum and took both my hands in his.

"I let the guinea pig loose."

There was no belt around the waist of Peter's red sweatpants that he could use to hit me with, as Poppa would have done. There was no anger in his eyes, only alarm, which moved like a virus, from one aqua eye to the other, and made his face rigid in a way that I had not seen before. And still, his first impulse was to console me with a "Don't worry, we'll get him," springing to his feet with a masculine power that electrified him all over, from the gray-blond sprinklings of hair on his arms, to his sandy-silver bangs, to his long, determined feet in their light, white sneakers. He quickly raced downstairs to fetch Ricky and Miguel, and when he returned, the three of us followed him upstairs, slouched to our knees, beginning the hunt. We looked under the bottom bunk bed; we cast clothes aside and invaded the closet; we inspected corners and checked under blankets. After we had checked everywhere else, Peter and Miguel hefted the bunk bed, and sure enough, the poor thing had balled up his body in the dustiest, driest, saddest corner. His glossy black, brown, and white fur was covered with dust and cobweb filaments that Peter carefully removed.

"This little fellow will be just fine," Peter said. "I'm glad we found him when we did."

"If we didn't find him," Ricky piped up, his voice taking on the thin pitch of boyish excitement, "his teeth might have kept growing. He needs to chew on wood to keep his teeth from getting long. Otherwise, they could grow right over his mouth and he won't be able to eat." He paused, and then, in a dire tone: "If a few months had passed, we might have found just a skeleton."

"Well, that didn't happen," Peter said hastily, returning the guinea pig to his tank, where he gratefully sucked on his bottle. "And it was kind of fun looking for him, like a game of hide-and-go-seek. The most important thing is that Margaux's birthday wasn't spoiled."

In my peripheral vision, I caught Miguel rolling his eyes. We watched Blackhead for a bit to make sure he was okay, and he was—he drank his water, kicked wood shavings into his usual nest, and went to sleep.

"Now that's the life," Peter chuckled, heading back downstairs.

Remesagil Jones Farm Market, the store that Peter took me to one Friday in May, was located on Bergenline Avenue across from the newspaper stand where my mother often bought her lottery tickets. It was one of the largest fruit-and-vegetable stores in Union City, boasting items with exotic names that, peering through his square reading glasses, Peter read off to me: Holland tomatoes, acorn squash, green and wrinkled chayote (which I said reminded me of Play-Doh), nanderines, Swiss chard, escarole, napa, knob celery. I laughed at some of the funny-sounding names, and when Peter started to bag some kale and turnips that were located toward the back of the market, I wandered off to rip the little plastic baggies off three at a time and press the scale to see the red arrows flit up like startled tongues. I loved this store—its fecund colors and dark crisp odors—I loved the giant cantaloupes that were like round bumpy suns but had surfaces that made me think of moons, and I wondered whether some of the swirling flies felt like astronauts when they perched upon them, eyelashlike legs lifting inquisitively.

Peter came up to me and said, "I almost forgot. Fiver is sick." Fiver was another rabbit; the half-grown son of Porridge and Peaches. "Do you think you could pick out a little something to make him feel better?"

"Oh, he loves carrots," I said, racing to those, but then I saw something green, shaped like elf slippers. "Actually, I want these!"

Peter refused me at first, saying they were pricey; then he gave in, as usual. I put the green beans in a baggie that he held open. Saying he couldn't afford anything more, he got into the long checkout line. His face seemed tight, impatient. Generally, he was always smiling. He had said a few times that I brought him total happiness, and that my love was the best thing that had ever happened to him. He had also said that he wanted to marry me when I was eighteen; I knew enough math to know that was only ten years away, and I was very happy about it too, because married people saw each other every day of the week, not just Mondays and Fridays. Married people could have babies, and they could live wherever they wanted. I told Peter I wanted to move to Westport, Connecticut, and live by a lake. When I told my mother I was going to marry Peter when I turned eighteen, she said, "You can marry him in heaven."

Peter continued to say how he felt sad that he couldn't make a baby with me now, because I had no working eggs. Sometimes he would say, "How's your belly?" a code that meant he was imagining me pregnant. Other times he would make a humming sound that meant he was picturing me naked. I didn't know why, but on occasion, it made me furious when he did this and I felt like hitting him.

I had entered the basement by only two of its three entrances: in the winter, by going down the soft wooden steps, or lately, because the weather had been warmer, through the heavy green doors at the back of the yard. But this time Peter, taking my hand, led me to the small cement slope at the front of the house and brought me to that narrow, oval-shaped wooden door. On the way, I glanced at the somber pink bear, even more covered in ivy than the year before, and the ivy now totally covered the mermaid's tail. Peter kept saying he was going to trim it before it hid the statues completely, but he hadn't gotten around to it yet.

"Are you mad? Are you mad?" I asked as we entered the basement. I knew by the way Peter was silent that there was something wrong with him. I felt a little afraid that he might be getting like Poppa, changing from happy to angry all the time, and that I'd never be able to predict or control him again.

Peter surprised me by saying Fiver was in the basement. He was sick all the time and, right now, he had to be kept quarantined from the other rabbits.

"Poor little guy! He's all by himself!" I said, rushing to the Pathmark shopping cart where Fiver was kept. "He must be sad alone here in the dark."

"No," said Peter, quickly. "He's not. Rabbits enjoy darkness. They live in warrens underground, in the wild, and when they're kept outside, the hutches need to be placed in shady areas. They like coolness and damp air. So don't think Fiver is unhappy here; he's really quite peaceful."

But he didn't look peaceful to me at all; he looked depressed. He was hunched in a corner with his head down, but not sleeping. He had a newspaper floor and a bowl of rabbit pellets and a bottle with a long metal tip. I took a bean from my pocket and stuck it through the mesh of Fiver's cart, but he wouldn't come over to take it no matter how I coaxed him.

"Is he going to get better? Or will he die?" I said, expecting the truth from Peter.

"Well, I think he'll improve," said Peter, though he didn't seem all that sure. "I've been buying the expensive brand of food, and giving him medicine from an eyedropper. As you can see, his home is tidy, his newspaper's changed every day, and he has plenty of water. I wouldn't worry about it. Sweetheart," he said, turning away from Fiver and taking both of my hands, "will you keep your promise to me?"

"What promise?"

"You said you would do anything. You made a promise."

"I don't remember."

"For the beans, remember? I said they were too expensive, just to feed to a rabbit; I said we should get carrots instead, and you already had them in your hands, a bunch of them; you said no, you wanted these, and that you would do anything in the world to have them. Remember?"

"Maybe. I guess so. I don't really remember."

"Well, you definitely said it," he said, softly.

"Okay."

We stood in silence for a second and then I began to talk quickly. "Remember the story of Jack and the Beanstalk? Do you think the pods are magic? They're like magic eggs. Maybe I'll get pregnant if I eat one."

Peter looked pleased when I said that, as I knew he would.

"Some kids at school were saying you can get pregnant from swallowing watermelon seeds."

"That's silly. Kids have so many misconceptions. Parents shouldn't lie to children about how babies are made. Kids should know the truth. The body is a natural, beautiful thing. I wish the world wasn't full of so much shame." He looked upset, as he did whenever he talked about the way the world was, and then he said, "Remember I told you how babies were made? I showed you my babymaker. My penis."

I didn't remember seeing Peter's before. "I saw Poppa's once. We took showers when I was younger."

"And why did he stop?"

"He said I was getting too old."

Peter shook his head and said something again about the trouble with society. Then I said, "Well, how is a baby made?"

He looked pleased with this question. "Human beings have organs that are magical. They combine with each other in this really beautiful, pleasurable way. Don't you remember anything I told you?"

"I don't remember."

"Imagine that: elementary schools teach children all about how plants reproduce but tell them nothing about the way human babies are conceived," he said. "Talk about repressing everything. I don't understand this society. Our body parts are beautiful and natural and we should be free to expose them wherever we go. I, because I'm male, have a penis and testicles; you, because you are a female, have a vagina and clitoris. These aren't dirty words; it isn't wrong to say them. It isn't wrong to speak the truth. I bet you didn't even know the names for your own reproductive organs until I told you."

"My mother calls it my private part. And she said once that no one should touch my private part. No one should touch my fanny either. But I don't think I agree," I said, hastily. "My parents are repressed."

"No kidding!" said Peter, looking even more wound up. "Think of a society that is so screwed up that you've got these untouchable parts and these are the same parts that happen to create the most pleasure, and everyone is brainwashed into believing that a perfectly natural thing is disgusting and wrong. And to think that these people pull their children's pants down to spank them and then they tell their children that no one should ever see them with their pants down."

"I know! I hate being spanked! And I don't know why I should take my pants down. Can't I be spanked with my pants on?"

Peter shook his head. "It's mixed messages, all of it. I'm sure your father feels perfectly justified telling you to take your underwear down, making you lie across his lap to be beaten with his belt; yet if he were to discover that anyone asked you to take down your pants, for the purposes of letting you know how beautiful you are, or to give you pleasure and joy, your father would probably kill that person. I have no doubt that your father would get his gun and shoot me if he found out I've seen you naked, yet he's nothing but a hypocrite and a child abuser. Oh, the big man, beating a defenseless child! With his belt, no less! Do you have any idea how sick that is? I know he's part of the culture; he was probably treated that way. Just passing it down. Generation to generation. No one stops to think."

Peter paused; I knew his question didn't require an answer. He lit a cigarette—which I thought was a little strange, since he rarely smoked in the basement—took a few puffs on it, and then ground it into one of the wooden ceiling beams. He began to pace.

"They tell you it's dirty; then they make you undress in front of them. When I was in a boys' school in upstate New York, the nuns used to whip us in the showers. In the showers, they would line us up and beat us! Yeah, like they didn't get some kind of a thrill out of looking at our naked bodies. You know why those nuns were so cruel? Sexual repression. Sexual repression and rage. This is what comes from all the repression in society. Do you know what I believe? I've even read literature on this. I believe that if children were to grow up with sexuality, as though it was normal and natural, which it is . . . If they were allowed to get joy and pleasure out of their God-given parts, this world would be a much better place."

"I agree," I said. I couldn't follow all the big words he said, but I got the gist. Like me, he hated rules and couldn't stand how adults were always trying to leave kids out of everything important. Yet something about this talk also made me uneasy.

Peter went on, "Mothers in certain parts of Africa massage their infants' genitalia before bedtime to help them sleep. There are tribes in the world that marry girls off at eight or nine. In certain tribes, you would be of marriageable age." He paused. "I love you. I want you to feel joy and I want you to be able to give me joy. There's nothing wrong with that. Can I show you? What I showed you before? My penis? You didn't really look at it. I think you were afraid. But I want you to know that our sexual organs are not ugly, they're not dirty, and they're not bad. They're beautiful and you don't have to be ashamed. So can I show you?"

I climbed into the cart with Fiver and said, "Look, Peter! I'm a rabbit!"

I started to drink from the water bottle, tasting the sweet metal and the sweet, warm water. I picked up the sad, curled pod, offered it again to Fiver, and when again he refused it, I ate it myself. It was so good, so crisp and green. I liked the feeling that the Pathmark shopping cart gave me, with its moist, strong-smelling newspaper beneath my hands and knees, its rectangular shape, the way the metal was crisscrossed, and the fact that it was on wheels. Peter came and picked me up gently, placed me on my feet; but I instantly sank again, to my hands and knees, to crawl on the ground like a baby, to feel the cold, hard floor beneath my hands.

"I'm a baby now, not a rabbit. No, wait, I'm a baby rabbit! Chase me!"

"Margaux," he said, looking disappointed. "You are eight years old and you know better." I hated it when adults told me I should know better, or that I already knew better. Peter had never told me that before, and I couldn't help but worry again that he was changing.

"Okay! Okay!"

He helped me up. "I'm sorry. I don't mean to sound like your father."

"Well, you are starting to sound like him."

"I'm sorry. That's the last thing I want. Anyway, it's true you're getting older. Not that you should stop playing childish games; I mean, you are a child, and I hope we can play children's games forever. But we can also do more mature things with each other, things that will give us both great pleasure. You made a promise earlier: you said you would do anything, and I would like you to try to do something very special and nice. Something that people in love, like we are, do together."

I stood there, as still as possible, and watched him take down his pants. He wasn't wearing any underwear. This time, I looked right at his penis, just to please him. The whole contraption looked like a bunless hot dog with two partly deflated balloons attached. The hair around his penis and testicles seemed stiff, like one of those steel combs used to groom dogs. I preferred my private area to his; it didn't have hair and looked like a woman's compact, the kind with the rouge and a little silver mirror. But I didn't want to tell him that; I was afraid he might get offended, so when he asked what I thought of it, I said, "It's nice. It kind of reminds me of a . . ." I tried to think of a metaphor he would like. "Of an ice cream cone. Since you've got freckles, it'd be the sprinkled kind, I guess."

"An ice cream cone with sprinkles. I've never been told that. Would you like to try to lick it, like you would an ice cream?"

"I'd rather have real ice cream, Peter."

"We can get one later. We can get anything you want. But right now, you can pretend this is ice cream."

I shook my head. "The problem, Peter, is that that thing . . ."

"My penis."

"Okay, penis."

"Don't be afraid to use the correct word."

"Okay, your penis, isn't that where you pee from?"

"Yes. Well, there's a little hole, see, and that's where I pee."

"I'm going to be licking pee. That's really gross."

"Well, why don't you just kiss it, then? Just kiss it right on the tip. It'll feel really good."

"No, I don't want to."

"Why?"

"I can't."

"Why?"

I knew that what I was going to say next would make Peter angry, but I was mad now myself. "It's disgusting, Peter! Just stop it! Just stop telling me what to do!"

"You made a promise. You promised me anything. Now you're going back on your word."

"This is unfair!"

"How so?"

"It just is!"

"How is it unfair? You made a promise and I'm asking you to keep your promise, and we swore we'd never lie to each other."

"I didn't know what you were going to ask for. You didn't tell me!"

"Well, then you shouldn't have said 'anything.' 'Anything' means anything."

"I can't do it!" I was on the verge of tears. "I can't! You're going to make me throw up if I do it. If you make me kiss pee, Peter, I am going to throw up!"

"There's no pee! It's clean. Society has brainwashed you with its rules."

"I can't stand rules!"

"No, you're like everybody else," he said, pulling up his pants, backing away as he spoke. "Don't worry, I won't make you do anything. The bad man isn't going to hurt you! I'm not going to force you to do anything! I'm not like that! What kind of person do you think I am?"

He opened the basement door and started to stride out.

"No, wait, Peter, wait!" I grabbed on to his T-shirt.

"Let go of me!"

"I can try, maybe, now that I'm used to the idea, maybe I can try."

"Let go! Don't talk about it anymore!"

"But I'm not like them, Peter. I'm my own person."

He snorted.

"I really am, Peter! I am!"

He turned to me, there in front of the house, in the savage sunshine, and whispered in a choked-up way, "You think my body is disgusting. You don't like me because I'm an old man. You think I'm ugly."

Fiver died two weeks later. The day after, I was standing in line in the big blue playroom where we lined up before the first bell at school, in my blue jumper, ankle socks, and Buster Brown shoes. I shifted my weight from one foot to the other. I felt my knees sinking so I straightened my legs, feeling my blood prickling and tingles shooting through my feet. To keep busy, I played with the hood string of my light spring jacket, which my mother had insisted I wear though the late-May weather was too warm. I wound the string around my finger, let it go, watched it snap back at me, then repeated the process. When one leg started to hurt, I pushed everything over to the other side. Sister Mary was nearby in her white habit; I hadn't realized I'd been sobbing until she put her arms around me.

"What's wrong, sweetheart? What's wrong?"

I couldn't stop crying enough to speak, and besides, I liked the sound of her saying "What's wrong?" I wanted her to keep saying it, and to hold my sadness close. She pulled my hand along gently, and I knew where we were going. Within my sorrow sparked a small delight, for I knew I would not have to go to class.

Inside the white room in her office, Sister Mary kept asking me what was wrong, but my mind drew a strange blank. I couldn't even remember that Fiver had died until she asked me to lie down on the bed and began to stroke my face.

"Do you feel dizzy?"

"Yes."

"Sick to your stomach?"

"Everything. I feel like everything is wrong."

"Are you having a problem? Or are you just sick?"

"My rabbit died yesterday."

"Oh, I'm sorry to hear that. Just keep in mind that the rabbit is in heaven. He's happier now than when he was alive. Because heaven is a beautiful place. With lovely gardens and streams and the most colorful birds you can imagine."

"What about things to eat?"

"Carrots and lettuce and grass and whatever rabbits eat; it's all there." She took my hand.

"I think I'm dying, too."

She held my hand tighter. "Don't say such things. It's not true. You're just grieving. We all grieve and then we get better."

"I drank from the same water bottle as he did, Sister. I think it's catching. I also ate something bad. It was something that wasn't mine;

that I didn't pay for. We were at the store, my mother and I, the fruit market . . . and, and I stole a green bean. I ate it when no one was looking. That's why I'm sick today."

"Well, I'm glad you told me that. I'm going to allow you to see Father John today and confess your sin. After confessing, you're going to feel much better. That's why we have confession, to wash the bad things off our souls so we can one day return to God. Stealing is a venial sin. I'm sure he won't give you that many Our Fathers, just a few. And maybe some Hail Marys as well. And you'll be as good as if it never happened."

"Sister, you don't think God would punish me by killing my rabbit? You don't think it's a penance?"

She stroked my hair. "No. This is your guilt speaking. I'm going to tell you a little secret. When I was a small girl around your age, I stole something from a five-and-dime store. I didn't confess right away, and I felt guilty just like you. My stomach hurt and I had a lot of headaches. You see, sometimes we don't always do the right thing because we are, by nature, sinners. We can't help that we're not perfect."

"I know I'm not perfect, Sister, but I feel like I'm the worst girl in the world."

"No, dear, it's not true. No. No, Margaux, no."

7

KAREN, MY SISTER, MY SISTER

After I returned from a three-week trip to Puerto Rico with Poppa that June (Mommy had to go the hospital, so she missed it), I discovered my days as the only little girl in Peter's household were over. Karen came to be my sister with her faded pink dress and her naked baby doll with its dirty face. She came with chipped front teeth and dirty fingernails. She came with a red Popsicle beard and a hippy sashay that I would never be able to imitate. She came with one white ankle sock pulled up and one crunched around her ankle and her hair in unraveling pigtails. We stood facing each other, each feeling superior to, and wary of, the other, in Peter's backyard by the cement birdbath. Karen carried a rusty green watering can: it was the same one I always used to water the tomato plants.

"Go on, give each other a hug," Peter said. "That's the best way to get to know each other. I can't think of a nicer way."

We did embrace, stiffly, and that was when Peter said, "Just like sisters. You two are going to get along fine."

I couldn't help but be shocked by the way Karen behaved. She spat on the ground. She cursed, using words that I had never even heard of, though I was eight and she was only six. Peter said that Karen had had a rough time and I should be patient with her—Karen's mother was a drug addict—and this was her fourth foster home. He called it synchronicity that Karen had arrived just when he was beginning to become depressed about me leaving for Puerto Rico. "I had no idea when you were coming home," he told me when we were alone together. "I wasn't even sure if we would ever see each other again. Karen really helped keep my mind off of it." When he saw the look on my face, he quickly said, "But of course no one can replace you, sweetheart."

I didn't understand Peter's need for Karen, but I knew that he would force me to love her. I had already disappointed Peter once, and I wasn't going to chance falling out of his favor again. Maybe Karen, despite her wild ways, or perhaps because of them, could be a lovable sort of girl. Peter seemed to adore Karen, and my mother took an immediate liking to her, often calling her a "sweet girl" regardless of her being from "a bad home." My mother was relieved to be out of the hospital; also, she was pleased when Poppa finally found another job as a jeweler, and began to work overtime to make up for the financial blows we'd suffered while he was unemployed. I could tell she was glad to be back in the routine of going to Peter's every Monday and Friday; she complained that the hospital had been boring, and that while she was there her medication was altered, which caused her to get severely depressed and even paranoid for a while. This kind of thing happened nearly every time she went. There were always new drugs coming out, and hospitals received free trial samples, which psychiatrists automatically considered the latest miracle breakthroughs. When the new drugs inevitably didn't work, my mother would end up back on Zoloft and Thorazine. Peter was outraged. "These people use you like a guinea pig," he said, "like you don't have any rights." My mother shrugged at that and said that the system was the system.

I could tell my mother thought Karen was the best thing in the world for me. "The teachers have mentioned how withdrawn Margaux's become at school lately," Mommy remarked soon after meeting Karen. "Maybe playing with another little girl will get her out of her shell."

Inès, too, loved Karen, as she had never loved me. She even took a week off work in July, and I remember seeing them together in the yard, bowed over the flower patch, under the white birdbath, showing Karen how to dig with the small metal shovel and tuck a petunia in like an infant. Sometimes she would end up dislodging earthworms or even a white grub, which caused me to scream though I'd never been afraid of insects before. Now I didn't much like gardening. Karen, however, wasn't afraid of earthworms or the occasional grub; she simply covered them back up with soil.

Peter hadn't taken me down to the basement ever since I'd disappointed him, and I was both relieved and nervous: if he wasn't taking me, did that mean he was taking Karen, and was she more daring than I was? Was she doing what I'd been too chicken to try? I worried about this incessantly, and kept a tight watch over Karen and Peter, so they couldn't slip off alone.

I specifically made sure Peter didn't use the humming code with Karen. I didn't want him picturing Karen naked, and I couldn't stand the thought that there was anything special between them. I told myself Karen was too young; Peter wouldn't want her. He had said eight was the most beautiful age, not six. He'd waited until I was eight to ask me for the special thing he'd wanted. Besides, he loved me in a different way than Karen; I could tell that he saw her as just a daughter. It was *me* who had the potential to be his wife and the mother of his children, because I was already so mature for my age, and though I'd let him down before, I was pretty sure he'd forgiven me by now.

Karen's pale eyelashes were spaced far apart, giving her a startled look, but then something in her eyes dismissed that impression; and you realized right away that this was a little girl who was rarely surprised, rarely afraid—a child with force, will, power.

Once, I poured a pitcher of grape punch all over the front of her dress at one of Peter's barbecues. We'd been fighting over a doll, and ripped it apart limb by limb. She shouted with horrid glee that she had the head, she had the head, the arms and legs were useless without the head! I never hit her, though I often wanted to, and she hit me at liberty. I learned that by controlling my temper, I would appear angelic by comparison. Peter would drag Karen, punching and kicking, to her room; he would lock the door on her, while I remained outside, with Peter. Peter would always say: "I hate to lock her in her room but what else can I do? She can't be allowed to hurt us or break things."

Karen's room was a portion of the living room; Peter had installed a wall and door so that she would have her own room, which was one of the requirements for having a foster child. Through the thin drywall partition, we heard Karen scream and thrash and throw things, and then finally cry and cry and cry. Unable to stand her sorrow after a while, I always managed to finagle the key to that room from Peter, though he said every time, "You're too soft on her, Margaux. She'll never learn this way."

Once inside Karen's room, I would do whatever was necessary to make her laugh, whether it was putting on a puppet show with the headless Barbie dolls (she always lopped off their heads during a tantrum) or tickling her on her belly and under her arms. Pretty soon, we were playing; sometimes, we played a game called Queen, and in deference to Karen, I always took the role of princess. In order to be queen, Karen would wear a cardboard Burger King crown on her head and wave a purple-and-white pom-pom, commanding me to bring this or that to her. Eventually, Peter would enter the room, saying, "Okay, Karen, you've been in there long enough!" Then out we would charge, grabbing his hands. Karen would often pass the Burger King crown to him, demanding that he be the king and start telling us what to do.

Inès's neon orange motorcycle helmet was only slightly too big for my head. The first time Peter let me try it on, Karen got jealous and started a tantrum. But Peter was firm with her, saying that she was much too young to go out on a motorcycle and, besides, there was no helmet in existence that could fit her tiny head. I felt a mean sense of triumph ripple through me when he said this. Let Karen stay stuck in the yard with Mommy, while I got to go riding on the bike. Let Karen be sad for a change; I was sad every time I had to leave Peter's house and she got to stay. I was sad that she was allowed to get real dirty in the yard, while I had to keep my clothes semiclean for Poppa. I was sad that she was like Peter and Inès's daughter, the sister of Miguel and Ricky, and I was just the girl that came two days a week, even though Peter said he loved me better than he loved her, but I was never to tell her that.

I always made a big production about how pretty the helmet was, just like a crown, with its glazed orange color that reflected white sugar dots of light, with its Pegasus and rainbow stickers. In reality, I despised the helmet and wanted to ride without it, so I could feel the wind winnowing my hair. At first, my mother was terrified that I would fall off the motorcycle; Peter showed her the helmet, and said that if such a thing were to occur, my head would be protected; besides, that would never happen, because he had been driving motorcycles for more than thirty years. I kept saying, "Only around the block," until she finally gave in. She stood by the curb, as I climbed on the Suzuki for the first time, repeating warnings like, "Don't lean over too far," and "Hold on to Peter at all times."

Peter taught me to lean whenever he did while tightly holding his waist, in the same direction, and only as far as he did, never farther. Going around the block, of course, I didn't need to know much about leaning, but later I would when we had to maneuver the bike around complex turns. This made me the driver too, and I would feel a great sense of pride when Peter would tell me I was the perfect passenger.

My hair was getting long, and by the start of August it was three inches past my shoulders, which meant Poppa hadn't paid much attention to it in a while; for years, he had insisted that it never fall even slightly past my shoulders. Whenever he noticed it getting longer, he would immediately take me to the hairdresser's for a pert bob, which he said was stylish for little girls, though this was a lie: most of my classmates sported hair that nearly reached the middle of their backs. It was a marker of a girl's social status for her hair to be styled differently every school day; while school was in session, my plain, unruly hair had often been mocked by girls who possessed French or Dutch braids and twists, pristine half and full ponytails, or fancy double buns. One day, I complained about this problem to Peter—mentioning how I dreaded another approaching school year when my ugly hair would be the laughingstock yet again—and he promised that he would find a comb that would undo my knots without the least bit of pain.

The first time Peter showed me the magical purple comb he'd bought at the flea market for a quarter, I was fascinated by it. It was unlike any comb I had ever seen, with two inward-curving sets of teeth. He said he would start at the ends of my hair and work his way to the top. So I sat on his lap in the kitchen and, gently, he began to work out the tangles. My hair was so badly matted it took over an hour of sitting still to untangle. But it wasn't as bad as I'd feared, because while I sat, we talked about "Danger Tiger." We also took breaks to eat chocolate-chip and oatmeal-raisin cookies.

Mommy watched Peter untangle my hair, and kept saying how amazed she was that he had gotten me to sit so still. When he was done, he put in two yellow plastic barrettes, one on each side.

"Go, honey, look in the mirror," he said, and I raced into the front room to look at myself in the full-length mirror that stood opposite the front door.

The large wooden mirror had carved birds. Peter had sprayed it with deep gold paint that made it look even more old-fashioned. I stood in front of the glass, touching my glossy hair. Peter came up behind me and put both hands on my shoulders.

"I'm going to start braiding it, like Karen's," he said. "It should be long enough."

"Peter, do you like me better with long hair or short?"

"It doesn't matter, sweetheart. But I guess I've always liked long hair on little girls."

We stared at each other in the mirror for what must have been a good minute; Peter was on his knees, so his face lined up perfectly with mine.

A few days later, at the dinner table, I saw Poppa squinting at me in a funny way.

"Your hair is getting long," he said, stiffly. "I didn't notice that."

I shifted uneasily in my seat. "It was a little bit long in Puerto Rico."

"My sister took care of it, unlike your mother. But I see someone is combing it out now. Let me see the back."

I reluctantly turned my head. He nodded and turned to my mother. "Have you been combing her hair?" He sipped his beer and cut his stuffed pepper in half.

My mother swallowed her food and then said, "Well, there's a new kind of comb out, you know."

"A new comb?" He raised his eyebrows. "Some kind of a break-through?"

"Well, at the flea market, they sell all sorts of . . ."

"You are buying things at some dirty flea market?"

"No, not exactly," she said, tightly holding her 7-Up, but not lifting it to drink. I had stopped eating.

"I give you enough money to buy quality things. I do not give you money to spend on used junk. I do not give you money to buy a comb that has been in some strange person's hair. My daughter could have lice now. She could have lice in her hair!" Poppa was the only one who was still eating; he ate while he waited for her answer.

"The comb was clean; it was washed. I didn't get the comb, any-way; Peter picked it up. It was only a quarter. It was a good deal. It was clean. It's a good comb. It was cleaned beforehand; Peter washed it."

I didn't know why, but I felt sick to my stomach as soon as she said the comb had been cleaned first.

"Who combed the hair? That man's wife? Wait, they are not even married. Okay, the woman, that woman he lives with. Did that hip-pie woman he lives with comb your daughter's hair? The reason I ask is because you are not capable of anything. You are not even capable of combing your daughter's hair. I have to keep it short because she will look like a rat otherwise. I have to keep up on it because nobody else does. So tell me, did that hippie woman, did she comb out the hair for you? Ask her if she can come here and cook one night. Do you think she can come here and cook me a nice roast pork?"

"I hate sarcasm. I would cook if you'd let me."

"And burn this house down? I do the cooking here. I am the one who cleans. I do everything here. I do everything and you do nothing. I am a slave for you people."

"I'm tired of hearing it," Mommy muttered.

"What was that?"

"Nothing. Anyway, Inès didn't comb her hair; Peter combed her hair. He did a good job: it's not tangled anymore."

"You let that man comb your daughter's hair?" Then louder, "You let *that man* comb your daughter's hair?"

"Yes, what's wrong with that?"

Poppa got silent and then said, "I need to meet this man; this man who causes such a great fuss!"

"He's not a fuss. Margaux spends most of her time with the two boys and the little girl."

"What little girl?"

"There's a little girl, Karen."

"There was no girl before."

"She's a foster child. I, for one, think it is wonderful for people to take in children from bad homes."

"This girl is from a bad home? What kind of bad home?"

"The mother was a drug addict. The poor thing."

"My daughter is around people who are from bad families."

"Peter's family is not a bad family. It's a very good family."

"These people are not even married."

"So what? They are a nice family!"

"Tell me, what kind of values are you trying to teach your daughter?" Poppa folded his arms across his chest.

"I would rather not talk about this."

"So, so . . ." Poppa was quiet for a moment. "Do you let her take a shower there? If she gets dirty outside you don't let her use their bathtub, do you?"

"No, I don't."

"She could get a disease."

"She doesn't use it."

"I want to meet this man, you know. I want to meet that man and the woman, too. I want them to come to Benihana."

"Benihana? They don't have that kind of money. You're going to have to pick a cheaper restaurant, something within their price range. It's not easy with three kids to support. They don't have it easy. Not at all."

"Well, you can tell these people that I will treat. I will pay for them *both*. I can afford it."

The next day, a Thursday, after work, Poppa told me he was taking me for a walk. I asked where we were going, and he said we were going to get ice cream. About two blocks into the walk, I sensed Poppa was lying; the Carvel was on the corner of Thirty-eighth and Bergenline Avenue, but we were on Thirty-ninth and Hudson Avenue. Poppa would have turned by now, since he preferred walking on Bergenline to taking the boring side streets. And there was no way he would want to pass Union Hill High School, where, according to him, all the savages gathered.

"Where are we going, Poppa?"

He hesitated. "To the beauty salon."

I stopped and just stood there, in the middle of the sidewalk, with Poppa tugging my arm.

"Let's go."

"My hair isn't tangled anymore!"

"Let's go. You be good. Afterwards, I will buy ice cream. I will get you a toy. Come on."

"No, I'm not going!"

He grabbed my arm and pulled. "Let's go!"

"Please! Don't cut it!"

"You want to make trouble for me. You want to humiliate me," he said in a low voice. "You want me to be the talk of this town. Do you see the people looking?"

By now, I was in a full-fledged tantrum, crying and begging and stamping my feet against the cement.

He pointed to a few teenagers passing Union Hill High. "Look at them looking at you."

We were standing in front of the building and I could see Good Fellows Barber Shop right across Hudson Avenue at Thirty-eighth Street. I thought of biting Poppa's hand and running all the way to Peter's, but I knew Poppa was faster than I was.

"Why are you doing this to me?" I screamed. "Why? Why are you doing this?"

He let go of my hand and we stood facing each other. "You. You. I'm ashamed to be seen on this street. Let them talk; they are talking about you. Let them laugh; they are laughing at you. Not me. You are the one making a fool of yourself on a public street. Now I see what that house has done to you. You have been going to that house for a year now, and the effects on your temperament are not good. You are turning against me. Tell me"—he lifted my chin and stared into my eyes—"tell me: what has that house done to you? If you do not listen to me, your father, I will make you sorry. You will cry; you will really cry when I take the privilege of that house away from you. I know you will cry then because that is all you care about. So you better watch it."

I began to walk, and he took my hand again.

"Good," he said.

While we waited for a hairdresser, neither Poppa nor I flipped through the magazines that were scattered on the small end table. Poppa clutched my hand, his leg jittering. I was afraid to talk to him at first, but then I said, softly, "Poppa, not much, please?"

"I will tell them to take off a little. You have split ends. It needs to be done."

"Just a little? You promise?"

"I promise nothing. These women are experienced; they know exactly what to do. I am a man; I know very little about hair. I will tell them to use their judgment."

"Poppa, you said you would tell them a little! Now you're saying something different!"

"You better not start up," he said, squeezing my hand. "You better not humiliate me."

I was silent, until he released the pressure from my hand. "Okay, but can I tell you something? School is coming soon; the other girls all have long hair. I'm the only one in school with short hair; they make fun of me. If you have them take off too much, I am really going to, it's going to, I mean, I am . . ." I cleared my throat and concentrated on not crying. "I am going to suffer, Poppa. It's hard looking different from everybody else. I want to look like all the other girls. I have to look like them, or they'll laugh at me. They'll call me a freak and ugly."

He didn't say anything.

"Do you hear me, Poppa?"

He still didn't say anything.

"I am going to suffer, Poppa."

"I will tell them just a little bit. If this makes you happy, I will tell them just a trim, okay?" He squeezed my hand, this time in a friendly way, and I was relieved.

A hairdresser with long white nails and a fluffy perm dressed me in the wide smock and led me into the shampooing room, where I lay back in the reclining leather seat, allowing my hair to fall into the basin filled with warm water. After the shampooing, I was led to the large swivel chair in front of the big, clean mirrors. I saw hairspray bottles, fancy combs, and brushes and hair dryers. Vidal Sassoon, Aqua Net. Poppa talked to the woman in Spanish.

"How much did you tell her, Poppa?"

"I told her to get rid of the split ends. Do not move while she does this. You might get cut. It might help to close your eyes. Sometimes there is a slip. I do not want you to move suddenly and get blinded."

I didn't close my eyes. But when the little hairs from the bangs began to fall into them, Poppa simply covered my eyes with his hand.

I felt the whisker tickle of the short brisk hairs on my cheeks. I felt her turn my head to the left and then to the right and hold my chin still. I felt the tips of her long nails and soft fingers. I felt the wide black smock, its stiff fabric, the way its cuff encircled my throat too tightly.

"Sit still! Do you want her to cut you? You are doing well. Sit still."

"Okay, all done."

The first thing I saw were my bangs. Then I noticed that the hair came only to my ears. I screamed.

"Shh. Stop. Behave yourself." He put his hand on my mouth and my teeth touched his fingers. "You look good. I am proud. You can wear this kind of haircut. It is called a pixie cut. This is the trend. You have a model's face. You can get away with this. Many Hollywood girls have these cuts. The runways of Paris are filled with short-haired girls."

"You lied to me," I said, as the hairdresser put the hand mirror in back of my head so I could see, whisking the hair up with her hand, and forcing a too-bright smile.

"Come, let's get ice cream now. Perhaps we can take a walk to Woolworth's; you can pick out a nice toy, some coloring books."

"You lied to me! You told her to take off more than you said!"

"You are embarrassing me. We will discuss this when we are alone. Let's go."

Outside, the summer heat came blasting against my neck. My back still itched from where hair had fallen into my shirt. "I look like a boy! Look at me; look how I look!"

"This is all the fault of that stupid woman. I told her to cut only a little. These people like to do things their own way. I gave her a bad tip for that."

"You gave her three dollars!"

"Normally, I tip five. This is why I like to get my hair cut by an experienced barber, personally. These young girls never listen."

"You talked in Spanish so I couldn't hear! I'm not stupid!" I was screaming. "You want them to make fun of me! You want me ugly like a boy! You want to ruin my life! I hate you! I hate you!"

"You hate me. Fine. This is inevitable. Perhaps you should cut down on going to that house. It is inevitable that you would rebel under the influence of savages!"

"No! You better not! You better not!"

"You hate me. This is the way it turns out. You hate me; well, okay, you know what, if you are going to hate me, I am going to hate you as well! I can hate, too! Let's go!"

"I don't care if you hate me! I don't care what you think!"

"You are an animal. You are a wild beast. You are not even human. No wonder they mock you! Let's go. It is not your hair; it is you! I feared that being raised by that sick woman, you would turn out bad, and I was right. You are a bad seed. Let's go. You take my hand!"

"No!"

"You take my hand right now!"

When Peter first saw my haircut, his eyes welled with tears and I could see he was saddened by my new appearance.

Later, when my mother was out shopping at Pathmark and Karen played on the living room floor with some Tinker Toys Peter had gotten for her from a flea market, he said, "I can't believe your father did this! This is child abuse!"

Karen looked up. "My hair is still long," she said.

Peter ignored her. "He has no right to cut your hair short! He doesn't own you! Nobody has the right to control your body!"

8

"ONLY IF YOU WANT TO"

Karen started first grade and I began third. I found that the cursive-writing practice books that bored everyone else were my heart's delight, and I even earned a penmanship pin that I would wear proudly. That October, with Peter's encouragement, I composed my first handwritten story on lined notebook paper. "The cat and the dog are the best of friends. They live together in a big house, with lots of furniture. Then one day the dog makes a big mess and wrecks the whole place. He scratches and bites everything up. But that night, Kitty sweeps and sweeps and dusts and mops. Until all the dirty dirt is washed away and they are happy again. The End."

I continued to write, but now for an audience. Carefully, Peter bound those loose-leaf papers in an album marked *Margaux's Stories* and kept them in the black trunk with the broken latch along with the two thick photo albums called *Margaux: Images*; and yet another album, entitled *Margaux's Art*, which was filled with my drawings. I wasn't a very good visual artist, but Peter seemed to think everything I drew was a masterpiece. There was this one drawing I had made him for Father's Day, of a tiger and an eagle (Peter's favorite animal) inside a large heart; underneath the heart were their children: tiger cubs with wings. One Friday, Peter took this drawing out of the album, put it in a dark gold frame, and hung it on the wall of his room, where it would remain for the next fourteen years.

Recently, I had begun having trouble sleeping at night. When I woke early, I took advantage of the time: descending the stairs quietly, turning on the soft kitchen stove light and working for hours on a paper ladybug play set. Since Poppa had to get up so early now for work, he wasn't creeping around the house anymore at odd hours, but one night on his way to the bathroom, he stopped in the middle of the kitchen and glared at me; I looked back at him. I expected him to yell, but for some reason, he didn't; he just stared at me like he wished I were dead, then darted back up the stairs.

In the backyard, Peter and I would sometimes lie in a white hammock under the giant ailanthus tree. Its trunk was so thick that it could have fit me, Mommy, and Karen inside it. I had never seen such a thick tree. Porridge and Peaches would be nestled inside their wooden hutch, their noses twitching against the chicken wire, after we had fed them baby carrots and brown rabbit pellets. On the opposite side of the yard, Inès had planted sunflowers; Peter said that she liked them best. Peter's favorite flower was the rose; the large white ones were called bourbon roses, and the smaller ones at the front of the house were ballerina roses. He also grew pink blessings; he said pink was his favorite color, and that maybe they would bring what their names promised.

I'd teased him about this, saying pink was a girl's color, but he didn't seem to mind; he said no one teased girls for liking blue, so why should he be ashamed for liking pink?

Whenever we were in the backyard, Karen would sometimes jump into the hammock with us and we would swing back and forth until we thought the thing would break. Every once in a while, we'd get rowdy, tickling or trying to push each other out. But most of the time, it was just Peter and I rocking back and forth, breathing in the flowers and the cool black dirt. Paws would dig a hole and lie beside us. I asked Peter why Paws dug a hole before he lay down, and Peter said it was because the dirt beneath the top layer of soil was cooler.

Ever since my haircut, I had barely even talked to Poppa, and often, when he wasn't looking, I would spit the food he cooked into paper napkins and then dispose of it later. Poppa didn't seem at all sorry about what he had done; his reaction to my ignoring him was to ignore me right back and to occasionally yell about me in the third person, calling me a beast and a demon child. If he'd known I was going to grow up just to turn on him, he wouldn't have wasted his time and money and life on me. One time when he was yelling at the dinner table, I got so angry that I slammed my plate down and the chicken and yellow rice and green olives scattered across the table. He grabbed me by the arm and my mother screamed, "Don't hurt her, get away from her!" He let go of my arm and struck her across the chest, nearly knocking her down. Then he looked at me backing away from him, and said, "You coward, go run away from me, coward!" He raised his fist and came at me. I backed up until the wall touched my back, and he started laughing. "You think I am going to hit you? I am not going to touch you. You are a coward. I am not going to hit you! Go, hide against the wall, cry like a baby!" Then he went upstairs to get dressed for the bar.

I didn't care about him anymore. I would go on ignoring him. I didn't even care if he saw me up at three, four in the morning: cutting, gluing, punching holes with a ballpoint pen. I didn't care if he gave me his mean look from the stairs at 3:00 a.m.; I could look mean too, and whenever I would give him a dirty look, he'd just quietly go back upstairs.

It took me two weeks to draw all the ladybugs, color them in, and then make paper clothes for them—jackets, pants, dresses, and sweaters. I'd punched out little holes for the arms and legs, and colored in fine details, like the buttons of a sweater or the polka dots on a dress. The ladybugs were all named; they were all part of my story. There was only one girl ladybug; her name was Mime, and I found it difficult to make her hair; I had to cut a small piece of paper into long straight pieces, and glue it on her head. I also included little paper carriages for babies, tiny paper roller skates with swirled specks of thread purloined from my mother's sewing kit to decorate the wheels, and a TV set made out of a Sun-Maid raisin box.

Then I presented the whole cast of ladybugs to Peter, who said, "Wow."

On the kitchen table, after spreading everything out, I started to show him how to dress the ladybugs carefully, without ripping them. "This is so nice. But, sweetheart, wouldn't you rather leave this at home and play with it when you're alone? It's too nice to waste on me. I'm an adult; I can't really enjoy it."

"You don't want them?"

"No, it's not that, it's just that I . . . Well, I thought you would really enjoy playing with them. More than I can at my age."

"They're for you! I made them for you!"

"Oh, okay, sweetheart. Of course I want them."

"If you don't want them, I'll throw them out."

"No, I'll play with them," Peter said. "While you're gone and I'm missing you, I'll play with them."

"Are you sure you'll play?"

"Yes, if you show me exactly how to take care of them and tell me all their names. I'll play with them with Karen."

"No! Karen will ruin everything; she won't be careful!"

"Yes, I suppose you're right. Karen won't mean to, but she'll ruin them."

Peter stored the ladybug play set inside the big black trunk with the broken latch, where he kept all his other "me" stuff. They might have lasted forever, inside the trunk, and yellowed with age, like the framed tiger-and-eagle picture, if Karen hadn't gotten into the trunk one night and ripped up all the ladybugs and their accessories. When Peter told me, there were tears in his eyes.

"I'm sorry, sweetheart. Karen did it while Inès and I were sleeping."

"Did you punish her?"

"Yes, I spanked her. I don't like to spank children, and usually I don't believe in it, but this was a horrible thing that Karen did. You spent so much time on those ladybugs. So I spanked her, and then made her stay in her room all day. All she did was cry, but I wouldn't let her out."

My mother now allowed me and Peter to drive all the way to Hudson Park on the motorcycle. In the woods surrounding a big lake, Peter would make sure no one was looking, and then ask for a fish kiss. A fish kiss was made by puckering your lips like one of those kissing fish at the pet shop. The fish kisses were not as gross as other kinds of kissing, since our lips barely touched. By now, I'd gotten used to most forms of kissing; the only kiss I didn't like was the Bazooka Joe. The Bazooka Joe was rare: we never did this in public, because it took too long. Peter would buy some Bazooka Joe gum, we'd read the short comic strip, and then I'd take the hard square of gum and chew it into mush. I'd pass the gum to Peter and he would pass it back to me. Our tongues couldn't help but touch, and to me, it felt like a fish flapping against my mouth. Every time this new kind of kissing happened, I would feel for a second that it was gross; then the emotion would die off as suddenly as it had appeared. Whenever I lost an emotion like this, I couldn't feel much of anything for the rest of the day, sometimes for the next few days. Lately, Poppa had been saying I was cold and heartless, just like "the bitch in Connecticut," and I wondered if he might be right.

This year, I'd be taking First Communion; I told Peter on one of our strolls at Hudson Park to see the leaves changing. I couldn't wait to receive the flesh of Jesus and be part of God. Some kids didn't understand Communion, though; they just thought that the whole thing was gross, and they even wondered why they couldn't chew the host.

"Idiots," I said, tearing a brownish green leaf off a nearby syca-more. "They think they can bite into the host like it's a wad of old bubble gum or something. This terrible boy in my class even said he was going to bite it on purpose. But the girls in my class are even dumber than the boys. We have to watch movies, sometimes, where Jesus dies, on the cross, and there's this moronic bunch of girls who always carry packets of tissues. And when Jesus is crucified, they all just start wiping their eyes as though they're sad."

"Your mother told me the other day that she thinks I was Jesus in another life."

"I know, she's always saying that."

We sat under a weeping willow and Peter put his arm around me. The air here smelled so sweet and different from the city.

"You know, my birthday's coming up. I know you don't have any money—you shouldn't worry about buying me anything. Have you thought about what you'd like to give me?"

"Well, I don't think it's good to talk about presents beforehand," I said, thinking of the new ladybug play set I was working on at home. "It ruins the surprise."

"I agree. But can I give you a hint on what I might want?"

"Okay. Give me hints, if you want, but I already have ideas about what I want to give you, 'kay? So if it's not exactly what you want, you can't be disappointed?"

"Of course not. How could I be disappointed in you, sweetheart?" He lit a cigarette. He tended to smoke more when my mother wasn't around to see him. "Okay, first clue: it doesn't cost anything. Not a single nickel."

"Okay . . . it's free. Next clue."

"Well, it's something I've been wanting for a while. It's something special and nice. It's something that people who are in love, like you are with me, people who are going to get married someday, it's something they do together as a show of love."

"Peter, do you want me to do that thing?" I said. It seemed easier to just ask and get it over with.

"Only if you want to and only if you're ready."

"I'd have to think, Peter. About whether I'm ready yet or not."

"No pressure. Only if you want to, sweetheart. No pressure."

9

"IT'S NOT WRONG TO LOVE YOU"

The night before Peter's birthday, I accidentally ripped a lady-bug in half while trying to dress it in a sweater. I would never be done with this new set in time! Never! With my arm, I swept all my newly created ladybugs off the table, and then I started pounding my fists against the wood. Suddenly, I sensed something and turned around. Poppa was behind me in his white undershirt and boxers.

"What are you doing? What the hell is this noise! Look at the floor! What the hell is this noise at this time of night! I have to get up for work, don't you understand! You are an animal! Get up! Get out of that chair!"

"No!"

"Get up so I can sweep! Look at what you did! Look at this! Are you proud? Get up!"

"No! Let go of my arm!"

"I have to clean this mess you made! Look at this! What is this paper?"

"Those are my ladybugs!"

I saw him glance at the ladybug house and then at the floor. "Why are they on the floor? Why? You tell me!"

"Sweep them! Go ahead! Sweep them! Throw them away; I don't care!"

"Pick them up! It is not up to me to clean your mess! Pick them up; put them back where they came from!"

"No, you sweep them! You sweep them!"

"I have to go to work, you understand! I have to work, you understand me! I work a ten-hour shift, goddamn it! I work six days a week sometimes! Nobody appreciates that I work! Everyone is a bloodsucker around here! Everyone is feeding off me like a parasite! I break my back to cook, to clean up after you people! I break my back!" As he yelled, he got the broom and swept the fallen ladybugs and their accessories into a dustpan. When he was done, he picked each item out of the dustpan, one by one, from the snarls of dust and crumbs, making an expression that was beyond disgust. Then he placed them on the table.

"Here are your things! Don't put them on the floor again! Show some respect next time for your own things; your own things at least, even if you have no respect for anyone else's things! I take care of my things; that is why my things last! Next time control your temper! I am going back to bed! I have to work! I have trouble sleeping as it is. There is no reason to keep me awake; shame on you! You are nothing but a selfish brat in your own world! Learn to think of other people, their needs, for once, for once!" He went back up the stairs slowly, eyeing me all the way.

Once he was out of sight, I dusted the ladybugs off and put them into the new ladybug house, another milk carton. Then I put the milk carton in my toy box with the rest of my stuff. Peter had been right; it was better that I keep the ladybugs at home—this way Karen couldn't tear them up—besides, he was a grown man, and I was starting to doubt he would play with them when I wasn't around.

————

Peter's birthday fell on a Wednesday, so we would be going to his house on a day we wouldn't normally. I should have been glad to be seeing him three days this week instead of the usual two, but instead I woke up with a terrible stomachache. Mommy decided that I was too sick for school and fed me a bowl of Campbell's chicken soup and saltine crackers in bed, while she debated whether we should still go to Peter's in the afternoon.

"We can't go if you're sick, you understand that, don't you?" Mommy said. "Peter will have to understand that. We can always celebrate on Friday."

"I think I'm not really all that sick. I think I'm more worried than anything."

"About what? What are you worried about?"

"I don't want to go to Peter's house without a present. But we don't have any money. Couldn't you have asked Poppa for money? Couldn't you have explained that it was for Peter's birthday?"

"You know how your father is. He's not too keen on Peter right now. Maybe your father is a bit jealous of Peter."

"Jealous of what?" I smirked.

"Your attention. Your father is a very jealous man. He likes to be everyone's favorite. At the bars, he spends money buying drinks for people, just to be popular. That's your father for you."

"He doesn't care about me. Did you hear him screaming at me last night?"

"I was asleep. The sleep drugs put me in the land of the dead. He didn't hit you, did he?"

"No. But he yelled really bad, and all because I dropped some paper on the floor."

"Paper on the floor? He shouldn't be walking around at night. He should be in bed, sleeping like a normal person. That man should be on tranquilizers like I am. He really should." She paused. "Is this why you're sick? Are you upset because he yelled at you?"

"No! He always yells. I don't care if he yells." I turned away from her, irritated. "I *told* you why."

We were silent, and then my mother said, "I have twenty dollars' emergency money. I could spend that; then later I could make up an excuse. Okay?"

I didn't say anything at first. "I don't know what Peter would want. I have no idea what people his age like. Maybe we should just stay home—you can call him and say I'm sick."

"Do you want me to do that? I can call right now."

"No, wait a second. Can you think of anything? Something that he would really like?"

"What about we get him a nice birthday cake? He has a real sweet tooth. We'll go to Sugarman's bakery and get him a nice chocolate cake with strawberry filling. We can have them write 'Happy Birthday, Peter, we love you' in red icing."

"Pink icing. Peter likes pink."

Mommy laughed. "Pink icing, then."

After Peter's birthday party was over, Karen wanted to watch *E.T.*, so we went into the living room and Peter popped it into the VCR. Inès, Miguel, and Ricky watched it with us to be polite, I think; and then, one by one, they slipped off. Karen lay on her stomach, ankles crossed, and I lay beside her for a while; she put her foot over mine. Mommy was perched on her usual red velvet chair; she loved *E.T.*

Peter motioned for me to climb onto the couch with him and I did. The blank feelings were coming over me again, but something else was mixed with them—a kind of raw energy. Peter had told me to wink at him, a code that we should go to the basement. But I had forgotten the difference between a wink and a blink. I heard low humming, and I looked at the red velvet curtains. The humming seemed to emanate from there, but it also seemed to come from Peter. For some reason, I thought of that purple comb. Then I thought of Poppa, the hairdresser's scissors, him saying he would hate me, too.

"Peter, I don't want to see this part coming up. The part where they stuff E.T. in that zippered body bag. I remember getting scared when I saw it at the theater." I winked at Peter, finally remembering how.

Peter asked Mommy to watch the rest of the movie with Karen; we were going downstairs for a second to give the cats some kibble and play marbles with them for a short while, since I didn't want to watch the movie anymore.

"I want to go, too!" Karen said, but Peter said, "I don't want you tripping on those basement stairs. You'll break your neck." He handed Mommy *Lady and the Tramp*. "If she gets bored with *E.T.*, put this one in." Karen pouted, but Peter gave her a stern, you-better-not-start look, so she settled down. Ever since Peter had spanked her, it seemed like she respected him more.

I was the first to descend the red-carpeted stairs; I led Peter by the hand. When we got to the wooden door by the first-floor apartment, he looked nervous. "Are you sure? Don't do anything you don't want to do. We can go back. We don't have to go."

"It's your birthday. This is my present to you."

For the first time, I didn't feel afraid descending the soft wooden steps. It was like there was nothing in me: no fear, no energy, nothing. Peter kept asking if I was okay. I nodded. As soon as Peter turned on the bulb, a few cats raced out of the shadows, mewing for kibble. Peter shoveled some Meow Mix from a giant bag into their ceramic bowl. I stood there, perfectly still, waiting for the tingles and prickles that meant my body was falling asleep.

Peter came over and faced me. "You are beautiful, you know that?"

I nodded, watching the cats eat.

"Do you love me?"

I nodded again.

"Can you say it?"

"I love you."

"You're not cold, are you?"

I shook my head, though it was slightly chilly.

"Maybe we should go back up," Peter said. "You don't look very happy. You're not smiling."

I shrugged.

"I mean, you don't have to do anything. Just being with you is enough. You don't have to do anything you don't want to do."

I still didn't say anything. I concentrated on trying to look happy and relaxed.

"I mean: what would you like to do? Anything in particular?"

"You tell me. I'll do whatever you want. It's your birthday and I'll do anything." I paused. "Happy birthday!"

He hugged me suddenly, almost too tightly. "I love you so much. Margaux, you don't understand. Margaux, Margaux. There is nobody else like you. No one in existence. You were made for me. You're my guardian angel. You're my love. It's not wrong to love you, not when it is so beautiful to be in love. It's not wrong to love someone so beautiful. We were made for each other; forget what the world says. Forget everything; we are the only two people that matter in this world: you and me."

I kissed him then, putting my tongue in his mouth. We kissed for a while. Then I put my hand on the crotch of his sweatpants.

"You're not afraid of me, are you?"

I shook my head.

"I'm in love with you. There is nobody else, Margaux. Nobody can make me feel this way. I love you unconditionally. You have great power, unbelievable power over me and I trust you. I trust you with my life."

I pulled down his pants; the sudden motion seemed to surprise him. His penis didn't look as scary and gross as it had before. It was a natural body part, not shameful at all; I knew that now. I touched it and it started to increase in size; Peter said not to be afraid—this was supposed to happen. The skin got tauter, the veins more rigid, those veins reminding me of terrarium plants, only blue. The hairy sac beneath it seemed tauter, too; I touched that and it squished in my hand like a bowl of refrigerated Jell-O. But what I couldn't believe was the other thing, which kept magically growing. I thought of Alice in Wonderland and her magic potion bottles and magic mints and mushrooms. Certain potions made her bigger; others reduced her size. She could be as small as my pinkie finger, or as big as Godzilla or King Kong. Peter's penis wasn't controlled by mints or mushrooms—I understood now that *I* controlled it. I knew enough now about how things worked to know that if I wasn't here, it wouldn't have gotten bigger.

I looked at the bright naked bulb. A fly was crawling on it. "Do you want me to kiss you there, Peter? For your birthday?"

"I would like that very much, sweetheart."

I kissed him where the sewn-up eye was. There was no pee there, no pee was coming out. Peter had told me no pee could come out while it was hard. No pee is coming, I told myself, as I kissed it several times, no pee, no pee. No blood, no blood. No wax or mucus, no sweat. Nothing could come from here.

"Can you suck on it? Like you would a lollipop?"

There was a story in an antique book my mother had when she was a child called *The Tall Book of Fairy Tales*; now it was my book. The tale I was thinking of was called "The Everlasting Lollipop"; it was about a boy, Johnny, who keeps licking a lollipop until it gets so big it's bigger than he is. The giant lollipop is used to decorate the street, since it's now the size of a lamppost.

I sucked on Peter's penis, still thinking of the stories in the book. There was another one called "Bad Mousie." Bad Mousie is the little girl Donnica's friend; he's a nice mouse, except he can't help but be bad and destroy things in the house. So Donnica's mother tries to kill him; she tries drowning him in a cardboard box, but the box melts and he swims out. She tries flying him away on a hang glider. She ties him up outside for an owl to eat. No matter how many times she tries to get rid of him, he keeps coming back. After a while, he decides that he wants to be good. He starts doing what he's told. He cleans the dinner dishes; he says his prayers. Maybe he drinks a glass of milk like the one my mother gave me for vitamin D every night. I wasn't sure if I was a mouse drinking milk out of the cat's bowl on the basement floor. I wasn't sure if I was a baby having a bottle or whether I was really upstairs having some milk and Oreos with Karen. Was I upstairs or downstairs? That was the first thing to concentrate on. Whether I was upstairs or downstairs. Or whether I lived now in the apartment on Thirty-second Street or in Poppa's new house. How old I was and what day of the week it was. Whether I was Karen upstairs drinking from a glass of milk or Margaux downstairs lapping from the cat's bowl. Suddenly, I felt like I was the size of a thumbnail. Then

I realized I was looking at a thumbnail. Peter's thumbnail. Then I realized I was looking up at Peter's face. As soon as I looked at him he patted my head.

"I love you," he said. "I love you so much, darling, so much. You should stop now, sweetheart. Stop now, sweetheart." His voice had a strange, choked sound. "You are so beautiful. So beautiful and loving; and this was such a beautiful evening. Thank you, thank you so much, sweetheart, thank you for loving me. Thank you for accepting me." He broke out into a wide smile and pulled up his pants in a quick movement. "This is the best birthday of my life!"

"Well, you owe me now, Peter!" I said. My voice all of a sudden sounded brassier, like the popular girl at school. "When my birthday comes, I want a big party! At Burger King!" I looked down; my voice fell to a mutter. "Poppa says . . ."

"Let's go back upstairs," Peter said suddenly, looking nervous. "Before they start calling a search party! Now, what did your father say?"

"That I shouldn't eat at Burger King because the hamburgers are made out of cows' crushed-up eyeballs and tongues and the bones of the cow, all ground up in a big machine . . ."

Peter shook his head. "He's crazy." We were approaching the wooden steps. "Take my hand, love. I know that these stairs are a doozy."

"Poppa's a liar, anyway," I said in that other voice.

"Speaking of Poppa and of your mother too, for that matter . . ." Peter stopped and turned on the wooden step, looking at me, a step beneath him. "You know better than to ever tell them about this . . ."

I rolled my eyes and wagged my finger at him. "How many times do I have to tell you, Peter? I can keep a secret!"

"I'm sorry, sweetheart, it's just that no one else would understand the way we feel about each other. They would attack us. They would separate us. They would say we were disgusting and bad for loving each other."

"I know, Peter, I know."

"I'm going to show you how I keep secrets." He took my hand in his. "I make a little lock, see, like this?" He put his pinkie on my mouth as if it were drawing a lock. "And then I give you the key, see?" He put the make-believe key in my left hand. "And," he said, taking that hand, "you lock the secret away. And here, I'm putting around your neck a little chain, and on the end of the chain, I'll tie the key." He pretended to fasten it. "So long as you keep that key with you at all times, and make sure no one steals it, you don't have to worry."

He kissed me on the forehead and I said, "I'll guard the key with my life."

I rubbed my nose against him. "Eskimo kiss!" He laughed.

"Fish kiss," I whispered, and we puckered our lips like fishes.

"Okay," he said, squeezing my hand. "Let's go, Butterfly Girl."

"Why are you calling me Butterfly Girl? You never called me that before."

"'Cause you're like a butterfly, always flitting back and forth, and you're so delicate I'd never want to hurt you; I'd never want to cause you pain, not like your father. And I'd never want to lie to you or make you feel ashamed, ever. I value what you've given me, I treasure it. And sometimes it drives me crazy that I can't marry you now, but I try to be patient. And I know we'll be married eventually; not a big wedding, though, I don't think, unless you become a rich lady someday. I'm sure your father wouldn't pay," he said, grinning. "Too cheap. Look at me. Look into my eyes. Let's look at each other, just for a moment." I looked at him then, really looked at him under the low light of the single naked lightbulb. I looked at his long, pointy nose, which he'd once said he didn't like; his eyes, which he said as a kid were baby blue but which had darkened and turned aqua; and his hair, once platinum blond, which had darkened into the sandy-silver it was now at fifty-two.

All I could think was that I was running.

When I got to the shed door, the door to the rabbit hole, with the hunter fast at my feet, the door to the milk carton house, the door at which the Hudson Park robin pecked, I was no longer the rabbit. Maybe it was the moment my sneaker slipped off, dragging my sock into the white snow. Maybe it was that moment when I first dropped to my knees and scooted under a low table. Maybe it was when his hands reached for me under the table, when my feet were kicking at his hands, and I was growling, hating him. I hated him because he was humming. Because the blue hat looked stupid on his head, and I hated it. Because he had sweatpants on, not jeans. Because I was a tiger now, not a rabbit.

"Go away, go away, hunter, or I'll kill you!"

"You've got nowhere to go, little rabbit! Nowhere to go . . . without your magic snowshoe!"

And he pulled my Kangaroo sneaker out from behind his back, and I loved him again, and started to cry.

"Don't be scared. I'll leave, okay?" he said.

"Don't leave me!" I charged out from under the table, banging my head again, more painfully this time, and clawing at his clothes. "Don't *ever* go away from me!"

He held me. "Why are you crying, my love? It's only a game, my darling."

I'm crying because. Because I hated him. It had hurt me so much to think that for a minute I had wanted to kill him. I had wanted to see him die in a million exploding blue hat pieces. I could not tell him this—that I had truly hated him.

"I'm crying because I banged my head. It hurts. And I lost my shoe and my foot is cold. See, it hurts."

"Oh, poor baby, I know it hurts, my love. And I will make it better; only I can. I have the sock, it's wet, but I have it. I have the shoe; it just has a little snow in it. Here, let's clear that out. Everything is fine, my baby, my little baby love, my little girl."

"It won't stop. Feeling this sad won't stop." The kisses came. On my hair. On my face.

He kissed each toe of the wet, cold foot. Then he put the wet, slimy sock over it. He slipped the Kangaroo shoe onto that poor, sad foot, and bound it with each strap of pink Velcro.

10

"THERE'S SOMETHING VERY WRONG WITH THAT MAN"

Lately, I had started thinking about the showers I had taken with Poppa up until I was five years old. These showers were great fun; we'd fling the washcloths on the tub floor, pretend they were roaches, and stomp them, singing the silly song "La Cucaracha." During the showers I had noticed the difference between me and Poppa but hadn't thought much of it. Now I couldn't remember if what Peter called his "babymaker" was different from Poppa's, so one Saturday when Mommy went to her therapy session with Dr. Gurney, I asked Poppa if we could take a shower together like in the old days.

At first, he muttered that I was too old for that now. But I begged him, and finally, he gave in. In the steamy, junglelike shower, I found myself staring at Poppa's penis. He saw me looking and covered himself with his hands. The shower grew louder with the silence. I felt like something needed to be said, but I didn't know what it was. Then I found a way to speak. I didn't know what my words meant, only that they had to be said. As I spoke them I used that popular girl's voice.

"Poppa, is that a toy? Can I touch it, pretty please? Is that your toy there for me to play with?" I wasn't sure where I'd learned those words, but it felt like I knew them by heart.

Poppa turned away, his skinny legs bent. "No," he muttered, nearly inaudibly. "No."

I reached over anyway to make him feel good. He shouldn't say no when that special part of him was mine, too. He was *my* father. Swatting my hand away, he squeezed the faucets shut. Poppa got out, dried off, dressed, all in silence. He put a towel on the floor next to the tub for me and then hurried out the door.

Sometime that winter after the shower incident, there was the drama of Benihana. We went there, the four of us; Poppa treated everyone, as he'd promised to earlier.

Inès decided not to go. Peter didn't seem to want to go either, but he knew that he had to. Preparing for meeting Poppa, almost a week before the actual Friday night, he tried on an old suit that he called his wedding-and-funeral suit. He looked so strange in a jacket and tie. He started to dab on some cologne, but I warned him not to; he had gotten it at the Dollar Store, and I knew one sniff of it would banish him forever from Poppa's good graces.

"Better no cologne at all than cheap cologne," I lectured. "And don't cut yourself shaving. Poppa says a man who can't hold a razor straight isn't somebody he trusts. He says anyone who cuts himself shaving is a nervous character."

"I'll use an electric razor," Peter said, as he stood before the gilt mirror.

Mommy called out from the living room. "Peter, if it's not a close shave, he won't respect you. You don't want to have a five o'clock shadow when you meet Louie. He'll think you're unkempt."

"Unkempt." Peter shook his head. "Unkempt and uncouth. Hooligans: the lot of them. Barbarians. Savages."

I giggled.

"Oh, and make sure you talk to Poppa," I added. "That's the most important thing. We went out to dinner one time with a friend of Mommy's and her husband. The husband didn't say much all night because he was shy. Poppa made fun of him when we got home. He called him 'The Mute.' Poppa says that he would rather stay home with some saltine crackers and deviled ham from a can than be stuck at a restaurant with a person who can't say two words to save his life. So make sure you talk a lot!"

For our big night out, Mommy was wearing a glitzy shirt with a snow leopard on a tree branch against a dark blue background. I had chosen it for her. She was also wearing lipstick and some rouge on her cheeks. I was in brand-new Mary Janes, white tights, a canary-colored Orlon sweater with large black flowers, and a black miniskirt. I had also put on some light pink Tinkerbell lipstick and nail polish, though Peter said he didn't like makeup. He liked nail polish only if it was chipped; I told him he was weird. My hair had grown out a little, so I looked less ugly than earlier, but I despaired of ever being pretty again; Poppa was already talking about cutting it. Inès noticed me sadly touching my hair in front of the mirror, so she offered me two metal butterfly-adorned bobby pins, but I knew I couldn't accept them: Poppa would know they weren't mine, and insist I take them out before I got lice.

We waited in the foyer a good twenty minutes before Poppa was due. "Louie's hair is thinning and he's very upset about it. So he grows it long in the back and combs it over," Mommy said. "He has a ducktail straight from the fifties. You'll see."

Poppa showed up five minutes early in a sharp black suit and freshly polished shoes, all decked out with his giant gold cross replete with precious gems and his thick gold watch. He reeked heavily of cologne. The first thing Poppa did was firmly shake Peter's hand; I could tell by the expression on his face that he was going to put on a big show that night.

The first thing Poppa did when the waitress came over was order sake. It came in a white ceramic jug shaped like an hourglass and was poured into tiny round cups no bigger than doll teacups. Poppa immediately offered Peter some, and I could tell Peter was afraid to say no.

"Maybe a little later," he said after a short pause. "After I've got some food in me. Sake, strong stuff, wouldn't you say? It's the drink of the kamikaze pilots, so it would've needed to be pretty strong."

"The strongest!" Poppa said, looking pleased. "Japanese rice wine! I love it!" He opened a cloth napkin and tied it around my mother's neck. At Benihana, eight to ten people would sit at a long hibachi table with a sheet of metal in the middle, used for cooking the food. Poppa had never minded sitting with strangers; he usually started conversations with them. Tonight, however, he was focused on Peter. "So I hear you fought in Korea?"

"I wasn't in actual combat, no. The air force used me as a carpenter. I imagine it was because I've always had an aptitude for working with my hands. I guess that's something we have in common. You're a jeweler, right? I was a locksmith before I hurt my back."

"You went to school for that?"

"Self-taught. Bluffed my way in, taught myself from books and on the job. I guess you could say I've always been a great bluffer. Could talk my way into anything."

Poppa nodded. "A good quality to have. I went to trade school. I made my wife's engagement ring myself. Also, you see the earrings on my daughter's ears? That is my work. My crucifix, too," he said, tapping it.

The waitress came and took our orders. Poppa encouraged Peter to order anything on the menu; it was his treat. Peter, looking uncomfortable, finally settled on the teriyaki chicken. Poppa ordered the Benihana Special for himself, and one for me and my mother to split. The Benihana Special consisted of teriyaki steak and a lobster tail.

Poppa got up to go to the bathroom, and as soon as he was out of earshot, my mother patted Peter's hand. "You're doing just fine," she said.

"I hope so," said Peter.

"Did you see how much sake he drank? And I think he was drinking before he left the house . . ."

"Probably," said Peter, too nervous even to bad-mouth Poppa.

"Here you go," I said, leaning over and kissing Peter on the cheek. "For strength."

"Aww," said my mother. "That's just what you needed."

By the time Poppa got back, the waitress was setting down our onion soup appetizer. Poppa thanked her for her promptness, and then said in a surprised tone, "Peter, I notice you are not wearing a watch! I could make you one, perhaps. I personally find it a crime to be late." He smiled and drank some more. He had pushed his onion soup over to my mother for her to eat. "Is there a particular reason why you don't wear a watch? Or any jewelry, for that matter?"

"I don't like the feel of anything on my arms. I've never been much of a jewelry wearer. As for being late, I usually make it to places way too early. I told Sandy that when I was a teenager, I got a call from the hospital where my mother was dying and I had to rush over there. I made it with only fifteen minutes to spare: ever since then, I never could stand to rush. In some ways, I thought it was merciful for God to take her after all she'd suffered. She was paralyzed on her left side and had been for four years due to a stroke. It was such a shame. She was a beautiful woman. Back in her day, she was a model for Barbizon."

"Really," Poppa said. The Japanese chef in his tall white hat had begun to douse the metal sheet with hot oil. It sizzled. "And your father?"

"My father was a lawyer. He had so much money he bought his own private plane. Had a heart attack one day flying it, died when he was only forty-four."

"Well, it is sad for one to die so young," Poppa said, watching the chef pour the ginger-and-mustard sauce into the octagonal bowls. "But it sounds like your father died like a man, at least. In his glory, doing what he loved, no?"

"He was a real bastard, my father, excuse my language. I'll have to be honest and say I wasn't sorry to see him go. I loved my mother, though."

"Well, it is not uncommon for a son to secretly despise his father, perhaps even wish him dead. It is not a requirement for a son to have affection for his father, only to respect him as the head of the household. I never questioned my father, or gave him a day of trouble. Then he died. My brothers were already out of the house, and I became a man at ten years old. When the father dies, a son must replace him with eagerness, honoring his memory but never weeping. I respected my father but perhaps did not love him . . . Anyway, it is different with the mother; a son must love his mother above all," Poppa said.

The waitress gathered our empty soup bowls and replaced them with wooden bowls of salad with ginger dressing. Poppa had taught my mother and me to eat with chopsticks, so Peter was the only one who had requested a fork—something I knew Poppa frowned upon.

"Hitler, for instance—I have read about this, it is well documented— Hitler loved his mother. Say what you will about Hitler: he was a maniac, a tyrant, responsible for insane cruelty, genocide, war—but he loved his mother. That is why I sometimes think even Hitler had a conscience. Because he loved his mother."

"Oh, Louie, please," my mother said. "People are nearby."

"So what? I am speaking the truth! The man, bad as he was, loved his mother!"

My mother gave Peter a look.

"Good and evil, what are they?" Poppa continued. "Can one say with absolute certainty that Hitler is an evil man? Can one say this *with absolute certainty*?"

"Well, I've read about Hitler myself," said Peter. "Didn't Germany represent his mother in his mind? Isn't that the reason behind all his atrocities?"

"Yes," Poppa said, his gold cross wagging with the force of his movements. "Exactly! That is the psychology! Hitler, for instance, loved German children. He would be seen petting the heads of little blond boys and girls."

"Can we please change the subject?" Mommy said.

"This woman," Poppa said, elbowing Peter.

We paused to watch the chef perform his tricks with the salt and pepper shakers. We watched him ignite the oil on the stove, causing a large fire, to the awe of the entire table. Everyone clapped.

"He's great," Peter said. "I always liked magic shows. I know a few card tricks but nothing fancy."

"Personally, I have seen better. Did you see him almost drop the shaker? He is inexperienced," said Poppa in a low voice so the chef couldn't hear. "I have been here so many times I have seen every chef; none of these tricks are new to me. I guess to you, Peter, this is a special treat." Poppa smiled. "Come here as often as I do and it will fail to impress. I come here so much that I have over thirty matchboxes; I have not gotten around to using them all. If I were you, Peter, I would have gone through them by now! I notice you are a big smoker. Myself . . . I like moderation . . . I smoke for relaxation, not because I am addicted. I suppose if I were in your position, home all day, with a lot of time to fill, I might develop more of a habit." Poppa paused to sip his sake. "Anyway, as I was saying before, no one in this world is evil. Not even Hitler. Pure evil is impossible. It doesn't exist."

"I agree with you there, Louie," said Peter. "It's like a straight line in nature. A perfectly straight line can't exist in nature. It's impossible."

Mommy looked horrified. "Hitler was an evil man!"

Poppa didn't answer right away. He concentrated on picking up his sticky white rice with his chopsticks. It was a nearly impossible feat, but Poppa always managed it without spilling a grain. "You miss the point. You miss the whole point of the discussion. Do you think I am championing ignorance? Do you think I do not watch the news? Do you think I am in love with criminals? The Manson murders turned my stomach. All I am saying about Hitler is that the man loved his mother . . ."

"I am not going to talk about Hitler anymore!" my mother whisper-yelled. "This is a sick conversation. Hitler is burning in hell, quite frankly, and I don't care to discuss him anymore in front of Margaux."

Poppa elbowed Peter. "Do you see what I have to put up with? Day after day? This woman has a simplistic view of the world. I, on the other hand, like to dissect things. I am a thinker. This woman already has her mind made up before a conversation starts."

Peter shifted in his seat. "All I know is that together the two of you have managed to produce a beautiful daughter." He smiled at me and then looked at their faces. Mommy was frowning as she ate her zucchini and noodles; Poppa was busy lighting a cigar. "I'm trying to think of which one of you she resembles more," Peter said, as he started to remove a King 100 from his pack. "It's pretty close."

"Everyone says she looks like me," Poppa said, lighting Peter's cigarette with his cigar. "Everyone says she has my nose. Her girl cousins all look like her. That is the look. In personality, she is very much like my sister, Nilda. Stubborn and defiant. Nilda was three years older than me. She would start fights with me and then run to my father and I would get the blame. I would be beaten for that child's sins!" He shook his head and was silent for a moment, eating. "My older sister was never beaten a day in her life, though a sound thrashing might have solved the problem. She was cunning, like this one. I do not trust this child sitting right here. She has my sister's blood. Capable of turning on the dime. I am trying my best to destroy this quality before it gets out of hand."

Peter took a long, speculative drag. "Louie, of course, you would know your daughter better than I, but perhaps you're judging her a bit harshly. Margaux is very kind and trustworthy. She looks after my foster daughter, Karen, as if she were her own sister. She does dishes and helps out in our garden."

"I believe you," Poppa said, putting up a hand to halt Peter. "Look, let's pretend Judas Iscariot is sitting here at this table with us. You want to talk about evil? Betrayal is the worst form of evil. If there is someone in history who really fits the definition of evil, it is Judas

Iscariot. Not Hitler. Not Charles Manson. They were just madmen. Judas kissed the cheek of Christ. Kissed him on the cheek, like a brother! Now, let me ask this: is betrayal not the worst thing you can inflict upon a person?"

"I'll have to think about that," Peter said, starting to eat his chicken.

"Good! You think! I like a man who thinks before he speaks! It is a rare trait!" He patted Peter on the back. "I like your company. I would like to invite you to the Belmont Stakes in June. My wife and daughter can go to the playground. You and I will make some wagers. Do you have a bookie?"

Peter shook his head.

Poppa turned to Mommy, straightened her bib, and ordered his dessert—pineapple slices. I asked for chocolate ice cream. My mother said she was trying to watch her weight. Poppa said to the young Japanese waitress, "More sake, my dear! I am in a good mood! I have had an excellent dinner! And I was served by a lovely girl; you are more beautiful than Cleopatra! I suppose you hear things like that all the time."

The waitress giggled and walked away.

"I have a way with women," Poppa said to Peter. "It is a gift. They fall in love with me, not knowing why." He laughed. "I have always known how to attract women. And I am not more handsome than the next person. I just have the gift. Come, Peter, let's have a toast. My wife cannot drink but we can have a toast. A toast to a fine dinner and to good company!"

Poppa poured the sake and offered the white flask to Peter, who didn't reach to take it.

"What is wrong?" Poppa asked, nudging him. "This is the best wine, I guarantee it! This wine will get you the drunkest! That is why I love it!" He laughed.

"Usually, I don't drink. Actually, I don't ever drink, Louie. We can make the toast but I can't drink this."

"Well, you can make an exception." Poppa smiled, but his eyes had soured. "We've had a good night. Some sake will relax you." He paused. "Don't worry, if you throw up in my car, I can forgive that! I can always get the upholstery cleaned! It is not like I have leather up-holstery! I wish I owned a Rolls-Royce but I have to be happy with my Chevy! A seventy-nine model like my daughter!"

Peter shook his head. "I'm sorry, but I don't drink at all. My father was a horrible alcoholic."

"You mean to tell me you drink nothing, not even a beer? I find it hard to believe!"

"Not everyone drinks, Louie, you know that," Mommy said. "It's not that unbelievable. With some people, it changes their personalities. My father was different when he was drunk."

Peter nodded. "My father was always drunk. He beat me and my brother every other night, for nothing. Whipped us with a cat-o'-nine-tails. Then he sent us to a boys' school where the nuns beat us. There were times when we ran away and were sent back to our father, who beat us for running away; then he sent us back to the school, where the brothers and nuns would punish runaways either by beat-ing them silly or sometimes with even worse punishments. One kid got his head shaved for running away ten times. No matter what my brother and I did, we just couldn't win."

Poppa was staring into his sake cup. When he saw the waitress, he quickly ordered the check. My mother and Peter kept talking.

On the way home in the Chevy, Peter and Poppa started talking again, this time about art. But I could tell Poppa didn't have the same spirit as before, and so I worried. When Poppa arrived at Peter's, he got out of the car, shook his hand, and said that we would all have to do this again very soon. But once Poppa got back into the car, he said, "That man is strange. I didn't know what to expect of him, but all I know is that I *never* want to be in the company of such a person again. What kind of a man refuses a cup of quality wine at a nice dinner that is the treat of someone else? What kind of manners does he have? He used me. That man used me to pay for his dinner."

"Louie, you insisted on treating."

"He didn't even offer money when the check came."

"That's because you said ahead of time that you were treating."

"But when the bill came, he was still supposed to offer to pay for himself. Or offer to treat us. At the very least the tip!"

"He couldn't afford it, Louie. Simple as that. They are poor, Louie. I don't think you understand that."

"I know that! That is no secret!" Poppa said. "I have no problem with paying! But there are certain things that are expected when one goes to dinner. Of course *I* paid. I am not a cheapskate."

"You're just mad because he wouldn't drink with you."

"I do not trust a man who cannot take one single drink! Fine, he doesn't want to be drunk, good! I don't want him sick in my car! Fine, but one drink!"

"Maybe he's afraid of being out of control," Mommy said. "Alcohol changes people. I respect him for not drinking."

"Oh, you respect him! The saint!" Poppa said. He was hunting for a parking space, but didn't seem to be looking too hard. This was the third time he had circled our block and the second time he had driven right past a space, not even seeing it. I noticed that the space was now taken. "Someone should give him a trophy!"

"You're drunk, Louie! You shouldn't even be driving! You almost hit that parked car!"

"These streets are too narrow! Listen, you want to drive? I will pull over. I will shut off the car."

"You know I don't drive! Just pay attention, please! I don't want Margaux dead because you're not paying attention!"

"Why didn't you tell me that the man was strange? I would have stopped you from going there a long time ago. Well, it is not too late. I want you to start breaking away from this man and his family."

I sat up straight in the backseat, my heart pounding. I was afraid to say anything. I was afraid to be silent.

Mommy gave him an incredulous look. "You would actually punish your daughter for an insult against you? What you *saw* as an insult? You would actually hurt Margaux to get back at him?"

Poppa laughed. "Oh yes, that is it, I just want to hurt *her*. *I* am protecting her. There's something very wrong with that man, I can tell. He can fool you at first because he is a good conversationalist. He has charisma, let's say. I was under his spell, too, at first. I thought: this is an intelligent man. This is a man of opinion. This is a man who knows about the world. He knew a lot about art, for instance. You heard him just before he left; he was quoting Renoir: too many artists spend time going to bed with beautiful women, rather than painting them. Good quote. I had a good laugh." He paused. "But then he tells me Renoir is one of his favorites. Over the greats: Matisse, Picasso. Renoir is no innovator: he painted flowers and babies. I dislike Impressionist art. This Peter—he likes—what was it?" He paused again. "Norman Rockwell. He likes Norman Rockwell. That is not a true artist. He painted the insides of doctors' waiting rooms. This Peter, this Peter, he can talk well, but you can tell he is not really educated. He is a manipulator. That is why I don't like him. Let's say he is about as real as his false teeth." Poppa laughed. "What kind of person has his teeth pulled in his fifties?"

"Now you're just being cruel," said Mommy. "You are just drunk and you're being nasty. Maybe that's why Peter doesn't drink. Drinking brings out the worst in people."

"Honesty is cruelty, sure it is," Poppa said, finally pulling up to parallel park in a space three blocks away from the house. "You can tell a lot about a man by how he cares for his appearance. A man who knows he has done right and has a clean conscience takes good care of his nails, his teeth. He respects himself and wishes his body to last forever. He smokes a cigar or cigarette occasionally but does not chain-smoke like that man. That man is self-destructive. The way he eats—he barely ate! He ate very little of his chicken and his noodles; did not touch his zucchini or watercress! Instead of caring for his teeth, he allows them to fall to ruin. He is a veteran. The veterans' hospital would have paid for what he needed, a root canal, whatever. This man will be dead in ten years, I guarantee it. His mother had a stroke, his father a heart attack. Yet he does not watch his smoking. I can tell that he is unhealthy; he probably has high cholesterol."

He turned off the car and folded his hands on his lap.

"Well, you can dislike him if you want," Mommy said. "Fine. Don't invite him out again."

"I never will. Do you want to talk about history? The worst men in history were those who insisted upon sobriety. Some of the greatest leaders were fond of drinking—Churchill, Roosevelt—while the worst tyrants through the ages abstained. Hitler, for instance . . ."

"Not this again."

"Hitler," he spoke louder. "Hitler did not drink. He lived very *cleanly*. Check your history book."

"I can't believe you're comparing Peter to Hitler."

"Again, you miss the point." He laughed. "I do not trust that man. I do not. You watch your daughter when you go over there. He and his family are bad influences. If it were up to me, I would not permit you to go there with her anymore. That simple. But *you do* what *you* want. *I* wash my hands of this matter. All I will say is I wash my hands."

11

CIRCLE, CIRCLE, DOT, DOT

"Good grief" was what Peter said when something surprised him. He didn't sigh; instead, he'd say the word "sigh." He painted the walls of the kitchen lavender. He started building me a wooden dollhouse. There was an afternoon (it must have been in the summer) when Peter asked Karen and me to strip to just our panties. After we did, he took several snapshots of us hugging and posing with our arms draped across each other's shoulders. Mommy must have gone to the Terrace Market for a Creamsicle or Dixie Cup or to Pathmark for a carton of King 100s. Or was Mommy actually there on the lawn chair while Peter, with all his talk of naturalness and nudist colonies and the way God made us, talked her into letting him take those pictures? Mommy might have been unsure at first, but this was *Peter*—I ran around the house in my underwear in front of Poppa all the time, and Peter might as well have been my dad. I couldn't remember if he tried to get us to take the underwear off. Hard as I still try, I can't remember much of anything concerning my time spent with Peter for the seven or so months following the dinner at Benihana.

The summer of 1988 I was only nine but already little breasts had started to form on my chest. I got pubic hair and was so repulsed by it that I took my father's razor and shaved with VO5 henna shampoo. I checked my face in the mirror compulsively, not to be vain, but because I had developed a fear that one day I would look and see nothing there at all.

I knew it was all my mother's fault.

We were in our bedroom a couple of weeks after I had been told I couldn't see Peter anymore and I was going ballistic yet again, tearing the sheet off the bed, throwing the pillows on the floor, knocking my stuffed animals off the mahogany bureau. Every time I asked her why I couldn't see Peter, she told me a lie about how she had once seen him slap Karen.

"No, that's not true! I heard you and Poppa talking! I heard it! You said it was over a kiss! It was over a kiss! Don't lie to me!" I came to her, my fist raised, and she backed up. "Tell me the truth!"

"Peter kissed you at the pool." Mommy started to cry. "He kissed you on the mouth."

"So? So what?"

"Peter kissed you! On the mouth!"

"So, I'm asking! So! So! So! So!"

"And some of the lifeguards saw . . ."

"What?" I felt ashamed that everyone now knew about my and Peter's secret world.

"It was right out there, in public, they saw it. One of the lifeguards asked me about it. Who Peter was. He said, 'Is he her father?' I said no, he's not related to us by blood. He was looking at me like I did something wrong. Like I wasn't a good mother. I tried to explain that Peter was a good friend of the family. He shook his head and said that this was serious. He said that he didn't want to confront Peter because, technically, he didn't do anything illegal. He said he would keep an eye on him, though. He said it was up to *me* to do something about what had already happened. When he said that, I wasn't sure what to do. I knew I had to do *something*."

"You didn't have to tell Poppa!"

"I had to," Mommy said, not looking at me. "He's your father. It would have gotten around anyway. Someone in the bar probably would have told him. Then he would have really been angry. Dr. Gurney said that what Peter did, kissing a little girl on the mouth, was outrageous. He said that Peter was a sick man. That your father and I should call the police. But your father said that wasn't necessary. So Peter got lucky."

"Poppa kissed me on the lips once! He came home from work and said hi and kissed me on the lips!"

"That's different! He's your father!"

"Peter's more of a father than him! Why are you doing this to me, why? Why are you punishing me? You're trying to kill me! You want to see me die!"

She shielded her eyes with her palm and spoke in a trembling way. "The psychiatrist said. Your father said. I have to listen to them. I have to do what's right. A man should not be kissing a little girl on the mouth at a public pool. Your father said he was worried that we would be the talk of the town and that people would look at him like he was at fault when all along he'd known Peter was a bad man, ever since that trip to Benihana. Please, let's stop with this! Let's just forget about him; we won't talk about him or what happened ever again. Let's never say that man's name again!"

"You call him *that man*, just like Poppa! You call him *that man*!"

"Don't speak to me anymore about this. I can't talk about this or I'll get sick. I don't want to go back to that hospital! Please, we can't talk about this anymore! It's done with, that's all that matters!"

The entire pantry was filled with boxes of cereal, packages of toilet paper and paper towel rolls, and canned vegetables. There was also a lot of junk food. I rarely ate dinner, and no amount of threatening or cajoling made any difference. Poppa started to make my favorite dishes more often: spaghetti with clam sauce, fried chicken, empanadas with chickpeas. These I would eat, only to throw it all up later. I didn't force myself to throw up; it just happened. I literally couldn't keep anything down except the cereal and junk food I ate throughout the day. At school, I ate only once a week, when the cafeteria featured my favorite food: chicken nuggets. During the rest of the week, I would buy packages of chocolate or powdered doughnuts. Then I would have to take my tray to a lone table with kids snickering at me. They thought I was a complete weirdo because I would constantly space out: during bake sales, recess, standing in line, in the library, at practices for Christmas shows. I couldn't follow directions at those practices and, therefore, had to be placed in the very last row of the stage, where the crowd wouldn't notice me. I couldn't help zoning out. I had done it for the last year or so, but had managed to keep the problem hidden before because I was able to snap back into reality whenever I needed to.

Now I just couldn't listen whenever people talked to me, even if it was a teacher or the principal. Kids would poke me and call me "moron" and "retard." There would be times when I would be in the bathroom stall on the toilet seat or washing my hands in front of the mirror, and I would be jolted back to where I was, unsure of how long I'd been gone. Our teacher, Sister Lenore, would occasionally send a girl in to bring me back to class. Every night, I'd fall to my knees and pray to be better, to be a normal girl who could concentrate and pass math and geography tests without cheating, who would have friends to sit with at lunch. Who would not be pushed to my knees in line when no one was looking. Who would not be chased down in the recess yard, wrestled to the ground, and hit by three boys and the tomboy who hung out with them. Who would not be chanted at, trapped inside a ring of my classmates: "Circle, circle, dot, dot, now I've got my Margaux shot."

I knew that I didn't deserve to be alive. That was why they hated me. It would never get better. I couldn't control where my mind went; I couldn't help that sometimes my surroundings disappeared and reappeared. God wasn't helping. Jesus didn't care.

It had been about seven or eight months since we had stopped seeing Peter and I had lost so much weight that my parents began to worry. When my mother brought me to the pediatrician, she said I had lost fifteen pounds but not to fear; it was probably a sudden growth spurt. My poor eating habits were just a phase. The bad test scores at school were likely due to my eyesight; she said I squinted a lot and probably needed glasses. The pediatrician pointed out that I was going through puberty rather early, and that this transition into womanhood was always stressful. She was used to my mother making a commotion out of my every illness, injury, or oddity. "Another thing," my mother said at the end, when the pediatrician was trying to rush her out. "She does this jumping thing. She never used to do that." While walking with my mother or during school lines, I would punctuate my regular tread with a sudden, spasmodic hop, or "skip," as Peter would have called it. It happened against my will, like a hiccup. It was more proof to me that there was something wrong with my brain. The pediatrician didn't see it as a problem, though. She told my mother to keep an eye on it and then went on to the next patient.

I'd been feeding the Thirty-second Street pigeons for a few months now with boxes of stale cereal from my mother's chronic overbuying: Fruit Loops, Lucky Charms, Cheerios. They'd grown to trust me. One by one, they landed on me. They landed on my shoulders, my legs; one even sat on my head. I'd feel their rubber feet graze against my scabbed-up knees, feel their beaks against the scratches on my arms, feel their throats in my hair as they sat upon my shoulders. They loved me. My pigeons loved me. They ate out of my palms and off my legs.

I wrote stories about the birds and decided I would put them all in a book entitled *The Trials and Tribulations of Pigeons*—an impressive title, I thought. Someday I was sure I'd publish the book.

Occasionally, though, I couldn't help but see the birds as one great gray machine. If one was frightened, they all flew away. If one decided to land, pretty soon they all came, pecking even when there was no food.

One gray day in November, I had an uneasy thought. The pigeons, for all their seeming love and affection for me, would not care if I were dead. There would be others coming with food. The more I followed this thought, the more disconnected I felt. I started to toss the cereal in heaps, not feeling anything toward my birds. All they did was the same thing over and over again. Suddenly, my hands jerked forward and I grabbed the closest bird. The pigeons took off all at once; all those beating wings together made a blast. The bird in my hand flapped his wings like crazy to get away.

"Let go of that thing! Let go of that filthy thing immediately!" my mother said.

I didn't let go.

"Margaux, you'll catch a disease! Let go of that filthy, disgusting bird right now! Let go or I will tell your father!"

I didn't let go, even though she kept screaming at me. The worst of it was hearing my name, Margaux. More than anything she could say to me, I hated the sound of my name on her lips.

Finally, I realized what I was doing and how afraid the bird was. I released my fingers, and I saw in the air a single slice of gray that kept growing smaller and smaller.

On our living room walls, Poppa had reproductions of Picasso's *Petite Fleurs* and Van Gogh's *Starry Night*. His Matisse reproductions especially scared me: my father had told me *La Danseuse Créole* and *Nu Bleu I* were supposed to be women but I thought of the former as a Martian and the latter as simply slabs of blue paint tossed together haphazardly. Eventually, I could see the female image in the green-headed, feathered being in *La Danseuse Créole*, but I spent quite a few years squinting at *Nu Bleu I*, hoping to glimpse the lovely woman that my father and Matisse had seen so effortlessly. Finally, that year, I kept looking at it closely, and after a while, I did see the upraised left thigh and the right thigh lying flat, like a smashed tube of lipstick, as well as her emaciated torso, her feet detached from her body, and her hand placed at the back of her head in a pose of despair. After I first saw her, I desperately wanted to go back to seeing random blue shapes but found that I couldn't. On the center wall, to the right of that picture, was a huge oil painting of a nude woman.

She was spread out on a maroon Renaissance-style bed and held a single white wheel-shaped flower. Her breasts were visible but her leg was arched to cover her vagina. I wanted to see her vagina to check if, like mine, it had hair growing around it. One of the things Peter had said about my vagina was that it was so beautiful and *hairless*. I couldn't stop worrying about this hair and shaving it all off with my father's razor.

Often, I'd sit on the plastic-covered couch, dressed only in an undershirt and panties, looking at the houses across the street. One day, I noticed a man on the front porch of one of those houses, staring at me. So I started to do things I thought would entertain him. I'd stretch one leg high in the air or toss my short brown hair (now grown into a chin-length bob). Or I'd pull up my shirt a little and gaze at my belly button. I did this every time I saw the man watching. Mommy was always upstairs, calling friends or 1-800 hotlines.

I felt like the nude woman in Poppa's painting: beautiful, so dark-eyed and haunting. I no longer felt ashamed. My too skinny body felt like a runway model's supple form. It was the only time I felt like I was worth anything, like someone could see me as something other than a freak.

One day, I waved to him. He waved back, and I didn't know why, but his boldness made me furious. I hadn't wanted him to wave back or react in any way.

I ran upstairs and barged into the bedroom Mommy and I shared. She was on the phone. I heard my name and figured she was again trying to get advice concerning me.

"Mommy, there's a man across the street; he's looking at me in my panties!"

She hastily ended the call. "He's looking in here, in this house?" She shook her head. "This is why you have to be dressed; you're too old now to be parading around half naked. Your father says and I say. I'm going to give this pervert a piece of my mind!"

My mother ran downstairs and stood on the porch and yelled across the street at the man, "You! You have got some nerve looking in here at my nine-year-old daughter! Do it again and I'll call the police!"

She slammed the door. "We don't have to tell your father about this unless it continues. We've got two sturdy locks on this door so I'm not worried. I don't want him taking it out on you, cutting your hair again, or anything like that. He worries enough about you as it is."

It was true. Poppa, drunk the night before, had taken me aside in the kitchen and asked me if I knew what rape was. I said yes. I had learned the word in school, when some girls had given me a note saying that they had hired a man to rape me. Poppa said that now that I was developing, I was a target. He said to be careful. Under the kitchen's fluorescent lights, he lifted my chin, looked me in the eyes, and said, "You know something, if a savage ever catches you, and gives you a choice between being raped or him killing you, you should choose death. That way, you still have your honor. You die fighting, like a real woman. You understand? You tell that son of a bitch to cut your throat first. You tell him you would rather be shot! You spit in his face! You call him a bastard and damn him to hell! You hear me? You understand? You never let yourself be ruined!" He was nearly yelling, and I was frightened, so I just told him what he wanted to hear. I couldn't tell him it was already too late; I was already somehow ruined. All I could do was hold my head underwater in the bathtub for as long as possible, trying to drown myself and in that way keep the family honor that meant so much to Poppa.

In the dark, though, I was not a girl at all and there was nothing wrong with me. At three in the morning, I would tiptoe down the stairs to practice my landings like a true cat. I did them in front of the big TV. Either I'd woken up in the middle of the night or I had never gotten to sleep in the first place. So I practiced. Under my breath, I roared, growled. Then I pounced onto the smooth linoleum again and again. Sometimes I got up on the second step of the staircase and leaped from there, trying as best as I could for a graceful landing on all four of my tiger paws.

12

THE FLOWERING NIGHTGOWN

Winter came, and Poppa kept the heat low, so we usually wore our coats in the house. He got stricter about the amount of time we spent in the shower, and he also started picking up the phone and listening when my mother made calls, opening Aunt Bonnie's letters from Ohio and reading them, and popping into my room at unexpected times. I still slept in the master bedroom at night; after my mother started sleeping in the kitchen extension Poppa had recently built for her, my father chose not to reclaim the master bedroom for himself, seeming content with the small room next door that used to be my room. Unfortunately, we still had the same problems caused by the fact that he needed to go into the master bedroom to get his clothes and I still needed to go into his room to get mine.

I usually watched TV only when Poppa was at work or at the bar. All other times, after I finished my homework, I read, huddled up under the quilt because the room was always freezing. I read a lot of adult romance, fantasy, and horror novels because I was bored by most young adult novels. I couldn't buy that the narrator of Judy Blume's

Deenie was so naïve she didn't even realize she had a "special place" between her legs until she turned twelve. That year, I read *Watership Down* twice as well as Stephen King's *Firestarter* and *Carrie*. One day, I even decided to read my entire pink leather children's Bible from Genesis to Revelation. Since I slept only a few hours a night, often waking up from nightmares and being unable to fall back asleep, I managed this feat within a few days. Poppa, too, would sometimes be up at these hours, and if he caught me reading under the tiny lamp when I was supposed to be sleeping, he became furious, saying it made him nervous when people were up when they weren't supposed to be. I knew he wasn't talking only about me. My mother often couldn't sleep either, and she'd listen to her radio half the night.

Mommy and I complained to each other that Poppa's rules weren't fair, such as the rule that no one but he was allowed to be up at odd hours. What does he think we're going to do, she once joked to a friend, slit his throat in the middle of the night? No one could use the bathroom in the morning until after he'd left for work, because he needed to get ready.

Poppa also became much more critical of my appearance. When I was younger, he had always said I was the kind of great beauty that had inspired the Spanish poets, but now he complained that my looks were going, in part due to my paleness and thinness, and in part due to my awful complexion. For Christmas, Poppa had bought me subscriptions to *Teen*, *YM*, and *Vogue* because he said looking at the models would teach me about posture, how to care for my hair, how to apply makeup, and most important, how to fight acne. I was approaching the age of ten and my face had really started to break out. Poppa made a big commotion about it, even going so far as to ban chocolate from the house, convinced that the chocolate doughnuts I always ate were the cause of it. Nearly every night, he asked me to stand under the fluorescent kitchen light while he looked at my skin through his jeweler's loupe. Whatever new evils he happened to find, he insisted on taking care of with a needle that he'd sterilized on the kitchen flame and cotton balls soaked in rubbing alcohol. He often praised me for being brave during these procedures, for standing perfectly still and not uttering a single cry. The strange thing was that the nights when Poppa worked on my skin were our only times of intimacy and, though I would never look forward to the sting of the needle and the stench of rubbing alcohol, I grew not to mind it so much because at least he wasn't screaming at me or my mother. I liked that he would touch my face with grace and care, and that sometimes, after the ordeal was over, he would touch my nose with the tip of his finger.

One night, I awoke to the sounds of shouting. I crept out of my room, hugging my body for warmth as I navigated the dark hallway to the balusters on the stairs and looked through them. The tiny night-light in the stairwell was on and it cast an unearthly glow over the faces of my parents, who were arguing by the foot of the stairs. Mommy was trying to get past Poppa; he was blocking her. Each time she tried to go past him, he laughed and raised his hand as though he was going to strike her. She was in a long flowered nightgown and he in a white undershirt and boxer shorts.

"Let me go by! You let me go!"

"Who else are you calling? I have a three-hundred-dollar phone bill, tell me who else!" Poppa shouted. "You tell me, goddamn it! Besides that bitch, who never invited us over for a Christmas dinner, that prostitute, that bitch who sat at the table with her legs spread out once at a dinner, that filthy bitch, she was coming on to me . . ."

"You shut your mouth!" Mommy said. "You're going to wake up Margaux with that nasty talk!"

Poppa was so drunk that he was slurring his words, which I had never heard him do. "She has probably heard everything already, thanks to you. Thanks to you letting her go to that dirty house, with wild boys and that sicko, that disgusting pervert, that man you loved so much! Are you calling him? It won't appear on the phone bill, because it is local. But I will find out if you call him! If you call him or she calls him, I will know! I have my ways . . ."

"I think it was a misunderstanding. It was blown out of proportion. Margaux is being punished for nothing."

"So you call him, then? You've heard his side of it? Do you know nothing about how men think? Do you know nothing about what thoughts men think?" He was speaking in a low, sneering way. "Did your father teach you nothing? Did he never take you aside and tell you things that girls must know about the world? Your father let you and your sisters run wild in the woods all day by the house. Your mother spent all day on a sofa, practicing her French verbs. This is how you grew up. This is how. Your father did not care for you. You speak of the man as a god, but did he tell you and your sisters anything? Any practical advice? Your father was a—"

"Stop talking about my father!" Mommy put her hands in her ears. "I won't listen to that talk! I won't listen to your nasty talk! You have a dirty mind and you are a sick man! You're the one running up the phone bill, with all your calls to Cuba, your girlfriend! I *do* wish I had been told something! I wish my parents had taken me aside! My parents were innocent. Unlike you! My father should have warned me about men like you, who run around with a million girlfriends. You took my whole inheritance from me, fifty thousand from my poor, dead father, who you have some nerve to bad-mouth now!"

"I used that for the down payment on this house! If not for me, you would be in an institution—the state would have your father's money. In a way, I did that man a favor by taking you on!"

"Look, I know you married me for my money; I overheard you once. You stole my whole life with your lies! Now look at me! Look at me!"

"Yes, look in the mirror!" Poppa bellowed with laughter. "Look in the mirror and you will see what I have to look at every day! A fat cow that no one wants to see! No wonder I have my girlfriends! I will not deny it! I have my girlfriends! So what are you going to do about it! Tell me your plan . . ." My mother was sobbing. "Tell me how the world is so perfect. Tell me how that man just wanted a playmate, a little nymph for his garden. I am not a fool. People may treat me like one, people may act as though I don't matter, as though I am just here to pay bills and cook and clean and sweat like a field-worker! Tell me if they were ever alone together. Tell me if they were ever alone."

"They were never alone!" Mommy shouted. "And if they had
been, I am sure his intentions would have been better than yours with
all your women! He's not a drunk like you. He loves his girlfriend.
He's faithful. He has a good heart. He had a good heart and that's why
you can't stand him! Because you are rotten!"

"You had better be careful what you say about me. You had better
be careful."

"It's *you* who'd better be careful, you bastard." I'd never before
seen a look on her face like the expression she made that day. "Margaux, come down the stairs! I want you to know what your father is
really like! About how many brothers and sisters you may have that
you don't even know about! Call the police! Right now! Call nine-
one-one!"

I panicked and went to the head of the stairs. Poppa looked up and
saw me standing there. He looked at me one last time, raised his hand
into a claw, and began to dig into my mother's forehead with his nails.
I started running down the stairs, screaming, "Don't do it! Don't hurt
her, Poppa!" I slipped halfway down and collapsed into them. My
mother was screaming. And when my father took his hand away, his
fingers were covered in blood.

She screamed at Poppa: "You fight like a woman! With your nails!
Your nails!"

Poppa looked dazed. After a minute or so, he went over to the
phone jack and removed the plug from the wall. "I want you to calm
down, both of you," he said. "I have had a little too much to drink
tonight. I have had a little too much and words have been said. Words
have no meaning at a time like this. I am under stress at work, I may
get laid off, I am hanging on by a thread, and this is a bad time. Your
mother has been getting sick for a while. I want you to both calm down
and collect yourselves. If the police come, you," he said, pointing to my
mother, "will be institutionalized, and you," he said, pointing at me,
"will be in a home. Everybody in this world fights. There are wars
every day, so do not look at me as though I am a bad man! Do not look
at me as though you cannot stand me! I have cared for you, both of
you! If not for me, you would both be out on the street!"

"Do you ever miss him?" I asked Mommy.

It was a Saturday night and Poppa was at the bar. Mommy and I were playing checkers at the oak kitchen table. She had a large gauze bandage on her forehead where Poppa had scratched her. Poppa had told us both to say that Mommy was trying to rescue our escaped parakeet from the jaws of a stray cat. Even though the story was ridiculous, no one questioned it—not the nuns at my school when Mommy dropped me off, not the owner of La Popular bodega, not acquaintances of Mommy who worked at J&J, Jelly Bean, Carvel, or Sugarman's drugstore not even the postman, who always chatted with Mommy.

"Do. You. Ev-er. Miss. Him," I asked again.

"Oh?" She blinked and tugged at the bandage. "This thing is itchy; it's driving me nuts. Miss who?"

"You know. Peter. Double jump." I took two of her red checkers.

"Well, I didn't see that coming."

"I tricked you."

Mommy sighed and said, "I miss going there, to Peter's. I miss the yard; it was such a nice yard. The little girl, Karen, she was a nice girl. I miss Paws the retriever, what was he, part retriever and part . . . ?"

"Collie. King me."

"Who taught you to play like that?"

"Peter did. He taught me chess, too."

"He taught you chess? When: sometime I wasn't watching?"

"Yeah, sometime you weren't watching."

Mommy was getting sick again. We knew it. She knew it.

"I don't want to go to that hospital," she said. "I won't go there."

They stood in the living room in front of the giant TV; Poppa was trying to coax her into her coat.

"I have already called the cab. He will be here any minute. Cassandra," he said, and I was shocked to hear him say her name, "listen.

We have been under pressure, all of us, including the child. Sometimes I feel like someone has cursed us recently, has wished trouble upon our house. Right now, I feel like the world is against me. My brain lately feels like a pressure cooker . . . Do you get me? There are certain moments in my life when I have felt like I am not equipped to deal with pressure; right now is one of those moments. I feel like any minute, I will explode. Do you understand me? I need to clear my head. You, too, need to clear your head. This is the right thing."

"What about Margaux? Who will take care of her? Will you take off work?" She put her hands on his shoulders.

"I already told you. I will call Rosa, down the street. She doesn't charge much."

"She doesn't do well with new people."

"I know. I know she does not. I wish I could be here. But right now, my hands are tied. I cannot take time off, not even a few days. I will get fired; I know it. They don't like me at this company. At Sanford, things were better, though it is the same everywhere. Always the same. The boss always wants me to go fast and I cannot! Don't these people understand that my goal is quality, not speed? Products—that is what these people want! I am an artist. I cannot do things fast; I must take my time. With me, everything must be exact; if I make a little mistake on a piece of jewelry, no one at work notices it but it weighs on my mind at night and I cannot sleep! I am the best man they have; they do not realize it. They don't give me any recognition, they treat me like a dog . . ."

"I can stay home with Margaux. Louie, please, cancel the cab."

"No," he said, shaking his head. "A friend of mine saw you walking with her on Bergenline the other day, not even looking while you crossed streets! He saw you two almost get run over!"

"I don't remember that. I'm always careful."

"I know you normally are, and this is why I know you are not well right now. Also, there are other things. You have been staring at the ceiling light while you listen to that record." He grimaced. "You have no expression in your face, no expression in your eyes. It scares your daughter to see you like this. It scares me. I am afraid something will go wrong around here. I cannot sleep with this fear. If I cannot sleep, I cannot work."

Everything Poppa had said was true. Mommy would laugh sometimes out of nowhere. She would call people every five minutes. She didn't sleep at all; and, because Poppa and I didn't sleep well either, we'd hear her calling hotlines or playing the *Sunshine* album all through the night.

After the cab took Mommy and Poppa shut the door, Poppa kneeled and took both my hands in his. "I must talk to you. I must speak to you as though you are an adult, my equal. First of all, you have not been watching her. That is a grave mistake. You have let her endanger your life. Suicide is one thing, but to bring anybody down with you is wrong. I do not trust that woman with your life. I do not trust her with my life, either. One day, I caught her handling my gun! Perhaps she wants me dead; maybe I do not completely blame her, but if she endangers you, an innocent, that is a mortal sin!" He paused. "Now, mistakes have been made on everybody's part but we must forget them and move on. Why must we move on? Because we are strong and we can, and if we do not, life will crush us like we are eggshells! Now listen to me, you are under the care of a sick woman. She is mentally ill. You cannot go to her with problems like you would to a normal mother. The problems that normal people shake off like crumbs crush her to dust. Your problems are making her sick. You are a strain on the family. I can handle you; I can even sympathize because I am a strong person, but she is being destroyed by you though you do not mean harm. Child, you must stop your antics! You cannot starve yourself and cry all the time in your room. You think nobody hears you crying, but I hear you."

I looked away in shame.

He lifted my chin. "Don't turn your face away, don't. You must have courage enough to face your wrongdoings. I am your father and I have no other choice but to tell you about the negative effects you have on us. You get sick and vomit nearly twice a week; no one knows why! You eat very little; you look like you are disintegrating!

You used to get first honors; now you are failing mathematics! You are a disappointment to us. To me. I had high hopes. People have children to bring joy into their lives, not pain and worry! No, don't cry; hold it back. You are strong. You will survive this. I promise you, Keesy. I promise you." He rested his head against my chest for a moment and then lifted it up, smiling at me. "Now that she is gone, we can enjoy life a bit, no? I feel guilty we did not go with her, that she must wait in that emergency room by herself for hours, but I know you cannot handle it, Keesy. All those hours with those bright lights and seeing her face like a zombie, it takes your soul from you. In life, there are sights you see that are indelible; they cannot be erased. I will see her face like that, with no expression, forever in my dreams; that look haunts me. But we cannot be sad all the time; we must live another second for every second we die! Come, Keesy, get your coat, shall we go out on the town? Just the two us, like the old days?"

"Okay."

Poppa stood up. He glanced at the time. He was still in his work clothes—a nice dress shirt and crisp trousers. "I don't have time to put on my jewelry. Well, tomorrow night. Tomorrow we will both get decked out for the town, since it is Friday night and I am free! Today we will just go to the place down the street. But tomorrow I will show you a bar across town that has a pinball machine. Remind me to bring quarters! I want you to wear a nice dress and good shoes and nice ribbons in your hair and some bracelets for your wrists, some perfume. We will go from place to place and I will show you off to my friends and they will remark on how beautiful my daughter is! They will say that *my* daughter is more beautiful than the moon! As for now, we go out to a little place, I order you a Shirley Temple, hold the rum. Now, get your coat, Keesy."

I was glad Poppa had called me beautiful. I couldn't help but love him now that Mommy was away. He was all I had. I got my coat from the closet and put it on. As I started to zip it, I realized the zipper was stuck. It made me angry, so I yanked on it, and the thing broke in my hand. Poppa came over and slapped me across the face.

"How many times have I told you not to be rough with things! You must be gentle, all the time, gentle! You cannot break things; things cost money! I cannot buy a new coat! I cannot afford it now that she is back in that hospital!"

"I'm sorry I broke it."

"Listen to me. Listen and hear me. You must never say sorry."

"What should I say?"

"Don't say sorry. Sorry, sorry, sorry, what does that do? You cannot take it back!"

The next night, Poppa kept his promise. We went to bar after bar, including the one with an old-fashioned pinball machine designed in the style of the Old West: horses clopping their hooves and guns firing. I kept running back to Poppa whenever I used up my quarters, almost slipping in my Mary Janes. I did look pretty, in a blue crushed-velvet dress and tights. A young woman was sitting on Poppa's lap. She had big hair and her brightly made up face was a carnival of color. She kept laughing at whatever Poppa said and he kept ordering drinks for her. But she didn't stay long, and when she left we went to another bar and then another one. I'd sneak some of Poppa's beer when no one was looking.

In a dark bar where we sat at a round cherrywood table in the back, Poppa ordered a Grey Goose on the rocks for himself and a Coke with an orange slice for me; he had remembered that I didn't like cherries.

The barmaid came over and set the drinks on the table. Poppa tipped her, complimenting her acrylic nails as he set the tip in her hand.

"Keesy, eat the orange slice," Poppa said when she was gone.

"Can I tell you something, Poppa? The other day, Mommy was slicing oranges for me. While she was doing it, she started cutting herself and blood got all over the oranges."

Poppa was silent and then he said, "I am glad I hospitalized her when I did. I made the right decision." He took a cigarette out of his pack of Marlboros and lit it. "I told you that when I was young, about nineteen, I ran with the bulls in Spain. While I was running, a man fell down. I wanted to help him up. But I had to keep running. You understand, Keesy? I had to watch out for myself, because if I had stopped, I would have been trampled." He paused. "This is biblical. Lot's wife, in the Bible, looked back and she turned into a pillar of salt. Looking back is salt. Looking back is tears. Looking back on the past is death." He cleared his throat. "Let us change the topic. Sometimes I, like you, think too much." He motioned to the orange slice and when I didn't reach for it, he ate it. "I will tell you something, Keesy, a fact about oranges. They originated in China. Everyone thinks they come from Florida, but no, oranges are Chinese. Pasta, too. It doesn't come from Italy. You know where I learned that?"

"No," I said, drinking my Coke through the straw. My face was hot and I felt a little nauseated but didn't have my usual sense of anxiety and dread. I didn't know if it was due to the alcohol, or just the fact that we were in a new place. "Where did you learn it?"

"Your mother's Fact Book. Her little book of disasters that she carries everywhere, her little guide that helps her through life, but not really. Not really." Poppa drank and then continued, "You must learn to smile again. No one likes a grouch. I myself have learned to smile in times of hardship. You, too, will learn this skill. So tell me, what is the problem, Keesy? Tell me why you are so sad. And do not say it is your mother. You are used to her."

My heart beat fast and then I blurted out, "I miss going to Peter's house. Not because of him. He was always busy when I went over there, so I never saw him. But I had a crush on his son, Ricky. We used to play together all the time. He was cute. I used to wish I could marry him. I miss him, Poppa. I miss the way I felt when he was in the room."

Poppa nodded. "I understand. I have seen the boy's picture. Your mother showed me his picture once. Very handsome, though a little unkempt. You are approaching that age now. That age when boys take on more meaning. But let me tell you something. Love is what you call a phantom pain. The poets write of it, our great art represents it, it inspires our musicians, but it does not really exist." He took a long drag from his cigarette. "Like an ulcer you think you have but the surgeon opens you up and finds nothing there. It is a chemical reaction, Keesy. Hormones. People die for it, but no one has ever proven it exists."

I drank the rest of the Coke and excused myself to go to the bathroom. As soon as I got there, I fell to my knees on the dingy floor, which was covered with toilet paper. I bent over the small bowl with brown stains on the sides of it and threw up until there was nothing left.

13

OUR LITTLE SECRET

Peter sent me a "Happy Easter" card and Mommy, recently released from the hospital, said I should phone to thank him. It had been almost a year since we'd last seen each other. When we talked, he complimented me so many times and told so many funny jokes that, after we hung up, I was beaming. After that first call, Mommy said, "I *knew* your father was wrong about him. How could a bad person send such a nice card?" She paused. "Your father has a control disorder, that's what Dr. Gurney says, but you know what: he can't control what he doesn't know. He's not even here half the time." Giggling like sisters, we discussed exactly how we would slide this by Poppa: I would call Peter whenever Poppa was at the bar. For the first time in almost a year, I felt close to Mommy again. We had a secret now, something that was just ours that Poppa couldn't know.

The first sign that Poppa was going to leave was the scent of his cologne erupting through the house. I would hear his feet slam the stairs as he charged up and down; he always went to the master bedroom and into his closet several times, and often I would hear him singing in Spanish. Poppa would fluff his shirt collar, repeatedly patting even the slightest crease in the fabric. He despised wrinkles; he got all his good clothes routinely dry-cleaned and never removed them from their plastic wrapping until it was time to dress. He still shined his shoes with black shoe polish and even repainted his one pair of Converse sneakers white every few years.

He would gather his rings and slip them on without the slightest sound—if one failed to sparkle, he prepared a solution to dip it in and cleaned it with a jeweler's brush—and out would come his gold crucifix, which he checked in the bright light for its shining power. It was not safe to call Peter until Poppa had left and the porch gate had snapped back into place. If the machine answered after the standard five rings, I would simply keep calling and hanging up on the machine. I assumed my constant calling didn't annoy anyone, because Inès and the boys were always polite when they answered.

That school year, in fifth grade, I made friends with a Dominican girl, Winnie Hernandez. People sometimes made fun of Winnie because she liked to read and her skin was considered too dark—just as blond Barbara Howard was thought to be too pale. Also, Winnie was a bit spacey, like me. She had a habit of walking around a blue pole during indoor recess; one day, I started following her and we made a game out of it. Then, a week later, Stacy Gomez told me pointedly after music class, "Winnie says to stop following her." The next day, I forlornly stared at the pole. Winnie motioned me to come over and Stacy said to her, "Don't play with her. Do you want to be just like her?"

A few weeks later, Winnie dropped a note on the floor for me to find. It said, "Meet me behind the auditorium stage tomorrow at Bake Sale." I did and we spent a long time talking. She said that she had overheard Carlos Cruz, the cutest boy in our class, say, "Aw, Margaux's not ugly. She's just weird." Winnie then told me, "I can be your friend, but I can never be seen with you in public. You can never sit with me at lunch or talk to me when people are around." I accepted the deal and, same as with Peter, we had a phone friendship.

On our new portable phone, I confided to Winnie about how a grown man had fallen in love with me and made me into a woman.

"Don't tell anyone. He still loves me and we talk on the phone when my father is out."

Winnie didn't quite understand. "A grown man can't be your boyfriend. That's against the law."

"He says the law's stupid. He's a rebel."

"Oh. We-ell. Do you still like Carlos?" Every girl had a crush on Carlos.

"But, you know. I'm not . . . Carlos is . . ." I felt embarrassed.

Winnie seemed to understand. "He can be your *secret* boyfriend. Maybe you can tell him you'll suck his balls." She started giggling nonstop. She'd meant his penis, but she'd said "balls."

She started in on her usual lecture: "You're pretty; you just need to try harder. You do things to hurt your own reputation." Everything you did and said, who you sat with at lunch and how you wore your hair, comprised your reputation at Holy Cross. "You know what the girls are saying about you?"

"What?"

"That you were sitting in class the other day with your legs wide open like you were trying to show off to the boys. Why do you do things like that?" she said.

"I don't remember," I said, feeling my stomach drop. "I don't always remember what I do."

Winnie sighed. She sounded sad when she said, "But that's *why* everyone says you're crazy."

The Story, a fantasy world that Peter and I went into every time we talked on the phone, was about people who turned into tigers. Even though I was older now, tigers still fueled my fantasies. The main character's name was Margaux. She hadn't been a tiger person originally; she had been a normal, happy girl in love with a pet shop owner, Peter. But then she met a handsome rock star and tiger man, Carlos, who made love to her, which passed the werecat curse on to her so she, too, would turn into a tiger. He got her pregnant with a werecat daughter, Desiree. She married Carlos and they moved into a townhouse in Connecticut. Peter couldn't stand being separated from Margaux, so she hired him as a babysitter for Desiree, and he moved in with her and Carlos. Carlos and Peter eventually became friends though they both loved Margaux. Peter was much smarter than Carlos, and he was the only nontiger person, so he took care of everyone. In part, the Story was influenced by my vivid memory of watching the bloody 1982 horror movie *Cat People* with Poppa when I was five.

Once I entered the Story, the fifth-grade Margaux, of the pimples and the brown bobbed hair, of the black eyes and the knees bruised from practicing landing like a cat, the Margaux who had no party to go to, no sleepover to attend, no boy who had a crush on her, that Margaux vanished. The only thing that came from that Margaux was her name. Margaux of the Story was twenty, she was rich from publishing novels, she had a rock star husband and an additional man who loved her so much that he didn't even care that she was married to someone else. He could not help but love her because she was so beautiful. I saw this Margaux clearly: she looked like Cindy Crawford. In the Story, she was standing by the eyelet curtain in the kitchen, watching Peter cook eggs sunny-side up as the baby Desiree cooed in the high chair, her long blond-streaked hair in a French twist (the kind you could easily make with a Topsy Tail), her arms and legs completely hairless and a velvet choker around her neck. Margaux also occasionally worked as a model and needed to go to photo shoots right after breakfast. There she was in the bedroom, undressing in front of a full-length mirror; there she was in the shower with Carlos and he was washing her hair; there she was driving her convertible; and there she was riding her horse, a beautiful, well-muscled palomino. There she was changing from human to animal: the bright fur was bursting like bonfires from her pores, her eyes were changing from brown to green, her dress was breaking apart. When she was her tiger self, Peter would chain her up in the basement so she wouldn't kill anyone. He would bring her meat and water, often rubbing her belly to coax her back into human form.

Often on Friday and Saturday nights, we talked about the Story from nine p.m. until two in the morning while my mother listened to the radio or her records. When I talked about it, I couldn't get tired, I couldn't get hungry or thirsty, I didn't see anything around me, only the scenes in my head. The only sounds I heard were Peter's and my voice.

Though I loved talking to Peter, I had a strange reaction at Hudson Park when my mother and I unexpectedly bumped into him, Inès, and the boys. With a huge smile, Peter waved hi but as soon as he did, I took off running. The next time we talked on the phone he asked why, and I didn't know, so I said it must have been because the sight of him was a sad reminder that I wasn't allowed to go to his house anymore.

One night during a Story marathon, I heard giggling in the background.

"Who's that?" I asked, not enjoying the fact that the Story was interrupted.

"Jenny and Renee. Oh, I didn't tell you about them yet? They're foster kids. I got them after Karen was taken from me."

"Who took Karen?" I said.

"Her mother. Karen didn't want to go back. They never do. She was gripping my shirt for dear life. The social worker had to pry her fingers off."

"Oh." I felt sad hearing this story.

"Wanna say hi to Renee? She's only a year older than you."

I didn't really want to but he put her on anyway. She was a silly, giddy type with a nasal laugh. She told me she collected plastic trolls. I considered them ugly, but for her I pretended to like them. I noticed she called Peter "Dad." She seemed to love him as much as I did, as much as Karen had. I would talk to Renee on the phone only once more and then Peter said that, just like Karen, Renee and Jenny had been returned to their mother. He also said it was starting to get too sad to foster any more kids and that he never would be able to do it again.

Only once during our separation did I make the mistake of calling Peter when Poppa was home. I heard him pick up the downstairs phone, press a few buttons, then pretend to hang up, trying to listen. I hung up and heard shouts erupting downstairs, but Poppa never once confronted me about it.

PART TWO

14

THE REUNION

Winnie kept her association with me secret up until the end of fifth grade, when I managed to befriend Irene Palozzi as well. Irene had started out teasing me one day during gym, but then I surprised her by actually standing up for myself. I didn't even remember doing it, but it turned out to be a charmed move because it won me her friendship, finally allowing Winnie to be seen with me in public. From then on, Irene, a big-haired, bigmouthed Union City cop's daughter, became my protector. That year, she even threatened to beat up a popular boy for saying I had bugs in my hair. At the start of sixth grade, our trio was joined by a fourth girl: Grace Sanchez. She was as good-looking as any *Seventeen* cover girl but far too meek to fit in with the class's four most popular girls, who had, at first, wanted to recruit her into their clique. She admitted to us she'd found the "in" girls so intimidating that, at their lunch table, she hadn't been able to get a single word out loud enough for them to hear. Irene was constantly telling Grace to speak up and was fond of making me over during recess with her purse's supply of blushers, lipsticks, eye shadows, and her travel-size bottle of Aqua Net. Our music teacher, Mr. Conroy, a Patrick Swayze look-alike whose attention every girl vied for, seemed to favor me even over the Cleopatra-haired Grace. "It's because she's a major flirt," Irene explained to our little group once, mocking the unconscious habit I had of looking down at the floor, then up at a man's face, always beaming the instant his eyes met mine.

Occasionally, this other, unknown side of me allowed me to assert my will against what I considered to be injustice. I was extremely mindful of Winnie, and whenever someone hurt her, even mildly, the part of me that rarely surfaced would immediately rise up to her defense. Once Winnie told me that she'd seen the most popular girl slip crushed glass into her soda, so in the hallway I came right up to the girl I'd been so terrified of for so many years. Our chests nearly touching, I demanded, "What did Winnie ever do to you?" She gave me a puzzled look and kept turning to glance at me as she made her way back to class.

With my new friends, there were sporadic moments when I felt myself to be like any other eleven-year-old girl. But deep down, I knew I wasn't. I still talked to Peter on the phone once a week, a secret I could never let them in on. I was closest with Winnie, but even she didn't seem capable of completely knowing me. Plus, she wasn't nearly as devoted as Peter. When I gave her half of a best-friends-forever locket, I noticed that she stopped wearing hers within a few days. She told me her mother wouldn't let her wear it, but I thought the real reason was that deep down inside she still thought I was a freak.

Instead of being happy that I had a few friends now, Poppa sometimes screamed, "Shut up! I hate your voice!" when I laughed or talked on the phone with Winnie anywhere near him. If my mother showed him one of my better report cards, all he would manage was a gruff "Good." Sometimes it was as if he didn't want me to exist anymore.

Protecting our house were two sturdy locks: a single-cylinder rim spring latch and a Yale 3000 residential deadbolt. Occasionally, Poppa bragged about his locks. He was fond of saying that if a burglar, rapist, or serial killer were ever to try to get past those locks he'd make so much of a racket that Poppa would have time to get his pistol, which he always kept fully loaded.

That fall we were on the bus heading home from Holy Cross when Mommy looked in her purse's usual compartment for her house keys and found they weren't there. We got off at our usual stop across from Washington School, walked over to the pay phone in front of La Popular bodega, and Mommy asked for Peter's number; she knew I had it memorized.

She must have registered the shock on my face because she said, "I think I remember leaving them on the kitchen table. Peter's a locksmith. If we could just get into the house, we could get them and your father would never have to know this happened."

When he didn't answer our telephone call, we walked to his house. We didn't talk; we were both lost in our own thoughts. I was so nervous about seeing Peter again that I took a package of Bubble Tape out of my schoolbag, opened it, and started pulling out the long band of pink gum without breaking off any to chew. I was still in my navy blue jumper with my light blue blouse underneath, my navy blue ankle socks, and Buster Browns. I looked at the overcast sky where the clouds made stark, disembodied shapes just like those in the paintings on our walls at home. "Wait! I think I see the house!" I sang in a strange bright voice. "There it is!" my mother said, her face breaking into a big grin.

The front door had been left wide open, so, on realizing that after all this time the bell was still broken, Mommy and I just walked in. Peter was coming down the stairs as we were about to start up. His hair was much more silver now than sandy. He was wearing paint-streaked gray overalls and a black Harley-Davidson T-shirt, and his vigorous, handsome face was flushed with happy surprise.

He squeezed me so hard that for a second all I could feel was that hug, and I tucked my face deep into his chest, the way I had always done. He smelled like Spackle mixed with dog fur. And when I lifted my eyes to his mouth I noticed it was pulled into an affectionate pout like the face a teenage heartthrob makes on a magazine cover. I felt like we were living in a romantic movie in which he had the starring role.

"I missed you so much," he said.

As we went upstairs to have a snack and catch up I could feel memories snatching and creeping at the edges of my mind. Right before we had stopped seeing each other two years ago, Peter had begun to hit me if I misbehaved. When no one was around, he had occasionally delivered a slap on the cheek or a blow to my hand—nothing compared to what Poppa did to Mommy, but it surprised me just the same. It was almost as if after we'd been to the basement that time for his birthday present, he felt he should treat me more like his wife.

When my mother went to use the bathroom he said, "You've got to find a way to convince your father to let us see each other again. I feel like I can't live without you. Don't you feel like you can't live without me?"

"Yes," I heard myself say, loving him again like we'd never been separated.

"I wash my hands of this matter," Poppa said. He had finally calmed down from his tirade and was now sitting at the kitchen table, working on a gold bracelet. His mouth was tight with concentration; his jeweler's loupe hid the upper part of his face. I sat on a chair perpendicular to his, pretending to work on terminating decimals. "That is what Pilate said to the crowd: 'I wash my hands.' The crowd had the final say. The masses always have the deciding vote. There are two of you and there is one of me. Therefore, I have decided to abstain from the ballot."

Mommy stood by the stove a few feet away from him in her long flowered nightgown and slippers. Her arms were crossed over her chest. "Well, I'm glad. Because Margaux hasn't been well and you know that. You can't always be so selfish and controlling. The boys have friends over, all the time. In the summer, neighborhood kids come into the yard to play in the sprinklers; that's what Peter says. I know you refuse to believe it, but they are a nice family! They're poor, but they're nice!"

Poppa shook his head. "So were the bitch and the banker, remember? But the bitch in Connecticut has a nice house in Westport. When the banker left her, she did not have to worry because of the size of the alimony checks. Some people get rich on the blood of others, they feed like parasites but yet they don't give anything! A simple loan to her brother-in-law! I would have paid her back! The nerve of her to think I would not have paid her back! I am a man of my word!"

"Oh, don't start, please, Margaux doesn't need to hear this screaming. We've been over this so many times."

"I could have put a down payment on that house in Nutley! Then she wouldn't have even met those savages! Everything would have been different. That bitch ruined my life!"

"Stop calling my sister a bitch."

"Oh, your sister. Your sister! As though that bitch can be called family. I trust that man Peter as much as I can trust that bitch to call us up right now and invite us over there. On a clear, bright Saturday, when the weather is warm and the driving smooth! That is how much I trust that man!"

Mommy sighed. "The whole thing was a big misunderstanding. About the kiss, I mean. I'm not saying I trust him, because you can't completely trust a man. It's not like I trust him with Margaux. But I do believe them, both of them, when they say she caught him by surprise; *she* kissed him. It was such a big deal over nothing."

Poppa held the bracelet in the light to inspect his work. "This is for Paula; a girl I know. I like to do favors for people. To fix things for free. It makes me happy to know I am of service. I am not a selfish person, like that bitch in Connecticut."

"Well, Peter tried to help us out. The only reason he couldn't get in here was because he didn't have his tools. He gave us some food, too."

"What did you have?" Poppa said, going over to his cabinet to put away the bracelet and his loupe.

Mommy hesitated. "Leftover KFC. It's good for Margaux. Protein. I don't care if it's fast food. At least she was eating."

"She ate a lot?"

"Two drumsticks and a container of mashed potatoes with gravy." Mommy was lying. I had eaten only half a drumstick and a bite of biscuit. Poppa opened the refrigerator, got an avocado, and began to peel it. "Your sister and that man. They love you. They all love you and your daughter. I am glad that man cannot get into my house! I am glad! He would probably try to steal my jewelry. Do me a favor. You bring her there, but you do not ever bring that man here. Just do me that one favor."

"You're a snob. That's what you are."

"A snob. Okay. I am a snob, because I keep my clothes pressed! Because my shoes are shined! I am a snob! Fine! You go to the pig house! There you can behave like animals with no one around to criticize! You are free now—to be pigs in that filthy place—both of you and I will know nothing about what you do there! Nor will I care!"

Bacon sizzled in a frying pan, shooting liquid sparks. Peter, dressed in his gray overalls streaked with white paint and a white T-shirt, flipped it over with a spatula. Paws sauntered into the kitchen, tail wagging. He seemed plumper than he used to be and his fur looked matted, like he could use a good brushing. I remembered him looking as shiny as those well-groomed dogs in Alpo commercials, but maybe he'd always been scruffy. He was still the friendliest dog in the world. He sat on the linoleum floor, tongue out, and offered Peter his paw.

"You're some beggar," Peter said, passing him a red Milk-Bone. "Pathetic." He petted his head and scratched behind his ears.

"You always give in to him, Peter," Mommy said. She was seated comfortably on one of the kitchen chairs. I, on the other hand, was too excited to sit down. I kept flitting from a spot by the hutch with the glass doors to the left of the stove where the cow-spotted pot holders hung on a wooden rack. Today I had a high ponytail held up by a plush black Scrunchie, supertight jeans with black lace on the pockets, and a gray bodysuit with a tiny metal zipper. The zipper was open to expose my cleavage, which I considered substantial for an eleven-year-old; I had a B cup, while Irene and Grace only had an A. Peter had said I was "filling out." He'd said that soon he'd have to beat the boys away with a stick. We'd been seeing each other again for only a few months, but my mother thought I had already put on a little weight. Even my complexion was better, we thought. Peter had convinced my mother to use her emergency money to buy me some L'Oreal foundation and Revlon pressed powder; both did wonders covering up my acne.

"Are you sure you want me to cook up all this bacon?" Peter showed me the package of pink meat with white lines running through it. "These lines are all fat. I don't know how healthy this is going to be. Are you sure you want all of this?"

I nodded. Peter had taken us to the Pathmark, where he said I could pick out anything I wanted and he would cook it. I had picked out a big package of Oscar Meyer bacon after debating between that and a frozen pan pizza. The bacon won because I knew I'd never be allowed to eat it otherwise.

"You're going to eat most of it by yourself?" he said.

"Yes!"

I heard a rustling sound. It was Ricky's chains; he was coming into the kitchen. The chains were hanging all over his jeans like silver tinsel; the jeans were ripped at the knees and he had on black Doc Martens. He had a tall Mohawk, which accentuated his pronounced cheekbones and the bony symmetry of his chin, nose, and forehead.

"Ricky, you gonna help us eat some of this bacon?" Peter said.

"No thanks," said Ricky, going to the refrigerator. Ricky was fourteen now and coldly polite. He hardly talked, but when he did, he muttered. He entered and left rooms as fast as he could, the chains on his jeans making the only noise. He was skinny and had gone through a major growth spurt, so he was tall now, about five-nine or '-ten.

Peter said he was now a punk rocker. And Miguel had grown his hair long, dyed it a psychedelic blue, and wanted to get a motorcycle, just like Peter had. We constantly heard punk and heavy metal blasting from the attic. Some of their friends had bad relationships with their families, so they ended up staying over for weeks or even months, all the while sleeping on the attic floor. The only thing that bothered Peter was that they ate all the food. He kept saying that Inès was always taking in strays and they used her without her realizing it. I didn't know what the inside of the attic looked like now, but since the boys often left the door open, I saw that the wall adjacent to the steps leading up to the attic was painted a vivid orange. One of the boys' friends had taken a can of black spray paint and written "Oi!" in about five different places on that orange wall, which Peter told me was a punk rock slogan. Whenever the attic door was left open, the steps leading up tantalized me: I knew I was not part of that world of girls in vinyl miniskirts, lace-up boots, and dog collars; or boys in studded leather jackets, toting guitar and bass cases. Ricky and his friend Vaughn had started a band, Rigor-mortis, which later changed to The War Dogs before the band finally settled on the name Prehistoric Defilement. They practiced nearly every day; each time Peter and I would pass by the attic while they were practicing, he would shake his head and say something like, "They call that music. But I call it screaming."

Prehistoric Defilement occasionally managed to get local gigs, and had attracted two adoring fans. Amber was a pretty sixteen-year-old in a studded dog collar who kept a Smurf fastened to the chain-link belt of her micro-mini at all times. She had painted-on eyebrows and called every older man she met Daddy. Then there was Vanessa, a gorgeous girl who sometimes wore a real black leather miniskirt, had bleached blond hair, and sported a dark tan from sitting on the roof in her bikini. Amber bragged about having two babies already, both C-sections. Vanessa worked as a barmaid in Manhattan—she'd gotten the job shortly after her cousin had made her a very realistic fake ID—and was so attractive that I was shocked when Peter told me she'd been stroking Ricky's Mohawk once and he'd kept pushing her away until he finally turned and shouted, "Get your goddamn hands off me!" "He's moody," said Peter, shrugging when I remarked that it seemed so unlike his personality to yell like that.

Peter knew that just like every other girl, I had a crush on Ricky. As before, we didn't keep any secrets from each other. I had even told him I'd written "I love Ricky" all over my notebooks at school and on my big pink eraser. Ricky sauntered into the room once and I could hear those chains swishing. He was all tallness and torn jeans and a beautiful boy face and long skinny hands; and I loved him so much then that I whispered in Peter's ear, "I want to die right now." Peter just shook his head.

Unfortunately, Ricky rarely glanced at me, but Richard, Inès's new boyfriend, looked up every time I went by. Richard, who was twenty-nine, adorable in his beret and shaggy brown hair, intellectual-looking with his crumply paperback science fiction and medieval fantasy novels and his horn-rimmed glasses. Richard, who was always stoned on pot or high on coke, at least that was what Peter said. He said Richard's charming and that's the thing that saves him, but he's like a little kid and can't hold a job or do anything but read and smoke and eat. According to Peter, Richard threw his cigarette butts in the toilet and ate all the spaghetti sauce and white bread without thinking of other people, but at least he was a good chess partner and he made Inès happy in a way that Peter had never been able to. When I asked why he wasn't able to make her happy, Peter explained that it was because he had told her more than three years ago that he couldn't sleep with her anymore. It was shortly after he had started being inti-mate with me, he said, and he hadn't wanted to be unfaithful. He told her the reason he couldn't make love was because he had grown up Catholic and he felt guilty about it. At first, Inès had said it was prob-ably best he leave because she wasn't ready to give up her life as a woman, but Peter cried and even got down on his knees in front of her, begging her not to throw him out. He had said that not only did he not mind if she saw other men, he wanted her to, and to please just think of him as a boarder from now on. She'd started seeing Richard sometime after that.

Peter told me not to go near Richard, but occasionally I did when Mommy and Peter weren't around. I liked to walk by him and have him say something like "Hi, Cutie," or call me "Preteen Dream," or say that if the girls looked like me when he was in sixth grade, he would've never wanted to grow up. But unfortunately, Ricky barely even looked my way. Even when I was wearing my silver bodysuit with the tiny zipper and my choker and my Revlon Stardust lipstick and my silver nail polish and the black kohl under my eyes like I was that day in the kitchen. I hoped he didn't find me ugly. Even though my chest was good, I was skinny and small-hipped compared with many of the more voluptuous Cuban and Dominican girls like Winnie, or the girls who were full Puerto Rican, instead of just half. Unlike Winnie and Grace, I hadn't even gotten my first period yet, and Mommy kept saying it wouldn't come until I put some meat on my bones. Now she had Peter agreeing with her. So I was at the kitchen table with Peter heaping all this bacon on my plate and calling me "the bacon queen." Ricky finished reheating a giant plate of spaghetti in the microwave and carried it to the attic, probably for everyone up there to share; now that he was gone, I could start eating. My favorite pieces were the barely cooked ones, pink and thick, oozing with grease and salt.

"Don't eat so fast, or you'll throw up," said Peter, and he pretended to hurl all over me, with lots of sound effects. At first, I said, "You are *so* immature." But then I grinned and opened my mouth wide to show him all the chewed-up bacon and he stuck his tongue out at me, laughing.

That winter, in his kitchen while my mother was picking up snacks Peter asked me what my friends were like. Smiling, I went into great detail about Winnie being the brainiest, Irene the protector, and Grace the great beauty. "Well, what about you?" he asked, and I explained that I was the entertainer. I'd tell my friends stories and act out roles that I'd seen on TV. I was the one who'd hatch grand schemes that never panned out, like running away from home and riding trains like Natty Gann or plans that did work like starting the Animal Love Club, a short-lived project that involved writing letters protesting fur-wearing and animal experimentation. Often, I'd imitate Poppa's rants for them and they'd all laugh (though Poppa's tirades were never funny to me when they were actually happening). Peter said that he wanted to meet my friends but I wasn't sure if that was such a good idea. I wanted to keep him separate from the world I shared with them. Unfortunately, he had the same habit as when I was younger, which was to pester me endlessly until he finally got what he wanted.

"Are you ashamed to introduce me to your friends?" he asked one day while I was brushing Paws. I kept up on his flea baths and grooming, so he always looked sleek now.

"Well, how will I explain you?" I said, gathering the tufts of fur and putting them in a grocery bag.

"You could say I'm a friend. They're your friends and I'm your friend, too," he said, caressing my back. I flinched for a second, then ignored it.

"We don't really see each other outside of school." This was only partially true. Winnie's mother didn't approve of any of us and Grace lived too far away. One time Grace and I had gone to Irene's to watch *The Exorcist*, which we made fun of by pretending that the possessed girl was doing Richard Simmons–type aerobics; this helped calm a terrified Grace. Another time I had stayed over at Irene's and we read ghost stories until two in the morning.

"Well, we could plan it. You could say I was your uncle. Why don't I take just you and Grace to the magic show this weekend?" That Saturday he drove me to the show on his motorcycle, which impressed Grace, whose mother dropped her off in a boring Toyota. Peter seemed to know exactly how to coax a timid person into feeling comfortable and relaxed. He snapped a Polaroid of us both holding the magician's python. Later, Grace would say how nice my uncle was and how much fun she'd had. Peter suggested taking us out again, but I said Grace's mother hadn't liked having to battle the traffic. When he persisted this time, I said we weren't good friends anymore because she'd started sitting with the popular girls at lunch. I didn't like lying to Peter, but for some reason I felt like I had no other choice.

Peter's house had changed over the past two years. These changes didn't appear to me right away. One day, I noticed that the rabbit hutches were gone. Peter said the rabbits had caught a virus and died. Then I found out that Warden, the caiman, had been kidnapped from his tank by an unidentified attic dweller and set loose in the yard in the middle of winter. The poor little creature froze to death. Now only the birds and Paws remained.

What we could do together had changed, too. When I was eight, Peter used to hold my hand and no one said anything. Now when he held my hand during a dog walk, we got strange looks. I didn't see how it was anybody's business what we did.

One March day, Peter and I were in the kitchen looking through a photo album. My mother was in the living room, calling the American Cancer Society to ask about when Peter should be tested for prostate cancer. There, under the photo album's glossy contact paper, was Karen with her head and arms locked inside a big wooden device. I asked Peter what that was, and he said it was a stockade, which was something used to torture people in medieval times. They had gone to the Renaissance Festival about a year and a half ago, Inès, Peter, the boys, Karen, and Richard.

I looked at Karen's picture again. She looked old, though she must have been only seven. Maybe it was the red streaky makeup under her eyes. Or maybe it was the stockade, enclosing her head and arms.

I noticed the picture across from hers, of a smiling blond girl. "Oh, that's Jill," Peter said. "She and her mother came over a lot last summer after Karen left, and she'd play with Jenny and Renee. She's pretty, isn't she?"

I shut the album.

My mother came into the kitchen from the living room and said to Peter, "I gave the American Cancer Society your address; they're going to send you a pamphlet about that test. I'm going to see if I can get Maria next. I'm not tying up your phone, am I?"

"Sandy, don't worry," Peter said. "I've told you people rarely use that phone. We might as well not even have a phone. So long as it's not long distance, it's fine."

My mother nodded and left to call Maria. Peter then said, "Margaux, do you want to see my room? I don't think I've ever shown it to you." That was true. We had always hung out in the kitchen, yard, or living room, so I was curious to see it. Peter's room was right off the kitchen; it had a wooden sign on the door that read, "Slave Quarters." "That's my joke with Inès," he said. "Because I do so much around the house."

The first things I noticed were the photos of me when I was eight. There were three large oval-framed pictures on the walls, and at the center of the main wall a larger photo of me and Paws hanging over a collection of potted plants next to a good-sized TV with a VCR and a Nintendo set. I was in my blue-and-white one-piece bathing suit, holding Paws's collar.

"Isn't that a nice picture?" Peter said. "And there's another one of you in that cranberry-and-gray striped shirt with the Peter Pan collar you always used to wear. Remember that shirt? Do you still have it?"

"No, I've outgrown it."

"And that picture," he said, pointing to the left side of the wall. "That's you and Karen and Paws clowning around by the Christmas tree." I looked happy in the picture, but for some reason I couldn't remember that last Christmas and thinking about it nauseated me. "Who's that?" I said, pointing to another picture.

Peter chuckled. "Believe it or not, that's Jill. The girl you just saw in that album; I know it doesn't look like the other picture. I put your picture on the left side straight across from Jill's because even though you're a brunette and she's blond, you both have that exact same *look*. That special look of love and, dare I say, adoration. That glow, that look, only comes once in a lifetime. You were both eight years old. And you know what? Both of you were looking *at me*. Two girls, the same age, one of an olive complexion and dark eyes and the other a very pale blond with blue eyes, but it's like you're two halves of the same person. And you're both filled with love and wonder; when I wake up in the morning, I see these two angels and they give me the strength to start the day."

In that picture, Jill didn't look like a real girl like me or my friends, even Grace. Peter's Jill was too flawless, too bright. In the photo album, she was just a regular girl with pigtails and chipmunk cheeks, but in this picture her face was slightly turned so it looked much slimmer, her curly hair was platinum blond, and her eyes were the faux blue of Christmas tree bulbs. She even had a dainty mole by her eye, which Peter referred to as her "beauty mark." I was both angry and awed by the sight of her; her good looks drew my eye back again and again with the urgency of thirst, and whenever I looked at her I felt bad because my picture on the left side was nowhere near as radiant.

"And you see how I chose a dark frame to offset her blond hair and a gold frame to offset you. And when I got the photos blown up, they were originally square-shaped. But I can't stand squares so I cut the pictures so they would fit into oval frames. It's an art of mine. You don't see any square or rectangular lines in nature so why should I have a room that's full of right angles? I don't even like to see squares on my ceiling. See what I did with the ceiling?"

I looked up.

"See?" Peter said, grinning. "I took this giant piece of blue fabric—Miguel, Ricky, and Richard helped me: they all held up part of it while I nailed the edges down. Anyway, I rolled it in such a way that it would resemble the waves of the ocean. I had a terrible ceiling before. Every day I would look up at all of these squares that look exactly alike, and the more I stared at those identical squares with their ugly cracks and stains the more depressed I got. But now I look up, and it's like the ocean is right above my head. You know what I'm thinking? If I get tired of the ocean, I'll make stars, white stars out of construction paper, Krazy Glue them, and it will be like I have the sky above me. Not like the city sky, but the country sky, like the sky of Bear Mountain State Park. Like I'm camping and the stars are all out."

"I've never been camping. I've never seen the stars." His ceiling did look like an ocean, so much so that I felt like I was actually swimming in it.

"You've missed out on so much; it's your father," Peter said, shaking his head. "I want to change that. I'd like to take you to Bear Mountain sometime. On the motorcycle, maybe. Wouldn't it be romantic?"

"Yeah," I said, staring at the ceiling.

Rubbing my shoulders, he said, "Margaux, tell me. Do you see one thing, even one little thing that doesn't automatically make you feel relaxed and tranquil? See, I have these anxiety attacks, I wake up in the morning and my heart is pounding and I feel like I can't breathe. The pictures manage to put me at ease, because they're all of children and children are innocent and carefree. When I look at children's smiling faces, I don't feel so sad anymore."

A few paintings of old-fashioned girls with plump cheeks and heavily powdered skin, their hair in ringlets, hung on the walls mixed in with the photographs. Peter walked about, showing me everything. On wood stands jutting from the walls stood girl figurines; Peter said some were made out of majolica, a type of porcelain. One blond-ringleted girl in a long white nightgown was holding her hand to her mouth to blow a kiss; another girl, barefoot and dressed in peasant clothes, was tending sheep.

I felt dazed, like I was in a different world. Trying to shake the feeling, I said, "So, do you always make your bed?"

"Well, in the air force, you learn those things and you never get them out of your system. Like your father: he was in the army, right? But he took everything he learned to a crazy extreme." He paused to light one of his King 100s. "I mean, I understand your father to some degree. It's important to be neat; not like Richard, who throws his clothes all over the place whenever he stays over, plus, his damn cigarette butts: he just can't put them in the trash can. The other day he threw them right in the kitchen sink! Your father would never be able to take him, he'd probably shoot him the minute he met him! Now, I have to admit that I like *some* routine in my life. It just makes me feel better. Inès says that every time we go out to dinner, I always order the same thing: pot roast, mashed potatoes with gravy, and green beans . . . Oh, you noticed that? You can't stop looking at that painting once you start. That's Norman Rockwell's *Curiosity Shop*."

He walked to the painting that was hanging in the back of his room to the right of an aquarium, situated above his bed frame, that contained plants. "See how at first glance all it looks like is a girl buying some dolls from a shopkeeper? But *then* you notice how the dolls don't have doll faces; they have the face of the shopkeeper."

"Oh, yeah . . . creepy . . ." The shopkeeper had a wrinkled face and gray hair that looked normal on him, but grotesque on the two baby dolls.

"Yeah, if you're just glancing at that picture everything looks normal, but then, as you look closer and closer, you start to realize nothing's the way it should be. It's funny; I feel like every time I look at it I find something new that's not quite right."

15

THE DOWRY

Shortly after my twelfth birthday, Peter started saying that French-kissing would be romantic. In my mind, it was nowhere near as romantic as cuddling, but I knew that once he started nagging, he'd never let up. On the phone recently, Winnie had mentioned that she had done it a few times with a boy on her block, and she'd started pestering me to catch up to her in sexual knowledge. We were the oldest of our friends, our bodies were the most developed, and now I finally had my period, too. I figured that after the kiss I could call her up and tell her what it was like, pretending I'd done it with Ricky. Peter's pestering had even jolted my memory: we'd done it before when he made it a game. Well, this time I said that if he wanted it done, he would have to pay me fifty cents; I had a mean impulse to somehow convey to him that if it were someone like Ricky it'd be free, but because he was old, he had to pay. I felt good about it then, like it would even out the fact that he'd gotten so many French kisses for free when I was too young to realize my own worth.

Peter paying me would be like a dowry, the fee paid for young brides in places like India; as always, Peter talked about how demented America and most of Europe were for not allowing men to wed young girls and had pointed out my period's arrival as nature's way of informing me it was time to marry and have babies. But in this sick culture, I was restricted from following my true instincts.

As Peter and I kissed right behind a white truck that read "Path-mark" in blue and red letters, I kept my eyes open even though one of my magazines warned that that wasn't romantic. Peter had his eyes closed. The bristles on his face scratched me a little. I looked at this truck, numbered 31186. All the trucks were coded like that. There was a large Dumpster and stacks of shipping crates. Peter's mouth tasted like ash and coffee and it was dry, like he didn't have much spit. I didn't want to think it, but I knew that I was grossed out. I loved him, but I didn't like the feeling of his tongue touching mine, and I tried to imagine it was Ricky's, but I couldn't. I knew Ricky wouldn't have stubble. I knew Ricky wouldn't taste like coffee.

"Fifty cents, please," I said with a smile when we'd finished.

"I love you, sweetheart. I really love you." He pulled me close to him, his body sucking in mine.

A month before the school year ended I found out some bad news. Winnie's mother was transferring her to an expensive all-girls prep school. We all wanted to transfer with her, but only Irene's family permitted it. I feared that I would return to my lowly social status at Holy Cross.

"If you want to transfer somewhere, go to public school and save me money," Poppa said, surprising me. For years he hadn't wanted me mixed in with public school kids, but now he didn't seem to care. I also talked the matter over with Peter, who thought it was a great idea; the public school was only a couple blocks away from my house, so there would be no more bus to take home from Holy Cross, allow-ing me to arrive at his house earlier.

Once school had ended and summer began, my mother and I began to head over to Peter's as early as nine in the morning. She even let me go to New York City on the back of Peter's motorcycle. I was dazzled by all the Mohawked, tattooed punk rockers in Washington Square Park. I adored the music stores in the East Village that blasted heavy metal and burned incense. Punk rock girls in high lace-up boots working in clothing shops told me I would look pretty if I dyed my hair purple. On the stands outside, people sold huge fancy silver and gold crosses tied to black shoestring necklaces. One day, I bought one for eight dollars and stopped wearing my black choker. Then I cheerfully gave the change from the ten to some runaways who were begging on Bleecker Street.

Old men always challenged Peter to games of chess on the granite-topped chess tables at Washington Square Park, and he was never able to resist them. There was one gray-haired black man whom Peter called the Grandmaster. He had eyes as dark as Inès's typewriter keys, and spoke in such a low voice that Peter had to cup his ear to hear what he was saying. As the Grandmaster was positioning one of Peter's King 100s in his mouth, I noticed that he, like Peter, barely had any teeth. It was then I realized that Peter had stopped putting in his false teeth. When I asked him about it, he said they were uncomfortable; he had learned to smile with his mouth closed and it didn't matter what people thought of him so long as he was comfortable in his own skin. To me, it made no difference whether he had any teeth, just as it hadn't mattered that there was a hutch in place of the turtle's tank or a piano where the iguana's aquarium used to be; just as it hadn't mattered that Rabbit was no longer fun and "Danger Tiger" was forgotten, along with Tickle Torture Time and the other games we'd played when I was eight. Just as I told myself it didn't matter that Karen was my sister once, but now I'd never see her again.

What was important was that Mommy and I were going to Peter's every single day now after school, not just two days a week. We never ate with Poppa anymore; he gave my mother fifteen dollars each day for our meals. Most of the time, he left it on the counter for her to take, but if he was in a bad mood he would throw it on the floor. When Inès came home she would cook things like chicken, rice and beans, or spaghetti for the "gang" upstairs, which was how Peter referred to them, while my mother, Peter, and I would head to the avenue and eat at a fifties-style restaurant called Yummy's or at El Pollo Supremo. Occasionally, we went down Palisades to Forty-second Street and had dinner at a crowded place called El Unico. It had the cheapest prices you could imagine, and we often got heaps of white or yellow rice, kidney or black beans, yucca, fried bananas, and chicken. Sometimes Poppa complained that we never ate with him anymore, but Mommy would remind him that back when we did, I barely ate, and that if I'd continued that way, I might have died of cardiac arrest, like Karen Carpenter. I assumed Poppa's complaints were mostly for show; secretly, he was glad we no longer ate with him. Plus, we had done things at the table that he said had made him lose his appetite, like chewing too loudly, or not wiping our faces properly; he used to say it was a wonder he could stomach any food at all, seeing my mother's blank look or watching me roll my peas or fried potatoes across the plate with my fork. But it was our silence that had bothered Poppa the most.

"I live in a house of monks," he would say. "They walk like monks; they stare into space like monks. They slouch like hunchbacks. Their faces are like ghouls."

When we'd come home from Peter's, around nine in the evening, Poppa would already be upstairs, watching his small TV in his room, or he wouldn't be home at all and we'd know he'd gone to the bar.

Sometime during the summer of '91, several months since our reunion on the steps, Peter began to dare me to briefly kiss, lick, or suck his penis whenever my mother was out. One day, he took me back to the basement. I didn't know where my mother was. Peter told me she had met a newly divorced man at Pathmark, Juan, but she didn't want me to know. Even though I'd never met Juan, I hoped my mother would divorce Poppa and marry him.

Mommy's new thing was to call hotlines and friends to discuss whether or not my spending all my time with Peter was healthy. She told them she kept a good watch on us, just as she'd told Poppa; I speculated that she might have lied because it was hard for closed-

minded people to deal with the fact that Peter and I were in love. I
wondered if she trusted me to make my own choices; if she understood that I had an unusually high maturity level even though my
physical age was only twelve. Instead of trying to destroy my will, as
Poppa had, Mommy was setting me free to live my life as I saw fit.
Peter and I had a fated love. Like in *Dr. Zhivago*. Like in *West Side
Story*. Mommy adored those movies.

As we descended the soft wooden steps I knew so well, Peter told
me this time he wanted to make *me* feel good. He asked me to lie
upon a wooden workbench. He went into the oak Victorian wardrobe, took out an old gray dress with pearly white buttons on it, and
put it over the bench so it would be comfortable. Then I lay down on
the dress like a patient on a bed.

"Margaux," he said, "I love you more than anyone else on this
earth. I want to pleasure you and try to make you feel good. Right
here in this place where I received the best birthday gift I could ever
hope for." When I didn't say anything, he continued: "When I was
about eight or nine, my brother and I went to a foster home. There
were these two girls there: Tina and Nancy. They were tap dancers."
He paused. "There aren't that many tap dancers now, but back then,
tap dancing was big. They were about thirteen and fifteen years old.
Tina, the older one, was the worst. My brother had a cowboy hat, and
she used to spit in it and then put it on his head. These girls forced us
to pleasure them between their legs. It was sickening . . . I couldn't do
it to a woman again after that. But for you, I want to try. I want to
pleasure you in that way. Is that okay with you?"

"How will it feel?" I said.

He started kissing my cheeks and the nape of my neck, my ears
and hair. Little kisses like chickadees pecking grain. Then he said: "I
just thought of another memory from when I was fourteen and was
staying with my father for a while. This is kinda funny. Me, some
girls, and another boy played strip poker . . . I lost the game and they
threw my clothes into a tree and I had to climb up and get them." He
stopped to kiss my mouth. "Anyway," he said, laughing. "I was a cute
boy. What'd you call a pretty boy. Like Ricky."

"Oh yeah? Were you prettier than me?"

"No, of course not. But I was cute, or what you girls would say nowadays . . . *I was to die for.* Do you want to know what I looked like? A little cherub, with my platinum hair. When I was about three, a woman came up to me and tousled my hair and said to my mother that I looked just like a seraph—"

"Is that the same as an angel?"

"Uh-huh," he said, kissing my hair. "The girls all loved me."

"What was your first memory?"

"My very first . . ." He started to take down my jeans, kissed my belly, then licked my belly button. I giggled at the sensation. "Riding a tire swing on a tree. I was swinging back and forth on a tire and I was happy. I felt like I was flying. What's your first memory?"

"Looking through the bars of my crib," I said, as he took down my underwear slowly, kissing me through the cotton. "And realizing I couldn't get out . . ."

"Don't ever wear nylon or lace or satin panties, Margaux, always wear cotton—"

"Why?"

"Because I don't like lace or satin or anything like that—"

"Why?"

"I just don't."

"You're silly. You like dopey baby things. You're a silly little boy." I was talking like that popular girl. I enjoyed feeling like her.

"Is that right?"

"Yeah."

"I love you, I love you so much. Is that silly?"

"Yeah . . ." I growled.

"What would you want me to call you? If it could be any pet name at all?"

"Cuddle Bunny. No, Snuggle Bunny. Snuggle Bunny."

"And what would you call it if I kissed your belly button?"

"Veening."

He pulled up my shirt and bra. "And if I kissed your bumps right here?" He kissed each breast and then sucked on them.

"Twiggling."

"And if I kissed you down here? In your place?"

"Snooking," I said. "That would be my word."

He started to lick me. "How does it feel? When I'm snooking you?" We both laughed at that. We couldn't help it.

"Seriously. Does it feel good?"

I didn't feel anything exactly, but I said, "Yes, that feels good. When you *snook* me, it feels *superfluously splendid*."

"So . . . you like it? I won't use the silly word, though, because I want a serious answer. I don't want to do what you don't like."

"It feels . . . pleasant."

"Okay. I like 'pleasant.' Everything should be pleasant."

But it still didn't feel like anything special; his tongue was like a paintbrush and he was asking the wall if it felt good to be painted. There was something about the basement that made me feel unreal, nearly dead; and then just when I felt deadest, life surged in again and I blurted out, "Peter, I'll never let Poppa separate us again. If he ever tries, we'll run away together; but tell me, where could we possibly be accepted for who we are?"

"Scandinavia," Peter said, as though he'd thought this through. "Or Thailand. I'd just have to figure out how to get you out of the country. And money. That would be a problem."

"We'd rob a bank. Like Bonnie and Clyde. Or I'd steal my father's jewelry and sell it on the black market."

"I feel like all this talk is taking away from the sensation. I want you to try to come. Can you try?"

"Okay," I said. "I guess words have no meaning at a time like this."

"Deep," said Peter.

"Well, Poppa said that once. Or maybe it was 'words mean nothing at a time like this.' It was after he scratched my mother's face. But when I say something like that, *I* mean it romantically."

"Margaux, concentrate on the sensation. You have to concentrate if you're going to have an orgasm."

"Okay. I promise to be quiet. I promise not to talk anymore. I am going to be as silent as a mountain or as speechless as a chair."

"Margaux!" Peter said. "Concentrate!"

"I am concentrating!"

"And stay still. You keep wiggling."

I pretended I was in a stockade, except instead of crouching over and sticking my head and arms into its locking holes, I was positioned under it. The dark oak clenched my throat like a punk chick's spiky dog collar. My mouth had been sewn together with black thread and my face was painted white like a mime's. I looked above to the white, flossy webs attached to the crossbeams and imagined spider's eggs starting to drop like rain. I looked at Peter's face. In the semidarkness I couldn't see his wrinkles, and the hair on his head could be platinum for all I knew. I touched his hair and it felt dry. I imagined the wood was getting tighter around my neck, chokingly tight, as I started to feel tingles between my legs. I looked down and envisioned Ricky's tongue on my vagina. Then I imagined it was Richard, then a boy in my class I had thought was cute. I couldn't think of Peter. He was just too old.

When he looked up at me briefly, his eyes were turquoise and loving, and his face seemed as large as the face of a president. He had a big Adam's apple, and I touched my throat to feel my lack of one. I loved him and hated myself for being so frustratingly unable to come. He was trying so hard and nothing was working, not the thought of being in shackles or the thought of Ricky doing it. Peter saw my face change and said, "What's wrong?" His arms came like long tropical ocean waves, and enclosed me like a mussel in a shell. I put my face in his shoulder; his shirt was terrycloth and felt so smooth against my face.

"You're wearing the towel shirt; I love it. I wish I had been able to come. You did such a good job and, as usual, I can't do a thing right. Maybe it's too cold here. Maybe it's too cold and too quiet and I'm too much like a ghost. Let's never come here again, never again. Okay?"

"Okay."

"I've always hated this place. I've always hated this basement."

"You never told me you hated it. Darling, princess, dear one, Snuggle Bunny, Butterfly Girl, just tell me the truth, always the truth."

"I don't hate it," I said quickly. "But now I feel like you're hiding me down here. I want to kiss you right in public. I want to take down your pants in the middle of Pathmark and have sex with you on the floor. I don't care what anyone says! People are so stupid! Why can't we just marry each other right now?"

"Don't worry what other people think," said Peter. "Of course they would object. It doesn't matter. We have our own world. Other people have nothing to do with us."

"But they do, Peter! You've even said it! You've said we should stop holding hands when we walk on the street because we're starting to get looks! Daughters don't hold hands with their fathers past a certain age! Any day people are going to start spreading rumors! Any day, you say, any day now! Well, I say let them talk! I wish I could make them live like I did in a hell worse than their worst nightmares. People like those lifeguards from the pool and Dr. Gurney and the police or whoever can stand and judge me when they don't even know me. Peter, if they could just live one day in my place and know how you can make me happy, how much you love me!" It was true, people were against me. They wanted to see me suffer. Even Winnie didn't care for me. A secret friend; that's what she'd wanted. I'd had to sit alone at a lunch table all that time because she didn't want to be seen with me. Better to have no friends at all!

"Sweetheart," he said, lighting a cigarette. "We've got to be careful. That's just reality. You don't understand what's at stake here. This is my life we're talking about. I could go to jail. It's no joke. We can be affectionate in private, like we are now. In the outside world, we've got to behave differently. I don't want to go to jail. Do you want me to go to jail, Margaux? You may not want it but it could happen. One wrong move, one wrong statement, and that's it! I'll kill myself before going to jail."

I shook my head. "Don't worry, I know I'd never do anything that would get you in trouble. You know that! I'd cut my own throat before I'd tell."

"Sweetheart," he said, putting his finger on my lips, "let's forget there are other people for now. Let's pretend we're on our own little planet. Let me see you as you are now, fully. I even want to see your feet, the backs of your knees. I love you so much that I want to see you exactly as God made you."

"No one can see, no one can judge," I muttered.

I sat up and took off my shirt and bra. I took off my socks and the velvet Scrunchie from my hair. I sat there, naked and shivering. My nipples were hard. There were goose bumps all over me and the hair on my arms prickled from the cold. I was both cold and hot at the same time, like I had the flu. I was beautiful, at least my body was, with its full round curves, long slender neck, and long legs and narrow feet and straight brown hair falling over my shoulders, bright as sap against my light olive skin. I was twelve and I was a woman. I was twelve and love burned in me like sap. Peter got down on his knees as though I was his goddess, as though I really was the only sound he could hear and I filled his head with miraculous ringing, as though I made him permanent, and for this he would always be grateful. He was so grateful, in fact, that he hugged my ankles and said, "Margaux, Margaux, all hail Margaux. All hail Margaux, Margaux, Margaux."

Peter and I started hanging out in his room and playing Super Mario Brothers 3, which Peter had just bought for his Nintendo. I had taught Peter how to make Mario jump and fly, how to find secret coin rooms, where to locate hidden mushrooms that would increase Mario's size or give him a second life, and how to use a special whistle to conjure up warp worlds. After a while I regretted teaching him anything because he became addicted. I was a far better player than he and had beaten most of the worlds, so the game had become dreadfully boring. Often, I would want to stop playing, while Peter wanted to keep going. My mother would sit in a kitchen chair while Peter and I played together.

Unfortunately, Richard had taken over the living room. His regular girlfriend, Linda, had thrown him out in December and he'd been here ever since and Peter didn't like it, but he'd told me in private that he couldn't say anything or Inès might start complaining about me being over seven days a week. Lately, Richard had started stealing money from everyone to support his coke habit: Inès, Peter, and even Miguel, who had a part-time job at Circle Cycle, a motorcycle repair shop on Tonnele Avenue. Richard had stolen money from Linda, too, which was why she threw him out to begin with.

Whenever Peter and I argued about the Nintendo, my mother would referee us, saying things like, "Margaux, let Peter play a few more rounds and then maybe you should go out and rent a video," or, "We should eat lunch soon; it is getting late." My mother wasn't always in the room, though. One day, Peter and I got into an argument over the game while my mother was at Pathmark. I got so furious over Peter's refusal to stop playing, even after I'd threatened to smash it with a hammer, that I took a bunch of cigarettes out of his pack, broke them in half, and put them in his coffee. Peter was so upset he went out by himself with Paws and didn't come back for an hour. When he returned, I was burying my head in a pillow. Peter swiftly took me into his arms and said he wasn't angry anymore. Mommy, who had been unable to calm me, said, "See, I told you, Margaux, that you two always make up. I told you that Peter wouldn't be gone for good."

Another time while my mother was out, we got into a fight in Peter's room and he hit me in the face and I scratched his arm, leaving a thin, jagged streak of blood.

"Look at what you've done! I'm going to clean this up," he said. "I sure hope Inès doesn't say you can't come over here anymore when she sees this."

"Don't go out there, then," I said.

"What's the alternative—stay in here with you? I don't have to put up with this abuse."

He went out of the room with his coffee, while I hid under the covers. I hated him for going out there.

I opened the door a crack and saw him washing the cut in the sink in front of Inès, who said, "What happened to your arm?"

"Margaux. It's nothing, really. We got into a little argument."

"And she scratched you like that? What was it over?"

"Ah, the Nintendo. Look, sometimes I think she's a little unstable. You know, from growing up in such a chaotic household."

"You have a lot of patience, that's for sure."

I wanted to shout at Inès that he'd hit me first, but instead I found myself despising her with such gut-wrenching force that I couldn't even be angry at Peter when he came back into the room, his arm freshly bandaged, saying we should go out on the motorcycle to take our minds off what had just happened.

Though the Nintendo was good for nothing but fights between Peter and me it provided an otherwise impossible chance for me to spend time with Ricky. On Saturday or Sunday, Peter liked to take Inès out for a ride or to eat; they were still good friends, he said, and needed to be able to spend time together. She needed someone to confide in about Richard and her job because both were stressing her out. To help me pass the time while he was out, Peter arranged for Ricky, a Mario 3 expert, to give me a run for my money while my mother thumbed through magazines, made calls in the kitchen, or talked to Richard. She didn't even seem to mind that he wasn't listening.

During those afternoons with Ricky I always dressed up in a tight baby-doll dress, short shorts, or one of my lace-edged camisoles. But he never looked at me or said anything; he just kept staring at the TV screen as though he was trying to block me out. I was always Mario and he was always Luigi; each time, he would defer the privilege of going first by wordlessly handing the main game controller to me. His eyes never moved from the screen, and I was afraid to look at him, even through the corner of my eye, lest he think I liked him. I was terribly conscious of both my breathing and his: mine sometimes seemed too shallow and I would try to swallow the sound, much in the same way I had tried to hold my breath underwater in the bathtub, hoping to drown. We didn't speak for what seemed like six or seven hours, though we were probably together only half that time.

Finally, one day after Peter's outing with Inès, I said to him, "I don't think Ricky really wants to play with me."

"Why? He loves Super Mario Three." Peter said, sipping his Taster's Choice and reaching for his lighter. I watched the lighter fluid swill forward, sparking a thimble-sized flame.

"I don't think he likes me."

"He's shy."

"I don't think that's it. He doesn't like me at all. He hates me."

"Why? Why would he hate you?"

"I don't know."

"Sometimes when a boy likes a girl, he can't talk to her. Besides, he's probably busy having thoughts . . ." He started to hum and I banged my fist against the bed.

"What are you doing? Margaux!"

I closed my eyes.

"I thought I was doing something nice by letting you spend time with the boy you have a crush on. Nice guys always finish last, don't they?"

Paws lay on the floor, his legs shaking from a dream like something mechanical. Suddenly, I had to bite my lip to suppress a crazy impulse to kick the sleeping dog. Shamed, I leaned over and rubbed Paws's belly.

Peter continued, "I was just trying to make you happy. I'm always putting you first."

"You just do it so you can go out with Inès," I muttered.

"What?"

"Nothing."

"I'm going to have a talk with Ricky. He needs to learn some social skills. I'm tired of the way he struts around, acting like he's too cool to talk to anyone. He and Miguel both need a good talking-to. God knows, Inès won't do it."

"Don't you dare tell Ricky what I said! Don't you dare humiliate me in front of a cute boy, Peter!"

He threw up his hands. "And what am I in your eyes? The dog's dinner?"

"No." I pressed a pillow into my chest. "I'm not comparing. Sometimes you twist my words."

"I'm sorry. Can't I get a little jealous? Am I allowed? I shouldn't be jealous," he said, stroking my hair. "If you love something, set it free. Free to live and love and be alive. It turns you on, doesn't it, when Ricky sits here? You can pretend I'm Ricky, you know. You can fantasize I'm him anytime you want." He got up and locked the door.

Then he returned to the bed and undid the top button of my jeans, starting to rub me.

"Where's my mother?" I said, my voice sounding strangely automatic. "Outside the door? She might catch us."

He laughed. "I like to take risks but I'm not crazy! She went to Pathmark to rent a movie for us."

"What movie?"

"Cheech and Chong's *Up in Smoke*. I watch that movie every year. Cheech wears a tutu and Mickey Mouse ears and they drive a truck made out of grass."

"Grass from the yard?"

"No, pot. The kind you smoke."

"Oh, Mommy wouldn't like that. She hates illegal drugs."

When I got dry, he put a little Vaseline on his finger. I pictured Ricky kissing me, then touching my neck and my soft breasts with their hard, nubby points, then putting his hand down my pants and touching the hot, moist motor between my legs. I remembered a belly dancer Poppa had once taken me to see during one of my mother's hospital stays, putting his hand down her hula skirt, slipping a roll of dollars down there, somewhere amid what I now knew was heat and wet—a pure, mind-erasing sensation.

16

CATHY AND PAUL

In late August, Peter began to renovate the first-floor apartment, which had remained vacant for years. Richard had moved back in, claiming the living room again, though he also liked to take over the kitchen, resting his feet on the table while he read and smoked. Peter said being able to work on the downstairs apartment was a godsend: it meant he would see less of Richard.

Since it was summer, I was all about belly shirts, short shorts (my favorite set of jean shorts had a pair of dice on each butt cheek and white lace fringing the pockets), tank tops and halter tops. "You're calling more attention to us with those outfits," Peter lectured. "Plus, if I leave you alone for one second a guy instantly comes over to talk to you. It's ridiculous. Back when I was a young man, we didn't approach women like that. We were respectful. These guys just come right up to you like mosquitoes out for blood."

Sometimes he talked to me like he thought twelve was young, but when we were doing sex stuff twelve was pretty grown-up to Peter. Even eight had been old. So why was he now treating me like I was a baby?

He went on, "I don't like the way Richard looks at you. Whenever you pass by, he always puts down his book and stares at you. I'm
sure it's just to annoy me. But you seem to get a kick out of it. Come
on, we're always truthful with each other: do you actually like it
when guys gawk at you like you're a piece of meat?"

"I don't know." I shrugged. "You're just jealous of Richard. What
if I had sex with him one day? I bet I could if I wanted."

"No, you couldn't."

"Why not?"

"He just wouldn't go for it, that's all. Richard likes to kid with
you. Sometimes it's not that funny. He has a knack for saying the
wrong thing, always the *exact wrong thing*. Do you know what he said
to me the other day? He was probably coked out of his mind, whatever mind he has left. As usual, he was bumming cigarettes. I was
going through my drawers to get him a pack and he saw the leopard-
print bathing suit you had worn all last summer, the one you out-
grew. He actually asked me if he could have the suit!" Peter shook his
head. "I said no, of course, but then he winked and said: 'Why are
you keeping it?'"

"He wanted my bathing suit? You should have given it to him. He
could rub it all over his face while he lies on the living room couch,
masturbating."

"Gross! Margaux, come on! That's the last thing I want to imagine!" He pretended to cringe. "Richard loves to aggravate people.
He's a real instigator. He needs to get a life. The other day I asked him
to help me with this apartment, but *God forbid*. That actually involves
work. Without me, this house would be in shambles."

That September, I started junior high at Washington School. I found
that I missed my friends terribly, and without them my shyness returned with a vengeance. Also, something had happened to me that
summer. I'd begun to suffer from mood swings ranging from euphoric
to despondent. My moods seemed to mostly follow the pattern of
whether Peter and I were fighting or getting along, but I'd also get

depressed thinking about my now defunct clique. Though I still talked to Winnie and occasionally Grace or Irene over the phone, it just seemed like there was less and less to say to them. As planned, I'd told Winnie about Ricky going down on me and I on him. She kept asking me what come tasted like. I told her it was like Italian ice. In truth, Peter, when we were alone in the room, had asked me to return the gift he'd given to me. He asked me to swallow and I felt like I should show him that I wasn't afraid to. Somehow telling Winnie it was with a boy my own age made it better.

I became something of an enigma at Washington School. I barely spoke, and when I did, I acted meek yet I wore makeup and sexy clothes. My homeroom teacher added to the mystery by periodically sending me to the school counselor, Mr. Trunelli, for seeming "antisocial." But he didn't notice any problems with me, because I soon became spunky, chatty, and witty. When I would come back into the classroom after these visits, girls would whisper as I took my seat about why I was sent to Mr. Trunelli's office yet again.

That winter, Justine, a gorgeous Filipina with long Doberman-black hair who'd been left back twice, noticed the dangling teardrop gems on my jeans; they were exactly like a pair she owned. "You're copying me," she said during gym class, which I was sitting out for my period, my second menstruation this month, though my male gym teacher didn't have the gumption to question me. Apparently, Justine knew the same tricks. She sat next to me, not bothering to pull down her white baby-doll dress, which rode up almost to her crotch. Such a glamorous, sophisticated girl talking to a nobody like me was unheard of, and not knowing how to react, I kept reading.

"I have that book at home," she said, tapping the dog-eared paper-back's cover.

I shrugged, not moving my gaze from *Flowers in the Attic*. The evil grandmother was about to whip Cathy now.

"You're copying me," she said again, and then her white acrylic fingertip ran the length of my arm.

I felt my eyes lock with hers. "Maybe it's because you're the only girl around who's worth copying."

Justine wrote her phone number in bold bubble letters on a slip of pink notepaper, instructing me to call that night, but I didn't want to call in front of Peter. When I was back at my own house, I lost my nerve. After all, Justine was the most popular girl in the seventh grade. The sight of Poppa, even if he wasn't anywhere near me, always made my self-confidence vanish.

In V. C. Andrews's books, brothers were always falling in love with their sisters and older men were falling in love with young girls. Everything was forbidden and secret and deliciously romantic. There was this young, beautiful ballerina named Cathy who had three men in love with her: one was another dancer, one was her own brother, and one was a rich doctor, Paul, who was forty years old. Cathy was only sixteen when she and Paul made love for the first time. Paul tried to resist Cathy's powers of bewitchery; but he was only a man, he couldn't control himself, so finally he succumbed. "Succumb," "bewitch," "seduce," "dazzle," "enrapture," "enchant": what wonderful words! I adored them and I adored Cathy. For one thing, the most important thing, Cathy was beautiful. Second, she was a dancer. No one could resist Cathy, not even her own brother!

Peter sanded the wall as I bounced from his right to his left side, telling him about Cathy's exploits. "So do you know what happens to Paul at the end of *Petals on the Wind*?" I paused. "He dies of a heart attack, right in Cathy's arms! He was making love to her and his heart *just stopped*. Isn't that romantic?"

"It is. But it's sad, too. Don't you think it's sad?"

I nodded. "But Cathy goes on."

"How old was Paul when this happened to him?"

"I dunno. About your age," I said with a grin. Peter swatted me with the sandpaper. "No, I'm just kidding. The first time we make love we'll be really slow about it, so you don't get too worked up. 'Kay?"

"Well, that's not gonna happen for a while." Peter said. "I'm in no rush for that."

We couldn't have had intercourse anyway; there was the danger of my mother returning unexpectedly or Richard knocking on the door for cigarettes. Richard had already interrupted numerous blow-job and hand-job gifts. "Why is this door always locked?" Richard once asked, and Peter snapped, "To keep you out so you don't rob me blind." In frustration, Peter once gave him three whole packs, but within the hour, Richard was back at the door, saying he wanted to borrow the motorcycle. (I was shocked when Peter handed him the keys!) Not only did Peter have Richard to contend with, but he was constantly on guard for the sound of my mother's shuffling feet; when she arrived, he quickly unlocked the door. Unlike Peter, I saw these interruptions as fun, for they added excitement; there was always the danger we could get caught and have to run away to Scandinavia or Thailand as planned. Meanwhile, I continued to tell Winnie of my sexual adventures with "Ricky," and pleasured myself at home fantasizing that my lies were true. Winnie kept asking me, however, when I was going to "do it."

Peter stopped working to light a cigarette. "Tell me more about Paul and Cathy. They're in love, right? Like us."

"Love *and* lust *and* passion, the devouring kind. But it isn't just Paul. All men want Cathy: young men, old men, middle-aged men, married men, single men, rich men, poor men, whoever. See, okay, Cathy's brother, Chris, is obsessed with her, as is Julian, her dancing partner. But Julian is mean, he hits her, and one day he beats her up so she can't even perform in a show. Cathy has Julian's baby, and a few years later, she marries Paul. Because Julian committed suicide! You see, she was married to Julian first, then Paul, and then she married this other guy who was her mother's husband! And all these men died!"

"Cathy sounds like a black widow spider. You know, the male spider of the black widow species, in order to avoid getting killed, has to tie up the female spider and then he, he . . . copulates." He made a face when he said that word. "But if she breaks out of the webs, she kills him, lays eggs on him, and when they hatch, all of his children eat his dead body. I don't think that's very nice, do you?"

"It's not so nice he puts her in a web either," I said with a shrug. "Anyway, back to Cathy—no, no, let's talk about the Story!" The Story had really grown in the past year. Whenever Peter worked, that was mostly what we talked about. New characters were starting to crop up. Carlos now had a mother, Arana, who committed suicide by flinging herself in front of a train, but then returned as a ghost to haunt the family. Then there was Victor, Carlos's brother, whom Peter animated in a rough, scratchy voice. Victor had gotten scarred for life after Arana had accidentally spilled boiling water on him as a baby; then, just because he wasn't handsome, she locked him inside a closet all day. The Story switched in time, constantly going back and forth from the boys' childhood to their future lives: Carlos's glamorous life as a rock star and Victor's miserable existence as a social outcast. I played Carlos; he was the most fun character for me because he was the handsome one, the one everyone loved. What I couldn't understand was that Peter actually seemed to like playing Victor.

"Let's see: what happened in the last episode? Was that the one where Carlos's cousin Tracy tries to break into the house and kill Margaux? Then, remember, Peter had to shoot her in the leg. Then they're all at the hospital. Let's see, we're at the hospital . . ."

"Sweetheart, don't take this the wrong way, but can we try to talk about other things besides the Story? I mean, every day we talk about it." I crossed my arms and glared at him. After everything I did for him. And not only did he continue to sand, he said, "It's all you want to talk about. For hours. For me, it can get repetitive; I'm not your age. I mean, I *like* the Story; it's just that sometimes it seems it's all we talk about."

"What else is there? There's nothing else for us to talk about!"

"Well, we were just talking about Cathy and Paul and their love for each other. How it was like us. That was interesting."

"Well, I'm finished with that!"

"I mean, you don't understand. For me, the Story can get tiring—"

"Then maybe we shouldn't talk! Maybe you should just sand."

"That would be peaceful. We could think. Enjoy some silent quality time together."

I turned away from Peter, arms still crossed. I would teach him; I would deny him what he wanted later.

"I don't think you could go ten minutes without talking."

"If I'm so good for nothing, then why don't I just kill myself!"

"See, I told you: you couldn't go for ten minutes!"

I screamed, "All you care about is your stupid sanding! And your stupid painting! This is all you think about!"

"Sweetheart, I'm sorry." He stopped sanding. "We can talk about the Story."

"No, I don't want to now!" I kicked the wall.

"Okay, later then?"

"No!"

"Please?"

"No! The answer is no, no, no, no!"

That spring, after Peter finished renovating the first-floor apartment and a family consisting of a couple and their three kids, plus the husband's nephew, moved in, we were outside almost constantly, in the yard, on the motorcycle, walking Paws, skating, or eating lunch at Woolworth's. Sometimes we'd venture all the way to River Road, where we'd take the motorcycle to a small hot dog stand, and then ride through a narrow badly paved scenic road with rock-studded hills and gushing waterfalls. I'd feel like I was out of time on the back of the motorcycle, singing "Papa Don't Preach," "Burning Up," and "Rescue Me," my favorite Madonna songs.

For my thirteenth birthday, Peter bought me a pair of black leggings that we referred to as my "Madonna pants" and a navy-and-white sailor dress at a yard sale that was for someone younger and smaller than me, so it was too tight and too short, but since I liked to look sexy anyway, just like Madonna, I didn't mind. He took pictures of me posing in the sailor dress on the motorcycle, holding the handlebars with my roller skates arching around the pedals; splayed out on the hammock with the skates on; sitting on the porch steps with my crimped hair loose and that silly sailor dress with its big silly white sash and long white kneesocks and the long red laces of my skates undone. Peter bought a small album just for these poses, entitled *Skate Girl*, but, although I didn't say anything, it upset me that he didn't think to use any new pictures to replace the blown-up ones on his wall of me at eight, or remove the Jill picture in order to put one of the Skate Girl pictures in its place.

Or maybe he didn't put a Skate Girl picture up because it was so sexy that it would have alarmed either my mother or Inès. As it was, neither seemed to notice the pictures he had up now, because they were so wholesome. Peter had even said to Mommy and me that because Poppa hung up works of art as well as pictures of famous race-horses on his walls but no photos of me, that it was more proof he didn't care. Mommy wholeheartedly agreed, and then I, too, started to take it as still more evidence of Poppa not loving me. "Just being his daughter isn't enough for Louie," Peter railed, and Mommy said, "Yes, he's obsessed with status." Poppa had one framed picture that I loved to look at, though, of his father's cousin, an important poet in Puerto Rico who'd gone insane and then died a penniless alcoholic in Harlem. I knew he respected her talent, despite her tragic life, and that was why he chose to display her picture.

17

RESCUE ME

At El Pollo Supremo, I tried to wear my mother down on the issue of going to Peter's alone. I waited until Mommy had finished her roasted chicken and tostones and had moved on to her favorite thing: corn on the cob. There was nothing my mother liked more than the sweet buttery kernels. From our orange-and-yellow booth, I watched a deaf man sell key chains. Opposite us, an elderly Hispanic woman in a kerchief peddled rosary beads. El Pollo Supremo attracted numerous peddlers, whose lives struck me as ideal because they weren't bound to any one place or situation. In my mind, peddlers, like rock stars, could go anywhere to make their living.

"Mommy, you need to let me have my independence. If you love something, you set it free," I said. Peter had been coaching me on what I should say. "I'm thirteen now. Don't you want me to do things on my own?"

Mommy sighed; she was so tired of this conversation. "Margaux, the main reason I don't want you crossing streets is because you don't pay attention. Even your teacher this year says you're always in a fog. You get decent grades and all, but it's like you're always in dreamland."

"Is that what she said: dreamland?"

"Dreamland or dreamworld, one of those, I can't remember. I should have written down exactly what she said."

"Well, that teacher is boring," I said. I thought back to a week ago when Justine and her friend Jocelyn confronted me in the hall. During history class, Jocelyn had seen me writing love letters to Peter. She'd told Justine, and in the hall that day, Justine asked me point-blank if I was still a virgin. I had gotten so angry that I'd started shaking and walked away without answering the question. "She's a loser anyway," sang Justine loudly, stomping her suede boots for emphasis.

"I think the reason that she can't concentrate is her father," said Peter. "Didn't you tell me that he gave her a hard time when she had to ask him for clothes?"

"A terrible time," said my mother. "At minimum, she needs about two hundred and fifty a year, and that doesn't include the winter coat."

"Let me tell it," I said, putting up my hand and looking into Peter's eyes. "Let's say I need two-fifty like she said. Well, I have to ask him for three-fifty just so I can talk him down to what I need. I have to argue with him for three straight hours!"

"She's right," my mother said. "He has nice clothes while I go around in rags. And Margaux has to beg like a street urchin for what's technically her own money."

"He doesn't care about us." I was in the midst of making a tiny hill of salt on my napkin. "I used to think he did, a long time ago. But then he did things, like when he scratched my mother's forehead open. It was like a horror movie, he just—"

"Living with him *is* a horror movie," said Mommy.

"No, living with him is a *horror channel*," I said. "Without any commercial breaks." I stuck my straw into my salt hill and licked the white grains off.

"He's afraid of her," my mother said, clutching her hands like a delighted little girl. "Her rages really disturb him. He sees her and it's like he's looking at himself."

Peter frowned. "That's no good. Two people in the same house with that kind of anger . . . Sandy, it's time. Really, you should divorce him right away. You don't have to worry about custody now. Margaux is old enough to testify in court that he's been abusing you both for years."

"I'm considering that," Mommy said, nodding. "Now that she can testify."

"If that happens you can stay with me for a while. Inès would allow that. We don't have much room, but you're always welcome."

"Maybe you can get the tenants to leave and we can rent the downstairs apartment!" We could then all live like one big family, I thought.

"You know what, Peter?" said my mother. "He's always had me brainwashed. He's like an evil sorcerer. The more you're around him, the more you'll feel you've got a spell on you that puts your brain underwater. You can't think. But today, talking with you like this, I feel stronger."

Over the next few weeks, I began to sense something *was* going to happen. I knew Poppa sensed it too, when around ten o'clock at night he took my arm. I was coming out of the bathroom; I had showered and put on my pink nightie with a family of teddy bears on it. My hair was damp and it clung to my shoulders. When Poppa took my arm, static electricity passed between our skin, and I jumped a little. I had thought he was just on his way to his usual ritual of mopping up the bathroom floor after me even though I'd already done it.

"Listen to me," he mumbled, avoiding my eyes. "Your mother is getting sick."

I tried not to panic. If he put her in the hospital, I might not be able to see Peter for weeks, even a month. Alone and without distractions, depression would eat me up. "I don't think so. She seems normal to me."

"She is hyper. That is the first sign."

"She's fine. No more hyper than usual."

He crossed his arms over his chest. "You know it and you are protecting her."

"No, I'm not. She just doesn't seem that hyper."

"I need your support on this. You are the daughter. You have to help me convince her that she has to be hospitalized. Otherwise, something terrible will happen. I can feel it. I have a sixth sense." He led me to the kitchen table and we sat down. "Tell me. What have you been noticing when it comes to her? You people are never around, so I have to find out secondhand. So, tell me. How has she been?"

"Fine, I think. She's happy because the last time she got on a scale she saw she had lost weight. She told me that."

Poppa shook his head. "Lost weight? It is from not eating, I am sure. Does she spend all her money on you? Do you *demand* things from her? Do you demand that she spend all her allowance on you? I am glad you have put on weight, but hopefully not at her expense. Not eating ice cream and junk. She will give you whatever you want; I know it. You are so difficult, such a difficult person that nobody has any choice but to give in to you. You bully your own parents—"

I stood up, feeling like I couldn't take it anymore, the constant put-downs. He never had anything nice to say about me, ever. "I have school in the morning."

He took my arm. "Wait." He tapped me and I slunk back down. He put his hands on his head and sighed. "I am under so much pressure. So much pressure with this woman who keeps getting sick."

"Well, I haven't seen her listening to the old records or staring at the ceiling. She hasn't been calling anyone more than usual."

"Oh, she calls people. I heard her calling someone the other night, talking about me . . . *My husband, my husband.* Imagine what people must think of me! I am ashamed. The people on the street, who knows what kind of garbage she tells them? Everyone knows by looking at her that she is not okay, but still . . . Still . . . I am ashamed. I think it is up to us to make a *concerted* effort. A *concerted* effort to keep her from collapsing. I tell her every day that she is getting sick; she says she has never felt better. She is nasty to me and *I* am trying to help her. I am the only one who cares for her. We are all she has. I will call Gurney tomorrow and tell him she is showing the signs. Last time, he increased her Thorazine. I think it is time for him to raise that and the Seroquel. Otherwise, she will start running around town, endangering your life, making a mockery out of me."

"She won't have to go to the hospital, right?"

Poppa's leg trembled. It was making me so nervous that I wished I could nail his slipper to the floor. "Maybe, maybe not, not if we make a concerted effort. This is what we will do for the next couple of weeks. I think your mother's blood sugar is out of sorts. I think she has not been eating properly. For a few weeks, I want you and her home by five thirty, before I get here. When I come home, I will cook for both of you. This way, her blood sugar will stabilize and I can make sure she is taking all her medication at dinner. I can keep track of her behavior and report back to Gurney. Also, the days are getting shorter. It is not good for her to be walking in the dark with you while she is sick. You could both get run over by a car!"

I felt like saying that Peter always walked us home, but I thought better of it. I knew I had better just go along. Still, less time with Peter combined with the thought of having to listen to Poppa's dinnertime rages made me feel sick inside. He saw my head drooping and lifted my chin.

"Your skin . . . I think I see a pimple starting on your left cheek. I can get the loupe . . ."

"No. I mean, no thanks. I feel really tired right now."

He nodded and I started to walk away. I sensed him staring and I turned around. He looked at me with an odd expression.

"You are getting taller. I just noticed that right now." He quickly turned away.

"He's in there and he's got guns!"

My mother wasn't just saying this. She was standing in the middle of the street across from the beige-and-red house, shouting it.

"Mommy," I said. "He's not home from work yet. He's not in there. Let's just go back to Peter's. If we run, maybe we can even catch up with him and Paws. Let's go back."

"He wants us home, remember? Home for dinner. So he can scream and bitch and complain about my sister and the dishes and how I'm a sick woman and how he's so *burdened*. I know that man is in there. He calls me *that woman*! Well, I call him *that man*! That man! That man! That man!"

"Poppa's not in there, Mommy," I said. "It's dark in the house. He's at the bar."

She ignored me. Her face was all lit up, as though she were having a religious experience. She started to shout again and I pushed all my long hair in front of my face to hide who I was. In Union City, whenever there was a fight, a fire, or some other unusual occurrence, an audience gathered. Elderly women with rouged cheeks, mothers with baby carriages, old Cuban men in hats, teenage boys in do-rags and chain-link necklaces wearing Nike and Adidas windbreakers, now they were all looking at us.

"Everybody listen! My husband is crazy! He has guns! He's going to kill me! He's a drunk! He's hiding in there; he doesn't want to be seen! He's in there with his guns! If we go in there, he'll kill us!" My mother's voice seemed like it was coming from a loudspeaker overhead and the people kept collecting the way Canada geese meet in the sky, forming their ominous V. "Someone, call the police!" my mother yelled. Nobody moved. Her face looked like a coal that burned so brightly it had turned into a chunk of white ash. "Somebody help us! My daughter can testify. She's right here! Tell these people, Margaux! Tell them what your father's like! Tell them he has guns!"

All the neighborhood dogs began to bark at once. They howled behind fences and gates; they moaned inside cages at vets and animal shelters; they wailed in doghouses all over Union City, Weehawken, North Bergen, and West New York. Usually, they could only hear one another, this network of dogs that started way back in the single-digit streets and traveled all the way to Ninetieth Street, but now I could hear them, barking in unison. I started to run.

"Margaux, Margaux, come back!"

I felt freedom blooming in my limbs; I was running faster than anyone's eyes could follow. I sped past Heaven on Earth Flowers, past

St. Augustine's Church, past the Chinese restaurant and the video store. Yes, I was fast. Almost there. Almost to Weehawken. To Peter's house. Up ahead, the police station came into view. I thought of stopping there, telling them about my mother. No, Peter didn't like police. Neither did I.

I crossed the street, walking past the bushes that grew poisonous ground cherries. I felt a pain in my side and a burn in my throat. The slower I walked, the more lost I felt; it seemed that as long as I was running I knew where I was going. But now that I had slowed, everything looked unfamiliar and I wasn't sure if I was in Weehawken or Union City. I couldn't figure out where Peter's house was.

It was garbage night and black Hefty bags sat in front of all the houses. I kept feeling like I was passing the same set of three bags, shiny and tied at their tops like sausages. After a while, I realized I was circling the same block over and over again. I decided to find a pay phone. I didn't have a quarter, so I called Peter collect and described my general whereabouts. Then I curled up on the hood of a car and waited.

I must have fallen asleep, because I woke to Peter's arms rousing me. The bike was making its usual crackling and spitting noises, heat lifting from its engine. Peter draped one of Inès's multicolored shawls over my shoulders.

"Hug it around your coat," he said. "It's always chillier on the bike."

Then he put my own silver helmet on my head, clasped the lock under my chin. In our helmets I felt like we were astronauts.

"Do you think you can ride okay?" Peter asked. I nodded. "Hop on," he said, which he always did when I got on the bike, and "Don't go to sleep. Sing to me if you have to. Stay awake, okay?"

On Peter's red velvet couch, I sipped Lipton tea that Inès had made for me. Paws snuggled at my feet. Peter kept talking, and at some points I understood what he was saying, but at other times he was like a TV newscast in the background that only occasionally filtered in. He'd said something about calling my house several times, and that there was no answer. He kept getting up and calling. I knew that I should be worrying about my mother right now—I should be afraid, but I'd long learned how worthless my fears were: I could never change anything.

I must have dozed off again, on the carpet next to the couch, because the next thing I knew Poppa was there. He frowned when he saw me lying with Paws, and even though he didn't say anything, I sat up. Poppa was in a green shirt with a black tie and brown trousers.

I had a strange impulse to run into his arms, but I was afraid he would push me away. I stood up anyway, started moving toward him, then stopped and sat back down on the red velvet couch. "Would you like to sit?" Peter asked Poppa, motioning to the couch, but Poppa shook his head.

"No, no, it's okay. I prefer to stand." Of course he didn't want to sit, knowing Peter got his furniture from yard sales and garbage nights. I had never expected to see Poppa in this house, and I couldn't get over the shock of it.

"K-Keesy, your mother fainted on the street. She was looking for you. She fell; she is okay. They took her to the hospital. The people were standing around. They took her on a stretcher. She did not get hurt, so do not worry. I will tell you something, though: it was humiliating."

"Poppa, I shouldn't have left her. I know I was supposed to be watching her. But she was screaming in the street and there was a crowd watching."

"I understand," Poppa said, nodding. "Come, let's go. Come, Keesy." Peter led us out of the living room and to the front door, past the piano with its broken keys, past the parakeets and finches that sat on perches or fluttered around in short bursts of movement. They were twittering, and Poppa stopped to glance at them.

"What beautiful things. But no cage?"

"Well, their wings are clipped."

"Oh! No wonder . . . Personally, I never believed in clipping the wings of birds or taking the claws from cats. I suppose I feel it is an indignity. However, maybe it is more of an indignity to be in a cage."

"I think so," said Peter, opening the door for Poppa and me. Poppa put his hand out; Peter took it. "I must thank you for taking my daughter off the street. My worst fears could have happened tonight: she could have been hit by a car or kidnapped by a psychopath. Her mother has no common sense. She stands in the street, yelling. Anyone would have run rather than be at the mercy of that crowd!"

"She feels guilty for leaving her mother," Peter said, nodding. "But it's not her fault."

Poppa nodded, then said, "Has she ever talked about me? To you or to your . . . To Inès?" He raised his eyebrows.

"I don't pay attention when she gets going on something. I know she's mentally ill," said Peter, lighting a cigarette. "What exactly is her diagnosis?"

"One doctor said schizophrenia, another bipolar, another said something about a borderline personality. Who knows? This Gurney, her psychiatrist, he writes 'schizophrenia' when he submits the claims to Medicare. But we don't know for sure. We never know anything. We live our whole lives that way. We spend our lives speculating on the causes of things. It is always an empty pursuit, right? It is like the question of mercy. Is there such a thing? I thought I was being *merciful* by sparing her from that hospital. By sparing the child. In reality, I was doing the opposite of whatever mercy is." He turned away and started down the stairs with me.

18

NINA

Poppa took a few days off from work right after Mommy's nervous breakdown. During that time, I managed to convince him not to drop me off at Rosa's. "For one thing, I'm too old for a babysitter," I said. We were in the kitchen; he was stirring rice in a pot. He'd been in a good mood ever since my mother had gone to the hospital. "And you'd be wasting your money. All Rosa does is leave me in front of the TV. But she doesn't even let me watch anything. I sit around while her son plays video games. It's so boring."

Poppa rubbed his chin thoughtfully. "What do you do at the other house?" By the other house, I knew he meant Peter's.

"Lots of things. Roller-skating. Walking the dog." I paused, and then started to lie. "During the summer, I helped Inès with the garden. We grew vegetables and sunflowers. In the fall, our zinnias bloomed; they only grow in autumn." I'd just made up a season for the zinnias to blossom, not knowing when they actually did. Poppa seemed impressed. "Also, Inès let me use her typewriter to type up some stories I wrote and she helped me study for my history test since she knows a lot about the Civil War. And once we made stained glass animals with a kit." As I said these things, I found myself wishing they were true. Though I mostly disliked Inès, there *was* something in me that was fascinated by her medieval-looking dresses, her books about casting Wicca spells, and the way she was always reading, writing in her diary, or clicking away at the keys of her old-fashioned black typewriter.

"She is nice," Poppa said, nodding. "An intelligent woman. She knows history so well she could be on *Jeopardy*." Poppa smiled. "We had a conversation in the kitchen while you were sleeping. I cannot figure out why she is with that Peter. He hardly contributed anything to the conversation! I am not sure why she keeps him around, except to work as a groundskeeper." He smiled again, and turned off the flame. "I pity that man for many reasons. He looked so much older than he did just a few years ago!" He scooped rice, chicken, red bell peppers, and okra onto my plate. Then he served himself and sat down to eat.

"Well," he said. "She probably needed a stable person to help with those two boys. I cannot say that he is not nice. Your mother was right about that. He goes out of his way to help people. It is a rare thing." He chewed thoughtfully. "While I was talking to Inès she told me many things I didn't know about this city. Its history. Do you know there are barely any elm trees in this town, almost none? Well, they all died of Dutch elm disease. I didn't know that. Pathmark used to be a reservoir. During World War One, American soldiers made an encampment by the reservoir to protect themselves from terrorist attacks."

He went on, "That woman is too intelligent to be stuck with someone who is so, so . . . *childish*. Does he not have a strange fixation with Christmas ornaments? Your mother mentioned that as though it was a good thing. As though being stuck in one season is not detrimental to a person's well-being." He shook his head. "And then he has that motorcycle! As though he is a teenager! I would have wanted a motorcycle when I was eighteen, but not now." Poppa played with the rim of his beer bottle. "A few weeks ago, your mother said that Inès had told her Peter is unable to relate to her *as a man*. His troubles are most likely connected to that back injury he has. I feel sorry for people like that, because they are somehow reduced. No wonder he needs that motorcycle."

Poppa paused, and when he looked at me, his expression was sheepish. "For a split second, I almost forgot who I was talking to—a little girl. A babe in the woods!"

"I'm not a child anymore, Poppa."

He made a dismissive hand gesture. "Anyway, with those two, it is a relationship *of convenience*, I can say that much. As all relationships are. Convenience." He laughed and drank his beer. "Except with your mother. With your mother, it is what I call a relationship of in-convenience! I am so saddled with duties and responsibilities. If I could have looked into the future as a young man, I would have moved to a mountain. I would have rather lived with the billy goats on some rocky slope. At least they would ask nothing of me!"

As Poppa talked, I made sure to eat everything on my plate, even the red bell peppers, which I didn't like. I wanted to make sure his good mood held.

"Things are not simple, not now. Everything is a complication! I don't even have a car anymore. I have to go back and forth to that hospital and I don't even have a car."

"What about the Chevy, Poppa?"

"I sold that car three months ago!" Poppa said, laughing, but then he stopped abruptly and looked into his bottle with a low smile that I couldn't interpret. "You did not even know that."

"You didn't tell me."

"When can I tell you? You are never here!" He looked directly at me. I looked away. "Anyway, when my car was towed I reached my breaking point. It cost me a hundred dollars. And for what? Parking with my bumper about an inch, or two inches, maybe three inches, about this much"—he indicated the distance with his hands—"about this much my bumper was sticking into a handicapped space. You know that woman down the street who has that Cadillac? That silver Cadillac? Well, she owns the handicapped space. Not because she is handicapped but because she knows people in City Hall. I've seen her at the nightclubs, dancing. There is nothing wrong with that woman. Those handicapped spaces are cropping up everywhere because everybody knows somebody. And they are almost twice the length of the car they are made for!" He shook his head. "Get me another beer, Keesy."

As I went to the refrigerator, he continued: "Well, those parking spaces are spreading like the Dutch elm disease. And the Chevy was a big car. You remember it, Keesy? A long car, strong, like the way they used to make cars. Now, if I had one of these Hondas or Toyotas, my bumper wouldn't have been sticking over her line. By two inches. Two inches! She could still park with me there."

"And they were able to tow you?"

"Yes, because it's the law! She was a faker, but on paper, *I* broke the law! Yet I knew she was the criminal, not me! She was breaking the law through corruption! So I would make sure she paid the price. It cost me a couple hundred dollars, but it cost her ten times more."

"What did you do?"

"About six months after I had finished my civil duty by paying the ticket and the towing charges, I went to La Popular and I bought a half dozen eggs. Then I drove to Sears and bought a can of red paint. And I took an ice pick and pierced a hole in each egg. I drained out as much of the guts as I could in the kitchen sink. Then I took a funnel." He made the motions as he talked. "And slowly, with my loupe on, I managed to fill each egg with bright red paint. At three in the morning, I drove past her house, checked that no one was around, and threw the eggs at her car! Then I waited a couple of months. When I noticed she had gotten a new paint job, I went back and did exactly the same thing. Because she had broken a law! Not *the* law! My law!" he said, jabbing his finger into his chest. "Anyway, another month or so and I run into Eduardo at the bar. He tells me the story of that woman. He doesn't like her any more than I do and he says, in a low voice, 'Louie, do you have any idea who would do that? What kind of a person?' Do you know what I said to him, Keesy?"

"What?"

"I said, 'I don't know who would pick on a poor handicapped woman like that. Whoever does something like that must have a criminal mind! He must be a real psychopath!'"

Ever since my mother had been hospitalized I had gone to Peter's house alone. During the walk, guys were constantly hitting on me; they whistled and hissed out of windows, told me I had nice boobs or a good butt, gave me beeper numbers on slips of paper or tried to get me to ride in cars with them. There were teenage boys everywhere when the weather got warm, hanging out on porches or car hoods or fire escapes, riding bikes and skateboards. These were boys with backwards-turned baseball caps, boys with loud, macho dogs, mostly Rottweilers or pit bulls.

Even after my mother returned from the hospital, I insisted on continuing to walk to Peter's by myself. Poppa seemed to understand that I had a phobia about her creating another scene in the street. She was on much higher dosages of Thorazine and Seroquel that really zonked her out, so she didn't mind staying home. Besides, I felt like I'd gotten addicted to the catcallers' attention even if it made me uncomfortable. Like I needed to be constantly reassured that boys liked me even if all they wanted was sex. Peter said all teenage boys were immature and just wanted to use me for one thing.

Once, I had my white denim jacket tied around my waist and a boy in a do-rag accompanied by his friends called out, "Show that ass, baby! I'm sure it's beautiful like the rest of you!" Blushing, I took the jacket from my waist and all the boys clapped. "You're pretty, mami!" another boy from the group shouted. "Don't hide that fine-looking face in your hair, girl! Don't look down! Smile a little, honey! It's spring!"

The boys were right; I should smile more. It was late May; another horrific school year was ending, and I was totally free now. And Peter treasured me more than ever; he now wrote me a daily four-page love letter, which he'd read to me as soon as I was safely inside his room with the door shut. He'd go over all the events of the previous day, emphasizing how much fun we'd had. Around this time, he had me write a journal chronicling our lives together, reminding me over and over again not to write anything even slightly negative in it. Sometimes if we fought or if I felt sad, he insisted I read the book to him.

Something I didn't understand was happening to me. I noticed my thoughts and feelings were drastically different depending on the day. One afternoon Miguel and four guys were gathered on the stairway leading to the second floor. I, who could normally barely utter the word "hi" to Miguel, tossed my hair and sneered at him, "Haven't you and your friends got anything better to do than to crowd these steps? It's a wonder anyone can get by at all." Miguel told Peter, who insisted that I call the house to say I was sorry (I was too mortified to apologize in person). "Don't worry about it," Miguel said, and even though he forgave me, I remained so disgusted with myself that I found thinking about that day unbearable.

Women liked Peter. Richard's other girlfriend, Linda, had flirted with him and invited him to her apartment a couple of times, though he didn't go. Jessenia, the first-floor tenant, often touched Peter's arm whenever she talked to him, usually to tell him about things that had broken in the apartment. Peter had said that overall, these tenants were a mistake. They were dirty and their place was overrun with roaches, starting an infestation in the second-floor apartment as well. Peter said that he had gone in there to fix a broken pipe and saw Jessenia's three kids, aged seven, five, and four, merrily keeping score of the roaches they smashed as a game. Jessenia was about twenty-six or -seven, beautiful with wavy black hair, a wide mouth, and very white, almost vampirelike skin. She moved nervously and chatted nonstop in repetitious yet endearing patterns. Peter was convinced that she was on coke, like Richard, and that she was having an affair with her eighteen-year-old nephew, who split the rent with them.

Everyone was having affairs with everyone else. Jessenia and her graveyard-silent lover with his black schoolboy curls, perpetual white T-shirt, and tattoo of a coqui frog on his knuckle; Richard with Inès (he still periodically moved in and out); Poppa with a pretty twenty-eight-year-old woman named Xiomara. After she had gotten back from the hospital, my mother said that she met Xiomara when Poppa brought her over once for dinner. I asked my mother what she was like, and she said Xiomara was extremely nice and cheerful, immediately making me think of Jessenia; and then I thought of the equally ingratiating Vanessa and Amber, whom Peter had taken to calling the "attic wenches."

All these women, despite their crappy lives, were always so sweet, so easy to get along with. This was the way of sexy women, I thought. They laughed without making a sound, just opening their mouths as though they were laughing, clasping a limp hand over their lips; they complimented and touched you carelessly, as though you were a dog or cat that they could pet at will. They showed girls the same affection they heaped on older men; there was no difference in their minds between young girls who looked up to them with wonder and older men who viewed them as goddesses. To be a sex goddess you had to view the world coldly yet treat it with overabundant affection; you had to be brashly childlike yet clearly womanly; you had to pretend you expected nothing, but in reality accept nothing less than everything; you had to tease and charm and flirt and whimper and coo and goad everyone you met.

Most men liked this kind of treatment, but not Peter. Sometimes it seemed like he thought everything about most women was false and crude. He hated long nails, particularly press-ons, mascara, and brightly colored lipstick. He hated fishnet stockings, perms, fake eyelashes, gaudy necklaces. He hated dangling earrings, hoop earrings, any earring that wasn't little and plain. He hated any bra that wasn't pink or white. He hated sports bras. He hated lingerie. He didn't like the color red. He couldn't stand shoes with fluff on them like the kind they sold in the East Village. He especially loathed high heels.

"Sneakers," he said. "That's what's sexy. Or bare feet. Not something you could use to stab a guy in the throat."

He didn't like big breasts. He said mine were a good size and that he hoped they wouldn't grow any more. I think he secretly wished they were smaller. He wanted me to keep my pubic area completely shaved. He let me use his electric razor. He didn't understand girls who had triangle patches or made other designs with their pubic hair. He couldn't understand piercings or tattoos of any kind, on males or females. He wondered why anyone would want to mark up God's most exquisite creation: the human body. Especially girls. Why did girls dye their hair? Why did some girls paint on their eyebrows? He didn't understand women who wore their hair short. Nor could he fathom the latest fashion of women wearing men's shirts and ties.

He'd developed a weird habit of judging girls and women he saw passing by, whispering numbers at random: "There's an eight. There's a six walking that collie. Two fives over by the mailbox." He wouldn't bother to rate women over thirty, but would rate girls as young as four. Every time he'd rate some stranger, he'd mention that I was a perfect ten, which should have made me happy but didn't always, because I worried that one day I would slip to a lower score. I could gain weight, or my breasts could get bigger, or what if my height increased? No, no, I reassured myself, that wouldn't happen. I'd developed early and I'd already grown to my full height. Hopefully, everything that could lessen me in his eyes was over and done with.

This was how Nina came about: from watching women like Jessenia, Linda, Amber, and Vanessa—all the while keeping in mind what Peter liked and didn't like. I put together a composite of those women along with the ones I had seen Poppa flirt with in bars over the years, every time my mother had gotten sick and we'd gone out on the town. I made Nina everything my mother wasn't. Coy and tough and pleasing to men, not "bad" but "naughty," not "cold" but "wicked." She was a hot coal; she was butter. A real sex goddess. Nina was a bitch. If she wasn't a bitch, Peter might feel bad about some of the things he did. He might feel guilty.

So, the summer I was thirteen I put Nina together—my master-work of womanness. She was so cool, she was bored. She was a paper doll. She was glue. She had nothing inside her. She was so beautiful.

She was younger than me, older than me. Fresh as a cornfield yet ancient as rain. She was me. She was not. Her hair was completely black, like Jessenia's, like Justine's. She was made out of stuffing. She was a wishbone. You could pull her in any direction and she'd be hard to snap. That's how tough she was. One tough cookie. No love inside her, but infinite sweetness. Patience. Light and witty. And careless. Most careless about herself. Her body didn't matter because she was outside of it. It was so beautiful, that tight, hot, perfect-ten body; she could watch that body from across the room. She was so sassy. So blah. She wore her nothing like it was something.

Nina lived to make Peter happy. To be happy, he needed a lot of intimacy. Intimacy meant hand jobs (which he called massages) or blow jobs.

Nina's crash course in how to please a man consisted of watching random porn movies in addition to Peter's homemade movie: a compilation of various X, double-X or triple-X clips of women doing whatever men wanted. He'd mute the porn so anyone who came into the kitchen to get food wouldn't be able to hear the moans through his thin door. He particularly liked to see women down on their knees, giving blow jobs, and men coming on a woman's face; the penetration was interesting for him only to a point, and after a while he'd fast-forward.

Some porn actresses had big fluffy perms, others had straight white-blond hair; another woman had purple eye shadow in streaks to make her eyes catlike, and another girl was naked except for pink leg warmers. There was one tanned, slender blond girl with a tattoo of a hummingbird on her shoulder. Every time the man put his penis in her doggy-style, the bird seemed to fly; I looked forward to this scene every time and imagined that the actress allowed the director to film her only from behind, so she could showcase her pretty tattoo. Sometimes porn could get boring, but I still found comfort in it, knowing that what we did together was no big deal.

What was happening to my mother at home was also happening to me, just in a different way. I could feel myself recede into the distance, but I didn't completely care. How could I care about someone who was so stupid, so unpopular? A girl who was weak, who had abandoned her mother in the street. Sometimes when I had nothing to occupy me I would imagine what my mother looked like the day of her nervous breakdown: sprawled in the street like the body of a chicken sacrificed in a Santeria ritual that I had once seen discarded on the curb. I would wonder if her fate was my fate, too. I was powerless to help her feel less depressed and I couldn't bear to think about her lying in bed despondent.

With Peter, I didn't have to think about my mother at all. He was always telling me I had to live in the now. Not the past or the future. Only by staying in the present moment and avoiding negative thoughts could a person ever hope to be happy, he'd say over and over. So whenever I had an uneasy thought about Peter, I'd seek to banish it as quickly as it appeared. Because he was being so well compensated, Peter finally stopped complaining about my compulsion to talk about the Story for hours on end. The problems of the characters became my sole focus. I was so blissful whenever we were in the Story world that the sexual favors Nina provided seemed worth it. We even started recording the Story on cassette tapes, and together we completed a novel version entitled *The Beast Within*. I watched the old Story evolve into a new Story with a different cast of characters, one that included Nina. And this new Story was an arena for her to act out her sexual fantasies toward boys her age. There was one boy who was forced to wear an electric collar that she controlled by remote, demanding oral pleasure from him every day. I played both characters—the boy and Nina. Occasionally I would insist on giving Peter his sex in the role of a boy pretending to be a girl. When I was playing this character, I experienced the same sense of freedom I used to get when riding the Ferris wheel with my mother as we reached the top. As a boy, I was further away from my own life than ever.

During Peter's massages, I always operated his penis like a yo-yo. A yo-yo is a curious creation because it essentially does nothing. It comes up empty, like a bucket sent down a dried-up well. Yet people can do tricks with yo-yos. I'd coil Peter's penis in my hand and make that same up-down motion. Coil my mouth around it, like a fangless rattlesnake devouring a live mouse. First the head: taut, pink helmet with its single alien eye. Then I took in the veins, the rough-clasped skin full of ridges, tight and bunchy at the same time, that skin down there that looked like the skin of someone who'd been burned badly, crimped the way it would be if you put your hand in flames and then pulled it out.

Since I had sinus trouble, I couldn't always breathe. I stopped to spit into tissues. I'd tap Peter's leg when I needed one. Sometimes I'd let him push my head down, even though it hurt my jaw and made me gag. He always felt guilty about doing it but I'd say it was okay, whatever made him come faster. My jaw prickled; then, when the protective numbness lifted, it felt like it was being pressed under a rolling pin.

He wanted me to talk dirty. Or pretend to be other girls besides Nina, which I hated. My favorite thing was to lie on my belly with my head down on a pillow and let him mount me from behind and rub against my butt until he came. This required the least work and energy; I was tired because ever since my mother had stopped coming, he asked for something sexual almost every day. If I didn't give in, he would go silent and start crying and saying I didn't love him or that I thought he was ugly or too old.

When he rubbed himself against my butt, he made me keep my face down; he didn't want to see my face at all. Usually, the bed was elevated so we could watch movies or read. But when he had me lie there, he turned the switch until the creaky hospital bed was all the way down. Then I'd take off my clothes, fall on the bed like a bunch of dropped jacks from a sack. I'd stick my head into the white pillow and breathe the sweaty scent of my own hair. I could feel the springs of the mattress beneath my naked rib cage; they always felt comforting. I'd let my hair fall over my cheeks and my mind go blank like a TV channel with nothing but snow.

It was at least peaceful then. His bones would come upon me like the bones of the whale enclosing Jonah. I would be nestled in this black stomachy sea. I would feel the arrow of his penis against the mushy-bread skin of my buttocks. His face would climb into my hair; his bones would link to mine. Then the soggy feeling. Then the tissues.

I would stand up and look at myself in the mirror. I would always look at myself.

"Admiring yourself again, Nina?" Peter would say.

Until I discovered Nina, I lived unplugged. I was like a food container, or the paper that held a Popsicle, a gum wrapper, cellophane, plastic, aluminum foil, a ziplock baggie. A disposable thing. Someone could eat the contents and the thing that held it would be thrown in the garbage. I was many disposable selves. I floated on the flat, sad shapes of ghostly girls, into a rotting shapeless bog until Nina, their queen and ruler, came to reign over them, over me. She told me I was pretty; I believed it. She told me I had power; I believed it.

Mr. Nasty, Peter's specter, was born around the same time as Nina. It started with the dirty talk Peter wanted to hear during the massages. Whenever I talked dirty, he asked me to call him "Mister." Never was I to call him Peter or any of the names I used to address him in letters or any of the series of names with which he signed his daily letters to me: Peter, Daddy, TBG (Teddy-Bear-Grizzly), Victor. "Call me Mister," he said. "Pretend I'm a stranger. I could be any man. Any race, any height, any age. I could be anyone at all." Peter instructed me what to say; a typical fantasy sounded like this:

Mister, can I see your big man-thing?

I'm afraid it's too big for you. Too big for your little girl hole.

(gasp) Mister, it is big! I'm afraid.

You've got a little tiny girl hole. I don't know if it will fit.

I'm afraid, Mister. Can I suck it first?

If you want to.

Can I suck your big huge man-thing?

It might be too big to get your little mouth around it.

I know how to open very wide. For my daddy.

Oh, you like to suck your daddy?

I know how to put it all the way in my tiny baby-girl throat. It's so tight. Just like my little baby-girl hole. Daddy likes to lay me on my stomach and then he fucks me so hard. It hurts me but I like it. I like to be hurt when Daddy fucks me because I've been so naughty.

And so it went: I played prostitutes, orphans, belly dancers, pixies, angels, nymphs, geisha girls. Peter played johns, fathers, priests, doctors, sultans, kings, as well as the infamous Mr. Nasty. When playing Mr. Nasty, he pushed my head down really hard and fast during the blow jobs. As Mr. Nasty, he pretended to have rough sex with me as I lay on my stomach and whimpered or pretended to cry.

Occasionally, I'd ask Peter to lick me again, thinking at least it'd be fair that way. He'd never performed oral sex on me, save that one time in the basement. But he kept saying he couldn't; I was younger then and now I was the age of the tap dancers who had forced him to do that. He said he would try to overcome his fear and when he was ready, he'd let me know.

Peter often "reimbursed" me for the sex, not just through my Story addiction, but also in deals, like agreeing to watch three movies in a row that I picked out from the video store or to take me three times around the scenic road instead of the usual once or to treat me to a thick vanilla milk shake at one of the many diners we frequented. He might have done these things regardless but I took them as more payment. I was afraid that if I did anything at all without bartering for at least some small thing in return, he might think I enjoyed it, and not understand that I paid a huge price to myself. After sex, I got the same feeling as I once had looking at the Garbage Pail Kids. Like something hideous was getting into me. I couldn't stand the sight of my face anymore. Neither could he, but he denied it. He didn't want to look at me. He said, *Sweetheart, you're beautiful, a perfect ten, what man would not want you, but we've pretended that we were father and daughter for so long that at some point it just stuck; you're my daughter. That's why I need to pretend it's not you.* But that was a lie. I knew it was because I was thirteen now, too much like a real woman for his tastes.

Whenever we used pretend names, it was easier for me, too. Names meant real characters, and that made our interactions more playful, more like a story. Mr. Nasty was graceful and clean-shaven and his face was always covered with a strange shadow like men had in film noir movies. But Nina was filmed in a different light, always a vivid kind of Technicolor. She didn't look like any actress or model I'd ever seen. Her eyes were a deep root-beer color, her hair a sleek, luxuriant black. She had a gymnast's body. Her hair took up most of her; it came down to her butt like the belly dancer I'd seen many years ago with Poppa. She *never* wore any clothes, whereas I was rarely ever naked. Since Richard was so fond of always knocking on the locked door, it was never a good idea for me to take off too many clothes, lest I had to hastily dress.

While I was Nina, I never got bored, because she filled me. Though she was smaller than I was, her presence was like a soda can that was constantly being shaken. She fizzed all through me, animating my blood and eyes. Her heart was so big it flushed my face. Most of Nina consisted of heart; not heart in a sappy-love way, but heart in the way a timber wolf is all heart. Nina was heart and mouth and hand. To conjure her, I would walk from Peter's bed to the wooden door, twist the little golden lock into place, stand by the door for about twenty seconds, and take three deep breaths. *Deep breath, deep breath*, Sister Mary used to say when she laid me down on that white bed in her tiny nurse's office; she'd put her hand on my chest, maybe to feel my heart, and whisper, *Deep breath, deep breath*. And for some reason, that simple thing was so hard, to gather all that thick air and hold it in me like a balloon being blown up; I'd almost cry with the fear that I wouldn't be able to do it and she'd be disappointed. So I took three deep breaths by the door, for good luck. I stood there and felt Nina ripple through me; I tossed my hair back, and strutted to Peter. Then I sashayed into the bed, slowly took out his penis like a sorceress releasing a genie, like Cleopatra awakening her asp. Cleopatra had died by snakebite, or so the story went—*she* died beautiful, as those who die by poison always do.

19

THE FALLS

One summer day, we climbed up a small slope to get to one of the waterfalls. It had rained a lot the day before, so the falls were filled with white foamy water that tumbled and charged over the smooth brown rocks.

We sat on a rock by the waterfall, listening to it hiss. "We'd better enjoy the time we have now. In high school, you'll probably find a nice, young boyfriend and I'll be out of the picture, right? Like that old saying: if you love something, set it free. Eventually, I'll have to do that with you, sweetheart. You can't be stuck with an old man for the rest of your life."

"Well, maybe I'll have a boyfriend here or there but nothing serious."

Peter smiled stiffly. "I'm not going to ever be able to support you. You know that, right? Not on my puny check. It's barely enough to keep me going. I'm totally dependent on Inès. I used to give her a hundred for rent but I can't even do that anymore. Thank God there's so much work to do around the house or I wouldn't be any good to her at all. And she's so compassionate that even then, she'd never put me out. I'm lucky to have her."

"Well, when I'm eighteen, we can marry. And I'll find a good job and support us both. We'll get away from New Jersey forever."

Peter smiled crookedly.

"You don't think I'd make a good wife?"

"No, I was just thinking maybe three would be the charm. It's always been my lucky number. I've been married twice before. The first time I was only twenty-one. She was fifteen. Anyway, I forged her parents' names on the papers."

"You could do that for me! Then I don't have to wait till I'm eighteen."

"I don't know. Those were different times. I mean nowadays I'd probably be thrown in jail for something like that." He grimaced. "Her parents eventually had it annulled. At her request. She met another guy. He was the manager of a movie theater. After they got together, I would find a tree to hide behind and look into their apartment windows with a pair of binoculars. Once, I saw them taking a bath together."

"Did they see you?"

He shook his head. "Another time I followed them in my car. I was planning to run their car off the highway. Anyway, I tailgated them for a while; they accelerated to try to lose me but I sped after them. I must've clocked about a hundred. Went on like that for a while—cat and mouse. All I could think about was the two of them in that bathtub. I hated her for that. But there was another part of her I knew I couldn't kill. I can't explain it. She was so pretty, with a face just like a porcelain doll. I just couldn't go through with it. I still loved her." He dabbed at his eyes with a tissue. "I guess I'm a romantic at heart."

He hugged me and we watched the waterfall. Then I asked him if that was the only time he'd come close to killing someone.

"There was one other time. My father used to beat me and my brother in an attic room. Once he knocked me unconscious. Then, after my parents divorced, it was relatives, foster homes, then the boys' school. I lived with my mother for a short time; she used to punish me by making me stand up all night. I would get so tired I would fall on the floor fast asleep. You know what she punished me for? Laughing in my sleep. She had to work in the morning, so she needed her rest. But it was probably the only time I ever did get to laugh."

I squeezed his hand, feeling so sorry he'd lived this tragic life. No one had loved him and he'd been totally on his own. He continued, "When I was thirteen and my brother was sixteen, he stole a gun and we went to kill my father in his hotel room while he slept. But he checked out early."

"And do you think you would have done it?"

He nodded. "My brother would've taken the first shot and then I would have shot him next, round after round. I would've felt like he deserved it. You know, he didn't even leave us a penny when he died! Willed everything to his sons from his second marriage." He shook his head. "But he wasn't all bad. When I was older, about eleven or twelve, he took me swimming a few times in the lake. That was nice. He also used to give me quarters, piles of them. Anyway, sometimes they passed and sometimes they didn't. They were counterfeit coins." Peter threw a rock into the falls.

At the waterfall, I discovered that Peter's second wife was a dark-skinned Ecuadoran woman, and when they'd traveled through the deeply racist parts of the South, they weren't allowed to rent a room anywhere. So they'd made love in the car. Peter said he and his second wife had four daughters. They'd used Catholic birth control—the withdrawal method. I asked him if he was in contact with them and he said they didn't live around here. He'd send Christmas cards every year but they rarely ever sent any back, and this hurt his feelings. He then started talking about all the odd jobs he worked. I could tell by the way his mouth tightened that his kids were a sore subject.

To support his large family, he'd worked as a parking valet, a New York City cabbie, and finally a window washer. He didn't begin his career as a locksmith until much later, after his second wife had divorced him. But he was used to moving around, changing careers. Even as a kid, he had to earn his own money; when he ran away from the all-boys' school (six times!) he worked as a shoe-shine boy on street corners, and washed dishes as an adolescent, starting out on a cross-country trip with only a quarter in his pocket. Before he met his second wife he had even worked as a male prostitute for a short span of time in San Francisco, where men paid to give him blow jobs. The best job he'd held was a short-term gig as a dance instructor, and by far the worst stint he'd ever had was the job washing windows. "You had to climb tall buildings held up by just this flimsy belt," he said, as we held hands by the waterfall. "I was dead tired from taking turns with my wife waking up at night and tending to our first daughter, who had colic. Oh, she used to scream and holler. And back then, things weren't easy. They didn't have disposables; you had to hand-wash the diapers. I had four kids, and all those years I was stuck in a job I hated to support them all and make sure *they* got to college. Boy, I hated that job. I'd have to start dressing at five to get there. I'd dread it every second. One thing you learn is *never look down*. I looked down once and the world went zigzag. It was as though an ant farm was being tipped over by some cruel kid and I was a little ant trapped at the bottom." He sighed and lit a cigarette. "Anyway, when I was about ten, my brother dared me to climb up the side of a stone wall, a wall about the size of the Pathmark water tower and just as steep. I wanted to impress him, so I did it. The problem? I looked down. That was when I froze, right in the middle of the wall. Just froze there like time had stopped. My brother had to talk me through it. 'Keep going. Don't look.'"

Hearing about his life got depressing after a while, though, and I just wanted to get back to having fun. So I said, "Peter, I'd like to climb up the waterfall. Right now: to show you I'm not afraid of anything."

"I don't want you to climb it unless you want to. Don't try to impress me."

"Well, maybe it is a bad idea," I said, eyeing the waterfall. "I don't have a swimsuit. I'll get soaked."

"Go up naked, then," Peter said, chuckling. "I dare you!"

"Okay," I said, and started to undress.

"I was just kidding! Margaux, no!"

But it was too late. I was determined to show Peter just how daring I was. Peter kept saying the waterfall was too close to the road, the cars going by could see me and my nudity could cause a serious accident. I wasn't concerned. Naked as a grasshopper, I started scaling the small waterfall, using the stones above my head to hoist myself up and keeping my feet poised on stones below me. The slowly trickling water was icy cold and the stones were slippery and mossy beneath my bare feet and hands. I liked that feeling, of the moss, and also the cold water; more than anything, though, I liked knowing Peter was watching me from below.

"Hey, Peter!" I called through cupped hands, sitting at the top of the waterfall. "Look at me!"

I was so triumphant about having conquered the waterfall that when we returned to Peter's house at early dusk to give Paws his evening walk, I leaped off the motorcycle, forgetting about the hot engine, which Peter warned me about whenever I wore shorts. I burned my ankle.

Peter helped me limp upstairs to his room, where I lay, leg extended on his bed. The burn had puffed itself into a large, clear bubble. He got a plastic cup and a roll of Scotch tape from the kitchen and said, "That bubble is there to protect and help heal the burn. I'm going to tape this cup over it to keep it from breaking."

I nodded, wincing as he taped the cup.

"Now what?" I asked.

"I'm going out to buy some antiseptic spray," said Peter. "Something to help speed the healing and take away any pain. In the meantime, just be very careful that you don't accidentally burst the bubble."

When he came back, Peter detached the tape and lifted the cup. The burn looked awful: the bubble had increased in size and was now oozing clear fluid.

"Everyone gets those. Everyone who rides," Peter said as he sprayed the burn with Solarcaine. Ricky came in and watched, which was rare for him. He was sixteen now and had recently shaved his head and gotten an eyebrow ring. Ricky and Miguel communicated with Peter only by grunting, but as it was, we rarely ran into them. The boys were so into their own business that, besides the occasional hi if they saw me alone, I was certain they barely even knew I existed.

I said to Ricky, "Do you think it'll scar?"

He shrugged. "Probably."

"Do you have one?"

He lifted the leg of his plaid pants and unlaced his Doc Marten. "Yup. See?" he said, pointing to a circular patch of skin that was whiter than the rest of his ankle. "You'll be branded, like me."

"Cool," I said.

Peter said, "Ricky used to ride with me all the time. Right, Ricky?"

Ricky grunted.

"Used to talk up a storm too, when he was younger. Now I can't get two words out of him."

Ricky reached into his pocket and handed me a Tootsie Roll. "Here, feel better," he said, and walked out of the room. I was so touched by his kindness that I never ate the candy, but instead saved it in the wooden keepsake box I'd made in shop class.

The air in Peter's room was blue with cigarette smoke. It was also blue because the only light on was the ghostly alabaster lamp, and the fabric that covered the ceiling seemed to cast everything in that strange, planetary hue.

I had called my mother and told her about the burn. Then I told her that Peter suggested I spend the night on the couch in Inès's room. "Is that Richard around?" she asked, and I said, "No, he's gone back to Linda." I could hear Poppa screaming in the background when my mother proposed the idea, saying that if only he hadn't sold the Chevy, he would have easily been able to pick me up. Then I heard Poppa say that if I hadn't worn shorts this wouldn't have happened; my mother agreed and said, "No more shorts on that motorcycle. Your father and

I have agreed to let you spend the night on one condition: no more shorts on that motorcycle!"

So the deal was made, and for the first time Peter and I had all night to cuddle and talk. Maybe he would decide it was time to complete everything by finally having sexual intercourse with me. I'd then have an excuse to call Winnie again and tell her about how I was a grown woman at last. We were talking less and less, and our conversations had become more and more stilted.

Since Inès and the boys didn't know I was in Peter's room, I had to be careful not to talk too loudly. Also, he gave me an empty vase just in case I had to pee.

"This is so exciting," I said. "It's like I'm totally invisible."

"Yes, and let's keep it that way," Peter said. "It's fun for me, too, you know? I feel like a teenage boy who's hiding his girlfriend from his parents. It's naughty, don't you think?"

"Peter, now would be a good time for us to watch dirty movies!" I opened the dresser drawer of his walnut commode, hoping this would get him into a romantic mood.

I pulled out a movie called *Loves of Lolita*. "This looks interesting. Let's watch it."

He laughed. "I'm almost afraid to let you watch that one. You see, this girl Lolita is unfaithful."

"To who?" I said, intrigued.

"To her dad. They're also lovers. Like us. It's very good for a porno movie, it's artistic." He slid the tape into the VCR. "And upbeat. What I don't like about porn is the girls sometimes look so sad and jaded, as if they don't enjoy anything. Instead of getting turned on, I start feeling depressed. But this movie is different. The actress who plays Lolita is cheerful; she honestly enjoys sex. When she gives a blow job, she doesn't treat it like a chore. Some girls in these movies have expressions on their faces like they're mopping the floor or taking out the garbage."

"Maybe to some people it's like that," I said, shrugging. "A chore."

Peter paused the movie, which was just about to start, and looked at me. "If I ever thought for one moment you weren't enjoying things as much as I was, I would stop everything sexual. I mean that."

We had this conversation often.

"You do enjoy it, right?" he said.

"I like being Nina." It seemed as though Peter's other self Mr. Nasty was dependent on Nina and that he needed her to survive. The favors she gave him made him feel guilty and caused him to owe favors in return. This all amounted to me being in charge.

"Nina," he said, shaking his head. "Nina is a naughty girl."

"Yes," I said, "and Nina would like it if you rubbed her between her legs while we're watching this movie."

"Okay. But don't you have to go to the door first?" Peter had grown more dependent on me going to the door than I was. It was easy for me to conjure Nina now, as easy as flicking on a light switch. Peter, however, liked the old ritual of me walking to the door, turning off the light, tossing back my hair, and sliding into bed with him.

"I don't want to walk because of my burn," I said. "Just call her and she'll come. Like a doggie."

"I don't think of her as a dog," said Peter.

"A cat, then. A wildcat."

"Ni-na. Ni-na. Oh, Nina. Where are you, Nina?"

"Help me, help me, I can't get out," I squeaked. "I'm trapped in here. It's all these clothes. They're suffocating me." I took off my clothes.

"Is it you now, Nina?"

"No," I said. "One more thing."

"What?" said Peter.

"This plastic cup on my leg."

"Margaux, you know that can't be taken off. The bubble might break."

"Oh! That name! Don't say Margaux! It's acid, dissolving me!"

"I'm sorry," said Peter. "But, Nina, do understand that the name Margaux is a beautiful sound to me. It's the name of the girl I love." He watched as I removed the plastic cup.

"Much better," I said as Nina and Peter started the movie. "I like pornography." I grabed Peter's hand and placed it between my legs.

He laughed uneasily. "We better be careful about that burn."

"Oh, you silly man," I said. I could feel that I was fully Nina and it was thrilling. "That burn isn't anywhere near my pussy."

Peter winced at the use of that word. "I'm sorry . . . Whenever I look at it, I feel bad. When I'm with you, I'm responsible for you. Can you please put the cup back on? For safety's sake?"

I shook my head no and we silently watched the movie as Peter rubbed me. Lolita must have been about nineteen in real life but she was made up to look much younger than I was. She had two floppy pigtails, a plaid schoolgirl's skirt, white kneesocks, and was even skinnier than I was. Peter was right, she was cheerful. She smiled and laughed as she had sex with different men: two guys who came to fix her air conditioner, a doctor who examined her, and later her father. He spanked her for seducing those men and she pouted because she didn't understand how she'd been bad. After the father spanked Lolita, he had sex with her to show her he still loved her and that she wasn't ruined in his eyes. After a while, I put Peter's hand back because the movie wasn't turning Nina on. Nina was aroused only by fantasies of domination over guys.

"So what did you think of the movie?" Peter asked after it was over.

"I liked it. Hey, someday we need to watch a movie of gay men." I said it casually, though I badly wanted to. I didn't enjoy seeing women give blow jobs or have intercourse; however, I found the thought that a man could substitute for a woman exhilarating. I wanted to see a male do to another male what seemed boring or even degrading when done to a girl. I wanted to be reassured that men and women were not so different. Peter's movies made it seem that the whole world was just women submitting to men, and I knew that wasn't true. Once I'd nabbed one of Richard's porn magazines from the living room and learned about dominatrices. I wanted more than anything to get a movie about them, but I knew Peter would never rent a movie about women controlling men.

Lighting another cigarette, Peter said, "I guess I can get a movie about gay men, though I'd be embarrassed to pay for it."

"Well, were you embarrassed buying this movie? Considering

that she's like a little girl and all?" I pointed to the cover. "She doesn't look like whatever her real age is at all."

Peter snorted. "Are you kidding me? Everybody buys movies like these. All men like young girls whether they admit it or not. Most guys are just dishonest about it. But if people didn't like it, why would there be so many movies with older girls dressing up to look so young or so-called underage girls dressing sexy? The whole society is hypocritical, if you ask me. If you were to openly admit, yes, I find young girls attractive, you'd be burned at the stake."

Nina was losing power; I'd already started thinking about the blood and pain Winnie told me accompanied a girl's first time. Winnie, my best and secret friend. Winnie, who'd always so graciously offered me tips on how to improve myself. As the image of Jill stared down at me, I could only think that she was a hundred times prettier; my movements were now graceless, my eyes without Nina to enliven them could only stare stupidly like a sow's. Peter's letters, rather than boost my self-esteem, sometimes damaged it, though of course that wasn't his intention. He'd always tell me: "I'm not your father; I'm not the kids in school who tease you. I accept you just the way you are." Which was what, exactly? Those words always hurt, no matter how he meant them.

"Peter, you know what I feel like now? Lying on my stomach so you can come on me." I knew Peter wouldn't want to do it with the burn because of being nervous about breaking the bubble. But the fact that he would be reluctant was now the exact reason I wanted him to. Besides, I needed him to feel guilty for coming on me so he'd then cuddle and hug and thank me afterward. I knew our barter system wasn't fair, but it got me some of the affection I needed from Peter, especially when Nina was gone.

Peter said, "With that burn, I don't think it's a good idea."

But after a bit more convincing, he put down the bed and got on top of me. I closed my eyes and ran my fingers through the sheet as if I were digging into the ground. When he got up the bubble was broken, leaking clear fluid onto the sheet.

20

"THE DEVIL MADE ME DO IT"

*T*een and *Seventeen* advertised the return of the sixties, and mannequins on Bergenline Avenue sported shirts splashed with patterns of large bright flowers and ankle-length hippie skirts tied in the front with long beaded strings. Also in style were stirrup pants, shirts with shoulder pads, and wide headbands. Crimped hair was out, curls were in; thin bangs were in, and hairspray was way in, especially for Jersey girls. For the first day of school, I picked out a black V-neck shirt and flowered spandex pants and gazed at myself in the full-length mirror in the master bedroom, where I still slept after all these years. I wore my fairy amulet for good luck and walked to school practicing fake conversations in my head. What did kids my own age talk about? If they'd seen me with Peter, who would I say he was? My father? He was so old he could have been my grandfather.

I took off my headband and let my superlong bangs fall into my face. I was afraid if I walked into the schoolyard with my face visible, they would point and shout, "It's her! The girl who spends all her time with that old man!"

St. Augustine's Church was right across from Washington School. I sat on the steps, hyperventilating. I took off the fairy amulet. They would think it antiquated: an old man's taste. I rubbed off my lipstick with a tissue. It was the wrong shade: too red. They would know I gave blow jobs. They would look at me and instantly understand that I was a whore.

I thought of myself facedown on the bed, just a body to come on, a rubber doll with a wide-open clown-sized mouth like one I'd once seen in Richard's porn catalog. My face must be ugly—no matter how beautiful Peter said it was—otherwise, he would want to look at it as he came. I knew that only he could love someone like me. I could say the dirtiest things when I was Nina. Even Peter was shocked by what I could come out with. Recently, I had even created a fantasy for him where a group of tiny fairies landed on the head of his penis and their wings buzzed all over it. A thousand pixies the size of hummingbirds. No, the size of hummingbird *hearts*.

But just because I had a dirty mind didn't mean I was a whore. I was still a virgin. Nina wasn't me. This thought made me feel better. I mustered the strength to cross the street and walk into the crowded schoolyard.

As usual, I ended up a social failure. I couldn't bring myself to approach anyone and start a conversation. In English class, when the teacher asked us to split into groups, I chose a table by myself in the back of the room. I was still able to manage good report cards and got the highest score in eighth grade on the CAT, which was a standardized test all Washington School junior high students had to take.

I'd not only stopped fantasizing about having school friends, I'd again failed to respond to friendly overtures. Two girls had given me their phone numbers, but as with Justine, I couldn't bring myself to call them. I was terrified they were trying to befriend me to get information out of me. Why else would they want to associate with a weirdo? After all, I had a big, juicy secret and I wasn't going to let them get to it. Not by bullying me and not by being friendly, either.

One Sunday in early December, Peter was out with Inès for a ride and I was in his room, cushioned under a carapace of thick blankets, waiting for him to return. I'd turned the radiator off because roaches craved its heat. I never bothered to kill them anymore: it seemed like altogether too much trouble to chase them down and dispose of their bodies. Sometimes it seemed as though if I stared at the radiator long enough there weren't roaches, like a trick of the mind had made them disappear. I was practicing this trick, staring at them until they seemed so still they didn't exist, then blinking my eyes to make them appear again, when I heard a knock.

"Come in," I said, figuring it was just Richard.

He was shirtless, wearing his usual green beret and army pants. "Just came to steal cigarettes." He opened the top drawer of Peter's commode. "Damn it, I can't find them." I started to get up to help but he held up his palm to halt me.

"Don't," he said. "I wouldn't want you to get up. You look so comfy under there."

It took me a couple of seconds to realize he was flirting.

"Yeah?" I said, flirting back.

"I mean, you really look cozy under there. Man, it would be a lucky guy who could get to cuddle up with you right now."

"You want to climb in here with me? Just for a sec?" I said.

Richard laughed. He looked sort of hypnotized.

I patted the spot beside me. Or rather, Nina did. I felt her power; it was a quickening all through my body. I liked the way he was trapped there, with his hand still in the drawer. Yet there was the other part of me, the non-Nina side, that just wanted to be held and cradled in his warm arms. Something about him understood me.

Finally, I said, "Please, just come."

"I can't," Richard said. "I'm sorry." Then, hastily, "Keep warm," and he left without cigarettes.

Strange people were all around us, but Peter and I tried not to stare; after all, we didn't appreciate being stared at. An old man a few houses up from Peter's spent all day looking out his open window with a nasty expression on his face. He always wore a stained white undershirt and the skin on his forehead was bunched up like the rolling-pin fur of a pug. Peter had nicknamed him "The Eagle Eye" and we made fun of him in private: Peter wrinkled his eyebrows, stretched his neck as though peering out a window, and said: "Whooo's out the-ere? Whooo can it beee?" But eventually I didn't want to talk about that man anymore, even to mock him, because I was sure his disgust was directed toward me.

Then there was "The Blesser." He spent all day making the rounds at various bodegas and at Pathmark, placing his hands on different items as though blessing them. Peter and I had once watched as he drifted through Fernandez Grocery, placing his hands upon the cans of Campbell's soup and Alpo dog food, the Santo Niño Virgin Mary candles (which, technically, we whispered to each other, should already be holy), the Fabuloso floor cleaner, the cans of Similac. Bodega owners were always tolerant of the Blesser. Who knows: maybe they were secretly grateful to him for his good wishes. Or maybe it was the fact that he wasn't badly dressed or unwashed: he was actually quite dapper, in tweed pants, carrying a small green umbrella with a wooden bird head for a handle.

After a while, it dawned on me that Peter and I were to other people what the neighborhood eccentrics were to us. People stared and turned away. I noticed whispering. When I finally brought the subject up he said that Inès had advised him recently that we shouldn't hang around Pathmark too much or walk together on Bergenline, because people were starting to talk. Miguel and Ricky told all their friends that I was their foster sister but they, too, must have heard the gossip.

"Sweetheart, Pathmark is where Inès's co-workers shop; that's where everyone around here goes. And I know for a fact that supermarkets are breeding grounds for gossip. All the bored housewives. Nothing better to do but wag their tongues," Peter said, as he watered the philodendron plant in his room. "I think Inès is right. We have to cut down on our public appearances."

"What is Inès saying about us? Do you think she knows?" In my mind, she had to have guessed the truth by now.

He shook his head. "I tell her how abusive your father is. She's even said, 'If her home life is that terrible, thank God at least she can come here.' She understands that I'm like a father to you. It's no different to her than taking in Miguel and Ricky's friends. She just doesn't like it if we raise our voices too loud. That's the one thing that bothers her. Other than that, what can she say?"

"Do you think she feels like she has to put up with me? Like I'm a problem?"

"Well, she said something about you being quieter when you come up the steps. And toning it down a little. Sometimes you get excited and tend to giggle really loud. And she said something about your clothes. I can't remember: did you wear a red shirt recently that said 'Sexy'? She didn't think that was appropriate."

"She hates me."

"All she wants is for you to tone it down, Margaux."

"Why don't you tell her to tone Richard down?"

"I'm the one dependent on her, not the other way around. I don't know what I'd do if she ever told me to leave."

Peter adjusted the philodendron's grow light and then went to water the plants in his terrarium. "You know, it might just be talking now, but it could get a lot worse. I didn't want to tell you this, but about a few weeks ago, someone approached me. It was very disturbing; he called me a bad name . . ."

"What was it?" I asked, sitting up in bed and pulling my knees to my chest.

"Child molester," he said, shutting the lid to the terrarium.

We were in Peter's room, watching Paws gnaw a rawhide bone. Suddenly, Peter said, "Why did you just say that?"

"What?"

"Just now you said, 'I wish that bone was your face.' Out of nowhere."

"I don't remember." This wasn't entirely true. I did remember a little bit, but it also just popped out. I thought of that day with Miguel on the steps, the irritation I felt; no, more like rage, actually.

"You don't?"

"Not really."

He sighed. "Then it must be somebody else. A demonic entity. This has happened to me, too."

"When?"

"A long time ago, I hurt my daughters."

I drew my knees up, hugging them. From the bed, through the window, I could see the ailanthus tree covered with frost. I loathed winter; I could never keep warm enough. Neither could the roaches, apparently. They crowded the radiator, more of them than I'd ever seen before.

"Wait, what do you mean you hurt them?"

"I don't want to talk about it."

Peter then explained about how demons strike when there is an open door, an invitation. Usually, they come when a person is vulnerable, like when drunk or doing drugs. If I had a demon jumping inside me at random, did that mean I could hurt somebody?

But, as I would learn later, my fears were groundless. My "demon" bothered only Peter, no one else.

At home in bed, I wondered what Peter had done to his daughters that was so awful he couldn't even talk about it. He must have meant he hit them, maybe even beat them. But he'd told me once that he'd never struck his children even though his wife had demanded it, so to trick her, he'd taken the child in question into his room and pummeled the bed with a slab of wood. I'd thought that was admirable, refusing to be violent. He was with me, but I provoked him. Poppa said I was a difficult person, too. Yet Peter still considered me his savior. I wasn't sure what he meant exactly—what was I saving him from?

The Devil? Years and years of studying religion had taught me that the Devil was behind every evil action we did. Since Peter's childhood was so horrendous, did that mean the Devil had even more sway over him than other people? But now I felt I was battling, too.

"You were born on Easter day," Peter often repeated. "The day of rebirth, new hope. You're my rebirth, my hope, and all I have in this world. You're God's special gift to me."

One January day, this mysterious demon threw an icy snowball right into Peter's face, almost hitting him in the eye. We were at "The Place," a small fenced-in meadow by Union Hill High School, letting Paw run through the snow and having ourselves a silly snowball fight. Peter's snowball, soft as cookie dough, had just struck my shoulder, and in response I grabbed a chunk of ice mixed with snow and pitched it like a fastball. It smacked his left cheek, leaving a red hoof-sized mark.

"Margaux!" he said, rubbing his cheek. "That really hurt! You could have blinded me!"

"I'm so sorry. My mind just went black for a second. You know. It happens sometimes."

Still rubbing his cheek, Peter asked, "Do you even remember throwing it?"

"No, it's like the other time."

We didn't say anything for a few minutes, just watched Paws bite the snow. Union Hill's eaves held up long, clear icicles, some of which had frozen strangely and were covered with tumorlike bumps, many of which seemed as sharp as sickles. Whenever I glanced at pointed objects, I would quickly have to look away or horrible thoughts bloated my mind: I would think of poking out my eye in the mirror and seeing the white jelly of my cornea burst, or I would think of stabbing myself in the breasts or vagina. I told Peter that I thought the Devil was putting thoughts in my head, sick images I would never have thought of on my own.

———

Peter had started reading self-help books, which he would quote to my mother whenever she said she felt like she'd failed as a parent because of her mental illness. "No fault, no blame," he would say to her. He picked her up a copy of *The Power of Positive Thinking* and taught her to pound pillows and yell in order to release her suppressed anger. Peter and I lit white candles and prayed for her to get well; we even performed a crystal healing spell from one of Inès's Wicca books. None of this worked: she was hospitalized again that February—her third time this year. Peter had ridden in the cab with us those last few times. In the emergency room, she confided to him things about her childhood she had never talked about before. When she and Aunt Bonnie were both nine, she said, a man had lured them into a barn, and, after raping my aunt, he put his fingers inside my mother until she bled. My mother's parents didn't call the police, because they hadn't wanted to go to court; they thought it best to just put it behind them. Mommy would faint in school or start screaming out of nowhere, so my grandparents took her to a psychiatrist, who started prescribing her Mellaril, an antipsychotic, which made her feel like she was sleepwalking. She didn't play anymore, but she caused no trouble either; she was, as she said to Peter, "a perfect angel" compared to Aunt Bonnie, who refused to take the pills; my grandmother disciplined Bonnie by sticking her in ice-cold showers. Her screams would reverberate throughout the house. "That was the way people raised kids back then," Mommy told Peter.

"You're telling me," Peter said.

Lately, I'd begun to grind my teeth down during my sleep to such an extent that I'd wake up with terrible jaw pain. Red scratches had started to appear on my arms and legs. My periods sometimes lasted for ten days at a time and I often spotted in between.

That winter, I began to feel like the scales were tipping. Peter owed me more happiness than he gave, and so he should stop going out with Inès, who hated me and wanted me dead. When he came back on Sunday, he had plenty to say regarding her bad-mouthing me. Why was this even necessary? I sincerely doubted Inès had demanded he take her out; Inès wasn't pushy about anything. It was he who was always pushing people beyond their limits to new ones. Did he even care that I went into long crying jags every Sunday because I couldn't stand the loneliness? Somehow I needed to convey to him just how much suffering he caused by putting Inès first. That woman did nothing for him, no sex at all. She supplied nothing so she deserved nothing.

I started to pretend I was the notorious demon, using a guttural voice to tell Peter, "You sicken me," or "You love your dog more than me," or "You used to be fun, but now you just act like an old man." These outbursts resulted in Peter's sobs and me blaming it all on the evil spirits. I then knew there never had been an actual demon possessing me, but this realization didn't stop me from dreaming about malevolent entities or fearing that I was in danger of losing my soul.

21

PRETTY BABIES

March heralded spring, which made Peter happy: when the wind died down he could take the Gold Wing out of the basement, where it had been corralled since the first snowfall. But March also reminded Peter of my birthday, which was a month away, and my birthdays always depressed him. This year would be the big fourteen. To Peter every one of my birthdays was another baby step toward the Armageddon of our relationship. As it was, he was always complaining about my age. He said that ever since I'd turned twelve and gotten my period, my vagina had gotten a scent. It wasn't a bad smell, he said, and would probably be exciting to most men, but because he had been molested by the tap dancers, he couldn't tolerate the scent of a woman's vagina, and so he wasn't able to go down on me. I didn't dare remind him that, unlike him, I put up with things I didn't like: such as the pain or boredom I went through every time I pleasured him, or thinking up hateful fantasies about prostitutes, street urchins, and the like. We had a new one in which he played a sultan and I was a slave girl who'd do the dance of a thousand veils. I really hated being slave girls. I had to get down on my knees and call him "Master." I had to pretend I worshipped his penis when, in reality, I thought genitals were the least appealing parts of boys and men. How could anyone adore something that looked like an anteater's snout with a hairy, baggy, vein-covered sack beneath it?

Only occasionally would he massage me with his hand while Nina entertained fantasies about gay men having sex. (We had finally watched a gay porno; sometimes Peter had to look away, but he didn't resort to fast-forwarding as he always did with lesbian scenes, saying two women together was boring.) Or boys my own age with hands tied with twine and dog collars around their necks who were sometimes forced by the infamous Mr. Nasty to eat Nina out.

Peter couldn't stand the sight of pubic hair on me. Once, I turned the tables on him. I told him that if he indeed loved me, he would shave his balls, which he did, carefully, with an electric razor. Though he declared his love to me every day in his letters, for some reason I kept feeling like I needed more and more proof.

Peter and I avidly devoured books about older men and young girls like Anne Rice's *Belinda*, written under the pseudonym Anne Rampling, Marguerite Duras's *The Lover*, the many V. C. Andrews books, and, of course, Nabokov's *Lolita* (though Peter complained that Lolita didn't love Humbert). We also watched the movie version of *Lolita*, *Baby Doll*, and *Pretty Baby*, a 1978 film starring Brooke Shields. *Pretty Baby* was set in early-twentieth-century New Orleans; it was about a photographer who fell in love with a twelve-year-old prostitute, Violet, and married her. "Now *this* is like us," Peter said after our first viewing. "This is true love." We watched it religiously, Peter pausing the movie at times to capture characters' facial expressions; we viewed it so many times we started to memorize lines from it, such as Violet's singsong declaration of love to her much older paramour: "I love you once / I love you twice / I love you more than beans and rice!" Peter always cried during the next-to-final scene, when Violet's mother took her away from the house where they were living and the photographer shouted, "You cannot take her!" and then softly, "I can't live without her."

Though we watched many movies about young girls, Peter also took my tastes into consideration. Again and again, we viewed the scene in *Risky Business* where Tom Cruise dances in his underwear. I had a huge crush on Ralph Macchio, which Peter said wasn't surprising since he looked like Ricky. Every time a boy was cute, Peter compared him to Ricky as though he were some kind of prototype. I didn't want Ricky mentioned; didn't want to be reminded of my crush on him anymore.

If Nabokov's Humbert Humbert was right and a nymphet was a charmed, charming, supple girl between the ages of nine and fourteen, I was fast reaching the end of my nymphdom. Since nymphets, for Peter, seemed to bud around seven, it was possible that, for him, they lost their luster even sooner. When Peter was out, I spent a lot of time gazing at the pictures contained within the oval frames on his walls, most of them taken when I was eight. Had I been prettier than other girls my age? I wondered this as I looked through three fat photo albums dedicated to pictures of me at seven and eight. Decently pretty, I supposed, with expressions ranging from drowsy contentment to schoolgirlish pluck (in some pictures I had a habit of lifting and furrowing my chin), to thoughtless, self-assured play. In some, I was full-cheeked and mousy; in others I was fox-faced, with kinetic eyes—girl of fast heartbeat, girl of rose-tipped cheeks and bark-rich hair. My most mundane actions were caught and fossilized: stooping to tie a grimy shoelace, clapping, feeding the parakeets, bending for a pinecone. So many pictures of me with Mister Softee ice-cream cones or Blow Pops. Then another fat album of me at eleven and a good-sized one of me at twelve. Then the Skate Girl album. But there were no albums containing pictures taken of me after the age of twelve. There were a lot of new pictures, but they were unbound, stored in the wooden box I'd made for Peter in shop class.

One picture stood out: a Polaroid of my eight-year-old, swimsuit-clad self clenching the edge of a wrought-iron picnic table in the yard. The nymphlike, bark-haired child stood with her wiry body crooked like a violin bow. The child's face had a strange expression that none of the other pictures contained: an uncharacteristic smugness, a keen, bawdy confidence. The expression was pure power: an awareness of her Slinky-thin body, its lucid, spanking-new appeal, with arms and legs as lithe as flutes, hair damp and mussed. This child's haughtiness, her knowingness in that picture . . . from where did it come? How did she learn that expression? Did she come to fourteen-year-old me one night with her dirty knees and rustic face, did that ghost of summers past drift into my bedroom like some succubus, touching her chest to mine like a live wire, waking that drowsy, jaded, and electric creature Nina, who bubbled inside me like a can of shaken seltzer? Like some enchanting and enchanted fairy godmother, Nina gathered into her hands the child's tanned face, kissed her full on her half-gaped mouth, and whispered: *Margaux, I am your future.*

Peter decided to paint the walls of his room after I complained that their pale yellow color was depressing. The new color he had chosen was a frosty green that resembled the inside of an avocado. "I don't want anything too attention-grabbing," he said. "The attention should be on all the beautiful faces in the room." By that, he meant me, Karen, Paws, and Jill. Jill. Hateful, adoring, flush-faced Jill, who was more beautiful than me because her eyes were blue and her hair blond. So many times had I stared at that eight-year-old specter who was probably now about my age.

"Peter, I can't stand it anymore," I said.

"What is it?" he said, moving the brush in a sleek up-and-down motion. The walls had been covered with primer the day before, and were now ready for a fresh coat of paint.

"School," I said, using the first thing that came to mind.

"They're still bothering you?"

"I was walking in line and I got hit really hard in the back. Some kids laughed. I'm not sure who hit me."

"That's real brave. Attacking someone whose back is turned."

"Yeah, I know. This school is no better than Holy Cross. Anyway, I think they've seen us together. They know you're not my father."

"Well, you're graduating in a few months. You can say good riddance to that school." I'd told Peter that Poppa was willing to put me in a Catholic high school in West New York, which might be far enough away for the gossip not to follow.

"Peter," I said, gathering my nerve. "I don't want you to put up that picture of Jill once the paint dries. She's from the past and that picture doesn't even look like her."

Peter cleared his throat. "I have several pictures up of you, one of Jill."

"They're outdated. You don't put any current pictures of me on these walls."

"Are you in a bad mood because of what happened at school? You shouldn't be taking it out on me."

"All I want is for you not to put up that one picture. Is that too much to ask? You're always saying you'll do anything for me."

"That's manipulative. You're trying to manipulate me." He kept painting.

"I'm not trying to manipulate you. Her picture bothers me. Every time I'm, you know, doing something for you, I have to look at that picture."

"Are you trying to guilt me? Is that what you're up to? Because you feel bad about something totally unrelated to me, some kids, some incident that has nothing to do with me . . ."

"Sometimes I think you're using me. Sometimes I don't think you love me."

"Using you for what?" He turned around; I'd finally gotten his attention. "What am I using you for?"

"Like I'm just a thing. Like I'm not really a person. Like I'm a doll."

"I can't believe this! For years, your father has been telling you either directly or indirectly that you're worth nothing. The kids in school make you feel worthless. I, on the other hand, have always tried to build up your self-esteem. Everything I do is to make you happy!" His eyes were tearing, and when I tried to touch him, he pushed my hand aside. "When I wake up in the morning, when I go to sleep at night, it's you! The first thought I have when I get up is to get a cup of coffee, smoke a cigarette, and write a letter to Margaux. Look at all these notebooks!" he said, pointing to a crate containing the notebooks of letters. "My room is a shrine to you!"

It was true. Everything that was me was stored in this room. Without Peter to see me, to adore me, how could I exist?

22

TYING THE KNOT

As I walked down New York Avenue, an old man kicked a beer bottle. Some pigeons pecked at a piece of yucca, rolling it back and forth like a hockey puck. *"¿Qué hora es?"* An elderly woman in black was tapping me on the shoulder. Black rubber shoes, black dress. *"¿Qué hora es?"*

"No español." I said, dragging myself out of my hypnotic state. *"No hablo español."*

She nodded and for a brief moment reached to pet my face. *"Qué linda,"* she said softly, and I realized she was saying that because I was wearing the prom dress.

I had gotten the dress from Yolanda, a woman who lived across the street from Peter. Yolanda had been our sole supporter amid the gossip-mongers; she always stopped to talk to us whenever she saw us on the street, and once she said it was terrible that we had to go through so much just because we had a friendship that people considered strange.

The woman in black walked away, leaving me flushed. She had thought me beautiful in my dress. Yolanda had given it to me for a prom or homecoming dance, but I knew I would never attend those.

I had worn the dress for my fourteenth-birthday party and now I was wearing it to my wedding. The dress was a white beaded poly-chiffon number with puffed sleeves and a partly see-through bodice. My shoes were also from Yolanda: white boca crepe sandals with pleated satin bows topped by glittery rhinestones.

In my fancy shoes, I had to be careful not to trip on the wide green steps leading to St. Augustine's doors. I wasn't used to wearing heels. In fact, I was accustomed only to sneakers, since I never attended parties or dances. Sneakers, the only shoes Peter found sexy. I suddenly worried about my choice of footwear.

But Peter showered me with compliments that day when he met me in the church's narthex. He was dressed in his wedding-and-funeral suit, the same one he'd worn to meet Poppa. His false teeth were in and he smelled of Brylcreem. We used the holy water from a small font to bless ourselves before entering the church.

Sermons were offered here in both English and Spanish, but there was no sermon going on when we entered that Tuesday afternoon in July. The church was empty, with the exception of a sleeping homeless man in flannel. "I'm glad he's here," I whispered to Peter. "He can be the witness."

We chose a pew in the middle of the nave. Peter picked up a black leather-bound Bible. He started to read the Twenty-third Psalm aloud.

I repeated the words after him: "He maketh me to lie down in green pastures / He leadeath me beside the still waters / He restoreth my soul."

I saw the Gold Wing, black and silver. I saw the bushes on River Road, bursting with dark red raspberries. I saw Peter's room, the girl figurines: dancing, tending sheep, feeding animals. I saw the world inside the brightness of Peter's terrarium and the brick house that contained the characters of the Story. All that was sacred was mine. I owned it. I was in church. I was a bride.

I was also a virgin, like the mother of God; I'd never had intercourse. I was wearing a perfect white dress. Peter had taken a picture of me wearing it in front of a cake with fourteen candles. The lights were off so the kitchen was dark, and in the picture there was only the dimmest outline of the hutch where Inès kept her dishes and bowls. Her tureen, her teakettle, her teacups, her coffeepot, her bowls and plates, all silent as ice. Oh, that picture was strange. My eyes were two spots of black; they looked like the holes left after fires burn into the earth. Normally, I looked fourteen, but in that picture Peter said I looked seventeen or eighteen. "Your body is a grown woman's in that dress. When did you grow up?"

It wasn't the body. It was the face that was grown-up. The eyes. Peter refused to take a picture of me unless I was smiling, and it was the barest ashes of a smile. There was an ice-cream cake, shaped like a heart, topped with strawberries. Peter and me. No one else came to our party. Inès's kitchen that day had been as quiet as the church was now.

We said our vows. Peter put the ring on my finger. We didn't kiss, though, because I was so afraid someone would see.

In the master bedroom of my parents' house, there was the queen bed, but it was too big for me. Or maybe not big enough. Every night, I went to sleep on the right side and ended up on the left, all tangled and twisted in the quilt, with small scratches on my arms, belly, and legs from where I dug into my skin while asleep. Even though my mother still slept in the kitchen extension Poppa had had built for her, she kept all her records in the master bedroom. It was there she'd lie in the day-time for hours on end, listening to those records and staring quietly at the circular fluorescent light on the ceiling.

One Saturday night, Poppa walked into the master bedroom, where I was reading V. C. Andrews under the overhead lamp. He didn't say anything at first, just stared at the record player. He was obviously drunk.

After a while, he turned to me: "Listen, between you and me, I am going to throw them out. Those records make her sick! Only you and I know what this is like, am I right? Well, at least you get to hide at the old man's house. But I am stuck here, in the inferno, with this sick woman. You look tan. You know something: I have not been to the beach in years. I am turning into a phantom of myself. I am giving you my money, my blood, so you can live. Do you understand? Your life is so carefree. You barely ever see her face. You have not the courage to face suffering. You are so weak; shame on you! You care nothing for your own mother; for shame! My father was paralyzed from diabetes when I was eight years old; I stayed by his side! I helped my mother cook. Shame on you for taking the easy life! If not for you, she would not be like this. It was the pregnancy and the post-partum hormones that caused her to go out of whack. Here's a piece of advice, take it from someone who knows: do not get pregnant, do not get married. Our blood has been tainted by hers. We are living in the confines of a curse. A curse has four walls and a window in which you can gaze out at the life you could have had."

Poppa sat down and stared at his shadowy reflection in the full-length mirror. He started speaking again, softly and calmly this time. "You have talked of demons in this room. In this room, right? The other night I overheard you tell your mother that there was a voice coming from the air conditioner. Don't be so quick to run to your mother next time. Listen: next time, just be still, and listen. You may find that it was only a garbage truck, a howling dog, or your own scream. It is only when the world goes deaf that it becomes unbearable. I have learned to embrace my nightmares. Your mother doesn't dream at all. She told me that once. She has no dreams, not a single one."

He was serious but so uncharacteristically calm that I thought it was my only chance to tell him about a mistake I'd just made: I'd bought jeans that were a size too small and had quickly outgrown them.

He sat on the edge of the bed, listening quietly in the gloaming of that wan reading lamp.

"I'll show you," I said, and rushed into the adjacent bedroom to get one of the pairs of jeans. I started to squeeze into them in front of Poppa, my eyes tearing up. "I thought I was three/four. I was sure. Anyway, I don't have the receipts anymore . . ."

Poppa stood up. "You act like this is my fault! This is your own fault! Why did you buy the wrong size! You have no brain, like your mother, you have inherited her stupidity! You know what? From now on I will buy jeans for you in the city!"

"No, you're not picking out my clothes! I'll pick out jeans myself on Bergenline!"

"Why, so you can buy designer ones?"

"You have designer clothes! Your clothes are really expensive!"

"I have to look nice to go to work! You do not work! You do not do anything except make misery for me! Your full-time job! To make my life a living hell! To make your mother sick and put her in the hospital with your bad behavior!"

"You shut up!" I couldn't stand it when he blamed me for my mother's condition. "It's you, you abusive pig!"

"You had better not talk to me like that! I will cut off your allowance! Then you will have to stay home!"

"I'll starve first rather than stay home with you! I'd be in the hospital too if all I did was listen to you go on and on about how much you hate us."

He put out his fist and I yelled, "Go ahead; I wish you'd kill me! I wish I'd never been born!" I meant it, too.

He turned away, closing his hands on the side of his face. "You are a brat, you hear me? You make your mother sick, you hear me? You ruined my life, goddamn you."

I ran downstairs and locked myself in the bathroom. As soon as I heard him banging on the door, screaming, I grabbed the radiator cover and started shaking it. "Hey, hey, hey! Don't break anything!" From the outside, he tugged on the doorknob. I kicked the radiator grill with my socked foot, feeling nothing. "You come out of there! Listen, I will give you the money! Just come out of there!" I opened the door and he stood outside. We locked eyes. He turned away, scowling, and went to his wallet.

"I am your bank," he said, slowly counting the money, stopping every once in a while to glare at me. "You have no decency. No pride. No dignity. No class. No conscience. No feelings. No self-respect. You are a monster."

I walked over to him and said, "Don't throw it on the floor; just hand it to me."

"You had better behave," he muttered, his face turned as he gave

me the money. "Now, leave me alone! Please! Get out of here! Looking at your face makes me sick!"

Late that night, I heard Poppa talking about me in the kitchen to my
mother when he thought I was sleeping. I had been going to the bathroom, but as soon as I heard them, I slunk down the stairs.

She was lying on her sofa bed in the kitchen extension, while he
worked on a pair of earrings at the table. "What did you tell them?"
I heard her ask.

"Look, to anyone who asks, he is her uncle, your half brother. Tell
her, too, so she knows."

"What are they saying, exactly?"

"They say: 'Louie, who is this man hanging around your daughter?
Is he all right, this guy? You trust him?' If it has reached the bars, it
means they are spending too much time together. Why is this? I thought
she was with the girlfriend, mostly, and the sons of those people."

"They walk the dog together. People love to twist things."

"Especially when it concerns me. People are so envious. Because I
am well respected in this town. I have a lot of friends. Everybody
knows me. I am popular. But now I notice the guy from the steak
sandwich place giving me a strange look. I go there all the time. I am
a good customer. Anyway, the point is, people are talking. She should
cut down on going over to that house. Maybe, after a while, she
should cut those people out of her life."

"They're the only friends she has, Louie."

"I know. If not for that, I would have forbidden her from going so
much. I thought it was a phase; she would outgrow it. However, it has
turned into an obsession."

"Well, what else has she got?"

"I do not understand it. What is the attraction? That crumbling
house is no carnival. What can a girl her age possibly do there for all
that time? He is nice, the old man, but he cannot be healthy for her.
What do they talk about during those walks? He probably laments

about his life before his accident, before his divorce. That kind of talk can depress a young girl. What can she possibly learn from it? And even though this man is not robust, not really well, what is going on inside his head? She is older now. More like a woman, less like a child."

"What exactly are you implying?"

Poppa laughed. "There is no way a young girl could possibly have feelings for someone so decrepit. That would be abnormal. But for the old man to have feelings for her, carefully hidden, this is possible."

"It's nothing like that. It's sweet and innocent."

"Okay, okay." Poppa put his hands up, then resumed his work on the earrings. "I believe you. I do not want to talk about this subject anymore. It sickens me. Anyway, the bottom line, you are the mother. You make her cut down on the time she spends over at that house."

"There's nothing I can do. You know I can't control her. You'll have to do it."

"Me?" Poppa placed the earrings on the table and took off his loupe. "I have no power over her."

"Well, neither do I. She broke my watch. She slammed it against the wall and broke the glass. I can't remember what we were arguing about."

"Sometimes I fear she will take the whole house down with me in it! I have seen movies! There are children who kill their own parents! She goes crazy, she starts to yell and she breaks things. I can barely speak to her. We never say two words to each other anymore. On the weekends, she does not even say good morning to me."

"Why don't you say good morning to her first?"

"She is out of control. She wants me to raise her allowance. So she can go spending money for pizza and hamburgers with that man! She can stay for dinner and eat the healthy food that I will cook for her."

"Well, I think they eat at places like El Pollo Supremo and El Unico. That's not unhealthy."

"I cannot afford it!"

"Louie, start saying good morning to her. Someone has to make the first move. And on her next birthday, make sure you say happy birthday."

"She did not say happy birthday to me this year! It was my birthday and she said nothing. For Christmas, she said nothing. I gave her a necklace, the one I made with the gold cross that has the diamond in the center. She did not even thank me."

"She wears it."

"She did not have one word of gratitude. I should call her the ghost because that is what she is like."

"Well, she will die if you try separating her from Peter. She will just die. She won't eat; I know it. She may run away from home. They are all she has."

"Like a ghost moving through here, except when she talks, her voice is so loud. Walking around here like she owns everything. Leaving her bowl of cereal for me to pick up after. Like I am her slave or something. Leaving her papers and books scattered all over the table. I tell her to clean up her papers, or I will clean them for her. She starts to shout at me: 'Don't touch my papers, get away from my things!' I did nothing to her. She is wild now. Completely wild."

After I told Peter about the conversation I'd overheard, we both agreed that we needed to take extra precautions about being seen, which would be even more difficult now, considering that Peter couldn't ride the motorcycle anymore. In addition to the chronic pain caused by his spinal injury, Peter thought he was developing arthritis. Inès suggested putting a FOR SALE sign on the Gold Wing and using the money to buy a car, and Peter kept saying he would do it, but never did. He kept hoping his pain would miraculously disappear and we would soon be riding again.

In addition to this problem our fights about him asking for sex every day or every other day without offering me pleasure in return and guilting me if I tried to say no, about taking Inès out on Sunday, about his insistent fantasies, became more frequent and violent. A few times Peter had even started choking me, which was a very strange sensation, my head flopping about as if it were made out of rubber, valleys of black dots exploding in front of my blurring eyes.

"I'm afraid one day I'll get so angry I'll kill you without meaning to," he said, laying his head against my breast and sobbing after a particularly bad fight. "Then I'd have to kill myself because I can't live without you. I love you so much, I never want to hurt you again! Don't ever get me to that point again where an evil spirit can seize control of my body! Don't bring me to that place I can't get out of, when I'm seeing red and I just want to kill you because you make me so angry. You can be so cruel to me, you make me feel like nothing. I just want it to be like it was when you were a little girl, and sometimes I think if we're both dead it could be like that again, and then I hate myself for thinking that because I love you and you're so young and I'd kill myself first before I'd ever harm you. Sweetheart, you have your whole life to live and I'm falling apart. I can barely sleep, and sometimes I don't even want to get up in the morning, and I think you'll go on without me because you're young and could have anyone while I'll rot here in my room with my pictures and memories of you." I knew it was that other part of Peter, the bad part, who had hurt me; the Peter who had been so abused that he couldn't help lashing out.

"It won't happen, Peter," I said, holding him. "We'll die first. You'll kill me by choking me or pushing a pillow over my face, and then you'll kill yourself. Like Romeo and Juliet. Then it's like you said, it'll be like it was, like a snow globe when you shake it and everything repeats on and on, it'll be so beautiful."

"I love you so much," Peter said, as I stroked his face and hair. "It's just that I can't stand it when you hold that ax over my head, when you're like my executioner, sharpening the blades. I could never go to jail. You know that."

The ax was our secret. Occasionally when we fought I lost control and threatened to go to the police and tell them everything. It would have been a self-destructive act because I knew that if Peter ever got arrested, I'd feel so guilty that I'd have to kill myself. I could never betray the one person in the world who truly cared about me.

23

THE CONFESSIONAL

We finally found a place within walking distance where we could be alone, even hold hands and say the romantic things I craved. To get to our new haunt, we had to walk down a long aluminum staircase framed by an ornate wrought-iron gate located on Boulevard East. We'd stop at a nearby food cart for a lemonade and hot dog and then we'd descend 221 circling steps with the dog. Peter got so tired during our arduous trip that he'd plop down on a step, jokingly lolling out his tongue like Paws. Whenever he did this, it was up to me to give him a kiss for strength, as I'd done years ago. Paws, whose muzzle had gone gray, would be glad to rest with Peter while I waited impatiently. The steps were built for commuters to reach the ferry, but for us they were a portal into a private nook in the woods where we couldn't be seen or heard. The Story could be as dirty as I wanted it with no one around to hear (the Story, unlike our sex life, never revolved around Peter's fantasies; it was much more focused on Nina and her exploits), so it was well worth both the difficult journey down and the equally grueling return trip: a long, circuitous route through Weehawken. Often, when we got home, I'd rub baby lotion on his back and he'd rest on his heating pad while I read to him. "Mommy, take care of me," he'd joke. I liked to feel that he needed me. If not for me, who would give him back rubs? Who would read for hours until her voice got hoarse, until he fell asleep in the crook of her shoulder? Who would go to El Unico to get food, as I always did when he hurt too much to leave his room?

The blow jobs and massages were part of this overall maintenance, in my mind. Peter often joked that he was like the Tin Man, needing the oil can of love and affection—as for me, being Peter's caretaker gave purpose and direction to my life, where otherwise there was none. I fancied myself as Peter's guardian angel. He said that I never looked so beautiful as when I tended to a pigeon whose wing had been broken; a peeping gosling separated from its mother; a turtle turned over on its shell attacked by ants.

I was just fourteen, but I often felt like I was forty. I took care of Peter as though he were my cub, a large, cumbersome, damaged, and worn-out bear cub, whose bawling baby face I would gather into my lap and whose tears I would sop up with tissues. His were the tears of a ravaged life as well as a life that had ravaged others. In our latest haunt, he revealed secrets he had never told anyone before; I tried to listen without judgment, as the Bible teaches. I tried to treat his stories as though they were part of our Story or a novel I'd read recently or a movie we'd rented together. Or a religious scene like Lot's two daughters seducing him in a cave, perhaps, or Jacob wearing goatskin on his neck and hands to fool his blind father into blessing him. Life for me had already lost much of its pulp; the edges were collapsing into the center, and in that gap was the sympathy Peter had sought all his life and never got from anyone. Or perhaps "sympathy" was the wrong word; what he was telling me was more confirmation of what I already understood in biblical terms: the bad Peter, under the influence of the Devil, did horrible things. His honesty was evidence that the good Peter was finally triumphing over the bad one, because to me, that was the whole point of confession—to figure out where you've gone wrong and to stop sinning. One particular confession that kept coming back to haunt me was his story about hanging a cat as a boy.

He had found the cat in the snow and brought him inside for warm milk and tuna, and the animal had scratched a bloody cut on his arm. He killed him because he couldn't stand betrayal, not when everyone in his life had proven to be untrustworthy. I said over and over, "Did you really murder a cat?" He assured me that afterward he'd felt terribly guilty, but I was still deeply disturbed by this. There was another story, of how he'd shot his own hamster. When he was ten years old he had wanted to buy a B.B. gun for five dollars but couldn't afford it, so he had sold himself to an older man who'd sodomized him in a hotel room. There was blood everywhere. He'd bought the B.B. gun and shot his pet dead and then threw out the gun.

On a different trip to the woods, he told me that his love for young girls had started with a nine-year-old named Sylvia, a niece of his second wife's. He said Sylvia had climbed into bed with him and started touching him and he hadn't stopped her. It had felt good to him, like playing, being naughty like the time when he was thirteen and he'd let in a pretty twelve-year-old neighbor, a virgin. They'd tried to have sex but her vagina had been too dry. After the incident with Sylvia, he had started being sexual with his daughters. It was innocent, he said, and they seemed to enjoy it as much as he did. His wife divorced him when she found out about it.

It was as though I was watching a foreign film and saw the drama, but was refusing to read the subtitles. Then I thought of something Winnie had told me about seeing a horror movie where a baby's lips were sewn shut, relaying that image to me as though it were nothing. Like she was proud. As though withstanding the film made her brave. But at what cost? To see it clearly, the most horrible of sights? Why ever did Winnie tell me that, passing it on to me? As though it were a stick of gum or a bobby pin.

"I don't understand," I said. "You used to say it was just me but now you're saying you did it with other girls before me. I thought I was special. You said you fell in love with me." Thinking about this, I felt like a power source with too many of its outlets in use, like my whole brain was having a blackout.

"I love you," Peter said, his voice cracking. "And you are special.

I loved my daughters, too, and I only wanted to show them how much. But now I realize that I was as sick an addict as any alcoholic, gambler, or drug user. There's no rehab for people like me and I feel so isolated from the rest of the world. I feel like I'm an outcast who can never fit in no matter what I do."

Peter gripped my hand. "I have to get better somehow. Even if it's on my own." He paused and then said, "Will you help me?"

"Yes," I said weakly, though I wasn't sure what he wanted me to do.

One September day I found a gay magazine in the woods, soaked from a rainfall, and I leafed through it, despite the ants sticking to its glossy pages. Peter looked on wryly while I paged through pictures of guys with bouquetlike genitals, musclemen whose bulging bodies were like mini–solar systems, young, girl-like boys called "twinks." I liked the twinks best, with their skinny chests, their pretty faces and wanton, sedated, jaded, perpetually turned-on expressions. In one of the pictures, a muscle-bound man held the hair of a twink, who enthusiastically sucked him off. There was tenderness in the picture, I thought, a cooperative energy; the scene was almost parental. The twink looked to the muscleman with wide, long-lashed eyes, searching for love and encouragement, and the man receiving his pleasure looked down upon the boy with benevolence. As I turned the pages, there were other loving scenes: men kissing without fear or shame, men loving each other with their mouths and hands.

Peter said, "Listen, there's something I have to tell you. About a dream I had a few weeks ago."

I was surprised he hadn't told me this dream before, since one of the first things we did when we first saw each other every day was go over our dreams and try to interpret them.

"In the dream I saw an angel standing in a blue light. She was wearing a white dress that was a little like your wedding dress. She didn't look at me with judgment." He swallowed, and I quickly handed him a tissue from my travel packet. "She didn't look at me as if I was disgusting, or a bad man. And I wasn't afraid. I stepped closer. And I saw that behind the angel was a ladder." At this point, he began sobbing, and I put my arms around him.

"Don't tell me anymore. It's making you too upset."

"I have to tell you about this ladder. It had a bunch of missing rungs. She stood there in her blue glow and looked at me with perfect calm. After a while, I was filled with horror. You see, I've been reading these books while you're at school, about how children interpret sexuality . . ."

"What about the ladder?"

"I couldn't really see it all because the top part was covered by fog. Like the fog that covers Manhattan and makes it look like it's disappeared. And as the angel kept looking at me, I knew what it represented. It was your life, sweetheart. And the missing rungs were the years you'd lost because of me."

"I don't understand what you're talking about." I felt like my circuits were overloaded again.

"Let me explain. Life occurs in stages, like rungs. First, you're a child playing with dolls. Then you're a preteen, getting into boys. Then you're a teenager, dating and such. But for you these stages were skipped. What we have to do is go back and repair the ladder. To do that we have to stop all the sex. Just quit cold turkey. Our love has to be wholly pure and spiritual. I'll be your father."

"You're already like a father."

"I mean, a father who doesn't have sex with you." He looked to Paws as if for support. "We have to stop. I've started rebuilding the dollhouse. You know, the wooden one I started building you a long time ago but didn't finish. I thought you could play with it. I would get you some dolls. And, eventually, you need to start going out with guys your own age. I'll be the proud father anxiously awaiting his daughter at home so she can tell him all about her date."

"There's this one guy I like at school. He doesn't like me. I told this girl in confidentiality I liked him and she went and told him. God, I hate high school. I want to drop out. But I can't; I'm not old enough."

"Did you hear what I said? We can't be sexual anymore."

"We're married!"

"Not legally."

"This isn't fair! This is sick! I can't be a little girl again! And now you're telling me I'm not allowed to be a woman!" I knew the most important thing was that I keep moving forward, that I leave the girl I was behind me, but now he wanted to stop me from doing so.

"We can start over. I know we can. This time, we'll do it right."

"You're just pushing me away like everyone else! I'm too old and this is your way of getting rid of me! You don't want the hassle! The people gossiping and Inès putting pressure on you! She wants me out; I know it! It was okay when it was in the basement! When it was just you and me, in the basement—"

"This is why it has to stop," Peter said, trembling. "Look at the effect it has on you."

"Are Miguel and Ricky saying anything about me?"

"No, I promise, they're not. They don't talk to me, not really."

"Because of me, I bet! Nobody can stand me! Inès, your precious Inès, never says one word to me!"

"Inès is shy. She's always been. And she hears us fighting sometimes and that makes her uncomfortable."

"Oh, I feel so guilty! I feel so bad for disturbing the peace! Defend Inès some more, why don't you? Why don't you live out your happy little life with her? And I'll just disappear. Don't worry, whether I'm dead or alive, you'll always have my pictures! And they never say a word!"

Before he could reply, I ran off into the woods, down the road, through the parking lot, and finally, to the boat docks, where I sat on the edge of an empty pier, over the gray water of the Hudson River, until Peter, limping, holding Paws by his leash, begged me not to jump.

24

STRANGER IN THE MIRROR

That November Peter bought a car, a 1978 Ford Granada, and my mother was hospitalized again for depression and paranoia. Poppa woke me up at five thirty in the morning to tell me she'd admitted to swallowing some 409 glass cleaner and was throwing it up; we would need to get her into the psychiatric ward immediately, so could Peter come even though it was an odd hour? I said Peter had a car now, and Poppa was relieved.

Before he left my bedroom, Poppa said: "I have stayed here constantly, you understand, because she was so suicidal. I could not go out at night for three weeks. Every night I listened to her nonsense. Even the drink could not keep me calm; I felt like the blood would leap from my pores. The talk of the Mafia. Oh, the Mafia is out for Margaux! I told her it was just prank callers. She insists it is the Mafia, whether she really believes that or because she wants to drive me mad, I do not know. Then she says that she sees people on the street wiping their eyes as though they are crying. And she thinks the police are going to arrest her. For what? I ask, and she doesn't answer. She sings to herself in the street, humiliating her family! Driving us to the point where we would need masks to go outside so no one would know we are related to her. She said she wants to climb to the roof and set herself on fire like a witch at the stake, not realizing she will burn us all away with her!" He was quiet for a moment, hunched over on my bed, shaking. "I was at work the other day. I went into the bathroom. I looked into the mirror at myself. I could not believe how pale I seemed. I had the expression of a two-thousand-year-old mummy. The scariest recognition is to look in the mirror and a stranger stands there wearing your clothes. I put water on my face. I thought: I must straighten my tie. I must go back out there. This is my lot. I should stop questioning it. But do you know what happened to me in that bathroom? Water ran down my face. At first I thought it was from the faucet but then I realized it was coming from my eyes, it was tears, and I was helpless to prevent them! What has happened to me? What has happened?" He got up. "Let's take her, all of us. In that car he bought—what did you say it was?"

"A Granada," I said, not wanting to go anywhere with Poppa; I couldn't stand talking about my mother, and that was all he did. Poppa had left me with the image of my mother on the roof, burning to death. I looked away, unable to block it out.

"Let us all go in the Granada, get her checked into St. Mary's Hospital, and then go out to eat together. What about we go to City Island?" The worst place in the world, I thought. Where we used to go as a family—me, him, Mommy.

He saw the look on my face and said, almost pleading, "We can feed the gulls French fries. We can eat fried shrimp. You can have piña coladas. When you were little, you saved the paper umbrellas. You had a tin container filled with about fifty of them. I found them all once and thought, 'What is she doing, saving them for a lifetime of rainy days?'"

I wore a floppy velvet hat to City Island that the ocean wind kept trying to snatch. Poppa and I were drunk; Poppa had tried to get Peter to drink but he used the excuse of being the designated driver. Poppa was so drunk that he nuzzled his nose to mine and Peter took a picture. On a wooden picnic table, Poppa and Peter sat discussing what would be best for my mother if she didn't improve: state hospital, electroconvulsive therapy? Or simply a change of medication? I let them talk alone. I blamed myself. If only I was home more often. And the prank callers from my high school had made her paranoid. Some boys had gotten my number from a snow list, which was a photo-copied sheet of paper listing everyone's phone number so students could notify each other of school closings. Despite our precautions of late, Peter and I had been seen walking together. The prank callers had threatened to rape me and asked if I was fucking the old man. I had gotten so upset once that I had put the portable phone in the freezer, where it couldn't be heard.

I stood by the wire fence at twilight as they talked, watching the gulls swirl over the green water, smelling the green air, the fried shrimp, and the crowds of people. I put a quarter in the binocular machine and turned it right and left. Sometimes I would capture a lone boat, sometimes a wooden post, one time a white gull floating on the water. Peter came up behind me and said, "Your father is so drunk that I hope I don't have to carry him back into the house tonight. You know something? He was decent tonight. I wonder about the person he could have been if his life had turned out differently."

"No point in wondering. He is who he is," I said, and silently we took turns looking through the binoculars. Every time the money ran out, Peter would put another quarter in; we did that until he was out of change.

We went back to the wooden picnic table behind Tony's restaurant where Poppa sat, running his gold toothpick through his teeth. "A gull took a French fry right out of this basket. He came down and snatched it with me sitting here. A rare thing to happen! Do you think it is good luck, Peter? Possibly a sign of better things to come?" he said, with a wry smile, and then entertained us by shuffling a dime under three pistachio shells he had gotten from the bar, testing how fast our eyes could follow his hands. I won every time over Peter, who said his eyesight and reflexes weren't as good as they used to be.

On the way home, Peter's favorite song, "Hotel California," came on the radio and Poppa drunkenly sang along about wine, knives, and a beast that can't be killed no matter how many times you stab it.

Winter passed with Peter true to his word: we were not intimate. I missed it intensely when Peter stopped even hugging and kissing me, saying that would tempt him. There was no more watching porn and reading lascivious novels. I missed the girls in the porn movies as though they'd been friends of mine; that was how many times we'd watched them. I'd imagined background stories for each one and reasons why they worked in the sex industry and ways that they were happy despite society's condemnations. He said there shouldn't be any more talk of violence and sex, even in the Story, because talking about violence had led him to be violent. Without the sex and violence, though, where was the story? I continued to write my novel while he was out with Inès, juicing it up in secret protest of these new rules. I tallied up my novel's mortal sins: five rapes including one gang rape, six murders, three suicides, three kidnappings, four cases of incest, and one threesome.

Peter even wanted me to dress differently now, more like a "young lady"; so, at a flea market, he bought me a baggy gray, red, and black striped dress that went past my knees. The other thing, which was almost too bizarre for words, was that he wanted me to play with the dollhouse and the gray felt mice like I was seven again. I did it once, to humor him, and then refused to do it ever again. I was more confused than ever, annoyed by the way that he completely controlled whether the intimacy happened or not, just as he had been in charge of starting it. What did he think I was—a windup toy he could play with to his heart's content and then toss into some dusty corner? I really missed him holding me, caressing me, calling me Snuggle Bunny, his sweetheart. There was no one else to do it.

Peter told me he'd been reading more psychology and self-help books and a memoir about a girl who'd been raped by her father, which particularly moved him. He said maybe it had even cured him of his addiction to young girls. Since he was tormented by the sight of it but couldn't bring himself to throw it away, he taped it under the mattress.

Perhaps inspired by his readings, Peter began a novel about abused runaways entitled *The Exploited*, which he asked me to write down for him in my neat, precise print. Our only arguments now were about this novel; Peter wanted complete creative control over it. He'd dictate what he wanted written down and I'd frill up the words in a poetic style that he deemed "flowery." I felt like complaining that his writing was colorless but was afraid he'd give me one of his relentless silent treatments. We played more chess now and occasionally Scrabble. Once, to his amazement, I nabbed his queen with my knight, defeating him. From watching him I'd mastered moving knights—the trickiest characters on the board. He shook my hand but said from now on he'd rather stick to Scrabble and gin rummy because my win was a depressing reminder that his mind wasn't as sharp as it used to be. The bed was an uneven surface for game boards but we had little choice since I refused to go into the kitchen. "You're not a leper," Peter had said. "Richard mostly stays in the living room now, and Miguel and Ricky don't bother anyone." But I couldn't even stand passing through that kitchen and front room in order to get to the Granada. I said that I would like to build a tunnel that led directly from the bedroom to the car.

If there was anyone in the kitchen and I had to pee, I would do so in a small vase that Peter kept in his room; he would dump the urine into the toilet at night after everyone went to bed. Peter's room was literally our whole world now, besides the parks and diners and fast-food drive-throughs. It had everything we needed: books, a tape recorder, a TV, our Ouija board, our Scrabble game, our chess set, our deck for poker and gin rummy. In place of sex that winter, we practiced meditation, visualization, and even astral projection. Peter said his spirit had already gone out of his body once and floated by the ceiling as he peered at his motionless form below. He was so determined to leave his body again that he consulted a book written by a guru who claimed to have done it more than a hundred times.

Peter would be the one to venture out into the kitchen to make himself coffee and get me a club soda or a cup of ice cream. Whenever he went out he shut the door immediately so nobody could see me. On my side of the bed I kept Oreos, Goya crackers, saltines, Fig Newtons, pretzels, Twizzlers, and packets of Big Red gum. I had a store of tissues, two changes of clothes including underwear, maxi pads, a string bikini, my roller skates, and my schoolbag containing my textbooks; I would do my homework or study for tests whenever Peter would go into the kitchen to chat with Inès.

The more time we spent in the room, the greater effort Peter made to pretty it up. He put up more permanent Christmas decorations: tinsel wreathes around each oval frame and colored lights around the TV. He even bought three tiny green lizards called anoles to liven up the terrarium. He bought more stands and more porcelain figurines so that it seemed there wasn't a single spot on the wall left uncovered. Only on my side of the bed was the wall empty, as though he was waiting for me to decorate it.

The inside of Peter's mustard yellow Granada was matted with dog hair, its upholstery stained with ketchup and sweet-and-sour sauce, and its glove compartment stuffed with packets of salt and sugar and napkins from various fast-food restaurants. The Granada was our second home, and I depended on the routine of our trips to provide me with a sense of daily structure.

Peter liked to play his cassettes, which were an odd mix: Willie Nelson, Neil Young, Fats Domino, Pink Floyd's The Wall, the Eagles, and Beethoven's "Moonlight Sonata." He said that the Beethoven gave him a feeling he couldn't exactly describe but the closest he could come was what he called "sublime hopelessness." Again and again, he'd rewind the tape and play it for me until I began to understand what he was talking about. Lately, giving up hope seemed like an easy and reasonable choice. During moments of pure despair, I was no longer trying to swim fitfully upstream; instead, I allowed myself to float. When trying to climb out of one of my depressions, it was just the opposite: I felt like a tortoise who had gotten a sudden and crazed idea to flee its shell, not realizing that its carapace was not simply an ornament, a topcoat, but tethered to its spine and rib cage, something one must claim ownership of if there was to be any peace at all.

The spring I was fifteen, Aunt Bonnie and Uncle Trevor came for a rare visit from Ohio but they were gone within three days, after Poppa took Uncle Trevor to the bar for a couple of drinks. Mommy said that Poppa had had too much to drink and words were exchanged. I was bitter at Poppa for ruining everything. I loved Aunt Bonnie. She was spunky and funny with a head full of bouncing curls and a faux Southern accent. I imagined Aunt Bonnie was the person Mommy could have been if she hadn't taken so many of the wrong medications. Whenever my mother had me sign a Christmas or Easter card for her, I always wrote "Mom No. 2." As a young woman, Aunt Bonnie suffered from alcoholism, but now she counteracted her low moods by doing volunteer work, putting together homemade cookbooks, and attending church events. She'd never had children, and said she was happy except for one thing: at fifty, she wanted to adopt a baby, but it was too expensive and the waiting lists too long.

Aunt Bonnie called Peter a "sweetheart" when she met him during our one lunch together at El Pollo Supremo that summer. She mentioned some boy she'd had a crush on in high school who'd also owned a motorcycle. Even though Peter had finally gotten rid of his, he couldn't stop referencing it at the lunch as though he were trying to impress her. Aunt Bonnie seemed to talk to him as if he were a ten-year-old, and when I thought about it, anytime I'd seen him with Inès she'd done the same thing.

Lately, Peter wanted to pretend the car's steering wheel was the old Suzuki's handlebars, and once he risked trying to roller-skate with me at a rink even though he said one good hard fall might very well land him in a wheelchair. As the rink's strobe lights blazed and the gem-studded disco ball shone, I noticed the manic look in Peter's eyes as he skated, even attempting dance moves after he caught me admiring a break-dancing teenage boy. I didn't know how to tell Peter that he was too old, that he was not only endangering himself but embarrassing me. He tried to hold my hand during the "couples only" skate, and I found myself feigning hunger so that, while Peter got me a pretzel, I could sit miserably alone as other girls whizzed by accompanied by friends or boyfriends their own age.

On non–school days, I used to get up early to type pages of my novel on an electric typewriter Poppa had bought me, but that summer I slept until one, which was when Peter picked me up for our afternoon ride. My skin began to take on a grainy appearance and my nails constantly broke. Worse than anything was the way the world became hostile. It seemed as if the too green blades of grass wanted to leap out and slash me, songs I used to like now scraped my eardrums raw, and my body felt disjointed, mixed up as though my bones were scrambled. I would stare at things like a crack in the wall or the palm of my hand and feel as if I didn't have enough strength to lift my gaze and set it elsewhere. I needed to escape my life, but I was afraid to kill myself. According to the Catholicism I'd grown up with, and to a degree still tried to live by, suicide was a mortal sin, met with the fires of hell. Yet it didn't quite make sense to me why somebody who was already suffering would be punished more. I lived in dread of the day when even this terror ceased to matter, when the pain would become so intense that I had no choice but to take action, like Mommy had.

My mother's second suicide attempt had just occurred in early June. She wandered off, found a wall in Weehawken, and jumped off of it, breaking her ankle. Our frequent visits to the psych ward made things worse for me; for Poppa, too. "I cannot stand to look at crazy people," he said one night in the kitchen. "To me, it is like visiting one of Dante's circles. The sounds of the lunch carts, the smell of the food and the unwashed bodies; it is enough to bring up the bile in my stomach. Those faces void of sanity, some sneering like pigs, some screaming like the undead, some staring at you as if you are the source

of their agonies. I tell you something, in those crazy wards, there are
many sick people, but your mother is one of the sickest. I have never
met such an upside-down, screwed-up person in my life. One thing
I have figured out about that woman is that she likes everything
topsy-turvy; she wants filthy instead of clean, broken rather than
fixed, chaos as opposed to order; to this woman, sickness is health. Do
you hear me? Don't you ever think like her, don't you ever be like
her. Maybe she doesn't mean it, but she makes everyone around her
as sick as she is." He was doing what he always did—blaming Mommy
when it was *his* fault she was so ill. His lies turned my stomach; he
didn't even realize my mother would be normal if only she were away
from him. He continued, "But, still you are no innocent. You are a
curse upon this household. You better listen to what I am about to tell
you next. Your carefree days are over. That man has a car: let him
bring you there several times a week at least! You show her some support! Some care! Though she did not care for you properly, she tried
her best. She carried you for nine months, so it is your duty. I am passing my burden on to you. She wants you! Her blood!"

I was thankful Peter always accompanied me, and every time we
visited, he played a game of Ping-Pong with Mommy. He once suggested we play a board game such as Monopoly, Chinese checkers, or
backgammon, but pieces were missing from every game. So Ping-
Pong was our only option, though my mother couldn't stand for long
periods of time on her ankle, nor could she move quickly. The psychiatric nurse said that she was lucky she hadn't died or become paralyzed. The nurse also said she was lucky to have such a devoted
daughter and caring husband, that if we kept coming regularly, she'd
soon be well enough to return home. I often wondered, though,
whether our visits did anything for her or whether she was happy at
all to see us. She could barely smile and her eyes had a wide, staring
look like a baby, except what is cute on a baby is disturbing on an
adult. Her laugh was unnaturally slowed down. She shuffled as though
her hands and legs were in shackles and her thinning grayish brown
curls hung in limp, unwashed clumps. I kissed and petted her, but it
didn't seem to cheer her up. I knew better than to expect it to. I tried

not to feel horrified, but here in the psychiatric ward, it wasn't possible to feel anything else unless you were heartless. Human suffering was everywhere you looked.

"She's so strong," a psychiatric nurse said once about me. If only she knew the truth. I came only because Poppa told me that if I didn't I was a bad daughter. Once the same nurse said I needed to help my mother take a shower, by handing her the washcloths and soap and making sure she shampooed her hair. The nurse said she knew I could handle it. I was so tired of acting like I was stronger and better than I was. And what good did these visits do? My mother wasn't cured by them but Poppa continued to insist I make appearances because that was the only thing he cared about: appearances. We could both die and his prime concern would probably be burying us with the right makeup. He was burying me right now. And these psychiatrists and nurses were no better than Poppa. They kept up their sick smiles and, instead of looking for a real solution, just kept stuffing her with drugs that never worked.

Over to the elevator she'd accompany me and Peter, staring with what the nurses referred to as "flat affect." "I'm coming back, don't worry," I'd say as I pressed the switch again and again. When the double doors closed, I would bury my face in Peter's chest while he pressed "G" for Ground. No matter who was in the elevator with us, I'd finally permit myself to sob as Peter held me. We'd then drive to a diner and I'd order a giant vanilla milk shake, which I'd consume within minutes. On some days, my anxiety was such that these milk shakes were the only thing I could stomach.

During the hospital visits, I tried my hardest to block out my mother's paranoid and delusional talk, but there was one thing she said that haunted me. It was her description of a hallucination she had in her room. She said she had heard drums playing. When an orderly heard her making grunting sounds, he came in to find that she had stripped off all her clothes and was squatting over a pool of urine, thinking she had just given birth to a brand-new baby.

Around this time, I started to develop a plan to get my mother and me away from Union City for good. I'd get pregnant, Poppa would return to Puerto Rico as he was now always threatening, and Aunt Bonnie and Uncle Trevor would feel sorry for us because we had nowhere to go. If pity wasn't a good enough reason, the fact that Aunt Bonnie desperately wanted a baby would be more than enough incentive to take us in. Apparently, my mother must have wanted a baby herself, or she wouldn't have had that delusion. Peter didn't want to have intercourse with me, but somehow I'd have to get him to change his mind. Poppa was always talking about institutionalizing Mommy and giving her shock treatments, which I was sure would turn her into a vegetable, like that guy in *One Flew over the Cuckoo's Nest*. I couldn't let any of this come to pass; I had to take action immediately.

As I'd predicted, Peter worried that if I went to Ohio he'd never see me again. I told him that when I was eighteen I'd come back and marry him, and as he was getting old, this was his last chance to do something meaningful—at least this way when he died I'd have a part of him with me forever. I didn't feel bad deceiving Peter, not when this was so crucial, and besides, he'd tried to trick me when I was eight by buying me those green beans. My mother and I were in crisis; life would crush us if I didn't act. Survival first.

One evening we were fighting again about Peter going out with Inès on Sundays. He shoved a pillow over my face after I threatened to tell Inès the truth about our relationship. Every time I tried to scream he pressed the pillow harder, whispering, "You bitch! You bitch! You bitch!" I could hear barking; then I felt something soft wriggling against my arm. When Peter lifted the pillow I saw that Paws had jumped up on the bed and was clutching Peter's arm in his mouth. Peter began to cry, petting the big dog in rough strokes. "Thank you, thank you, you're my best friend," he said to Paws as he went out of the room.

He came back with a butcher knife, which he handed to me, then fell to his knees while saying that I should kill him.

"Put it right here," he said, and I held the knife to his Adam's apple. "Do you forgive me? If you can't, maybe you should slit my throat. I deserve it."

I couldn't speak, or I didn't want to. I started to put the knife down.

"Do you forgive me?" he said again, firmly clutching my wrist.

I managed a nod and he released my hand. I rested the knife beside his cigarette pack. I was so relieved to be rid of it. The plant lights seemed so white that they were almost blue. I felt a strange calm that bordered on euphoria. It was a feeling I got a lot after we fought like this.

"Sweetheart," he said, still on his knees. "I used to make you smile. You used to laugh. How can I make you happy again?"

I didn't answer. I stared at my hands, then at my long, tapered fingers that were spread out to expose the webs in between. Peter had once remarked that I had a pianist's hands. I examined my left palm, remembering how Grace had once told me that if the lines formed an "M," it meant the Mother Mary was protecting you. I found the "M," and hoped to God it was true.

When Ricky and Richard moved out that summer, I took it as more proof that people had to be willing to take huge risks and make radical changes. Ricky decided to live with his girlfriend, Gretchen; Peter didn't like her although she seemed more stable than Ricky's previous girlfriend, Audra. One day, Miguel had rushed home to get Peter, saying Audra was fighting with Ricky and she had a pocketknife. I'd gone with them. By the time we got there, Audra was threatening to cut her throat in front of the large crowd that had gathered to watch. Ricky tried to wrench the knife away from her and somehow she slashed his hand. After that, the two made up, as though it took the sight of blood to remind them of how much they actually loved each other.

When Ricky moved out (an end at last to the shame and torment I felt every time I saw him), the attic became as quiet as a crypt. His new girlfriend, Gretchen, was a Cuban Goth chick who wore only black except, Peter said, for funerals, to which she would wear white; she also wore wigs though her hair was perfectly fine, which Peter didn't understand. He sarcastically referred to her as the "wig witch." She had a three-year-old son her parents helped her support (they also paid for her apartment). Early in their relationship, she'd insisted that Ricky spend nights at her place. I sensed that there was some kind of bad blood between Peter and Gretchen, but I wasn't sure how they could have even managed to interact without me knowing about it. As for me, I'd talked to her a couple of times and found that she was as sweet as any of the other attic girls.

Richard had moved into a tent at Bear Mountain State Park, hoping nature would cure his coke addiction. He'd been going downhill for a while—hanging around the house shirtless with a Charles Manson beard, army pants, and a necklace made of eagle talons. He had gotten into Native American spirituality of late, had stopped taking baths and talked about searching for his spirit animal. His final move had been to pitch a tent at a camping ground with loads of canned goods and a pair of binoculars to catch the sight of a red-tailed hawk or double-crested cormorant. I wished him well. Inès occasionally went away on weekends to stay in the tent with him, always looking flushed and happy when she returned. Peter said that no one could make Inès feel joy the way Richard could; he was her drug, just as Ricky was Gretchen's; just as I was his drug and he was mine.

Miguel remained by himself in the attic. Every time I saw him he seemed quieter and paler. He no longer wore his hair long and came downstairs only to eat or to go to his job at Circle Cycle. Whenever I passed him, he would utter a low hi or offer a solemn wave that was almost like a salute. I was grateful to him for that.

25

THE DROPOUT

That August, Peter and I made several trips to Coney Island to eat Nathan's hot dogs, ride the Cyclone (even though for days later he would be confined to bed), and swim in the ocean. Peter said he wanted to see me ride the carousel, but I didn't want to; didn't he realize I was too old for that? As usual, I let him have his way because it was easier than listening to him nag. As the lighted mirrors and pastoral scenes turned under the pavilion, I hid my face in my wet hair, smelling the salt of the Atlantic in its tangled strands. I'd gotten into this habit of draping my long hair over my face like a sheepdog and wearing dark sunglasses even on overcast days.

Every time we went, Peter repeated his stories of a Brooklyn gang he'd run around with when he was fifteen. The initiation was to stand perfectly still while the gang shot at him with homemade guns that never fired straight; it was terrifying to stand with their tiny bullets whizzing all around him. He told me of how they beat him up every day until he'd agreed to join; how they robbed women walking on Mermaid or Neptune Avenues, to get money to ride the attractions at Steeplechase Park.

Once, Peter left the beach to walk to the bathrooms, and as I stood with my feet in the surf, a good-looking Hispanic boy in drenched basketball shorts came over. The ocean seemed too loud at first to talk so all I did was peek at him. As the tide churned, it sucked in the smallest grains of sand by my feet, which were tingling. The clouds were white and flimsy, almost engulfed by the enormity of the blue sky and ocean. From far behind us, we heard the rickety Cyclone climbing, plummeting.

The guy finally spoke. "I wish I hadn't worn these," he said, pointing to his shorts.

I could barely talk around such a cute boy, but I managed. "Why did you?"

He shrugged. "The matrix didn't give me time to find my swimming trunks."

"The matrix?"

"My mother." He had no facial hair but the softest-looking peach fuzz on his upper lip that I imagined would feel good if I kissed him. I felt a bit like a mermaid who had landed on the shore by a human boy's feet. He seemed to squint at me like he saw something that made him curious.

Ahead of us, three children dashed into the ocean, carrying pails of water to fill and bring back to their sandcastles. Seeing kids play often made me sad though I wasn't sure why.

"What's your name? Do you have any brothers or sisters?" I asked, realizing my speech sounded halting, unevenly paced.

"Danny. One brother."

"I'm an only child."

"Oh. You're a princess. Spoiled, spoiled, spoiled." He smiled and shook his head. "I didn't get your name."

"Michelle," I said, instantly comforted by my lie.

"Oh, snap! Look at that jellyfish. That's mad huge."

"Where is that thing's mouth? Does it eat through its body?" I said, unable to think of anything better.

He was looking away. "Is that guy coming over to us your dad?"

I didn't say anything, just stared at the sand. My worst fear was that Peter would yell my real name in front of Danny.

"Your dad looks pissed. Told you you're a princess." Danny smiled as he darted into the ocean.

Peter drove me to the Catholic high school in the neighboring town of West New York every morning, until a winter day came when I simply refused to go there again. I was only a sophomore and fifteen was technically too young to drop out. I sat on my father's staircase dressed in my "Beary Sleepy" nightgown and white cotton ankle socks. My mother had already been bussed to a day program for the mentally ill at Mount Carmel Guild that her psychiatrist had insisted she attend even though she said she was too depressed to leave the house for the music, art, and group therapy classes.

Poppa, dressed in his work clothes, was pacing and yelling at the bottom of the stairs when there was a knock on the door.

"Peter," he said. "Look at her. Look at her sitting on those steps. She has gone crazy, like the mother! She will not move from that step! You take over! I cannot handle this! I am going to die of a heart attack! You convince her to go! You get her off that step, please! I cannot stand the sight of her sitting there as though she owns this place! She does not own a single part of this house!"

"Margaux," Peter said evenly. He was dressed in his leather jacket. "I'm parked by the fire hydrant. You've got to let me know, are you going or not? If you're not going, I'll move the car."

"Of course she is going!" Poppa charged over to the step and grabbed my arm. "Get dressed. Get dressed. I have to leave for work."

"Leave for work, then, because I'm not going. Peter, move the car."

"Are you sure?" said Peter.

"Yes, I'm not moving."

"Okay," Peter said, starting to the door.

"You! You wait!" Poppa yelled, pointing at him. "You tell her to go! You put some sense into her head; she will listen to you!"

"I can't force her to go. Once she has an idea in her head, that's it."

"Whose side are you on?" Poppa said, glaring at Peter. "The side of reason and good sense or do you want this child to destroy her life? Do you want her to become like her mother? What is your motive here? Are you not out for her better interests?"

Peter was silent. Poppa turned back to me. "Listen to me, listen to your father. I will raise your allowance. You will have more money. Just be a good girl and get dressed."

"No, I won't. I won't go back."

"Why? Is it the teachers?"

"No, it's the students. I don't fit in. I don't fit in anywhere I go."

"Ignore what people say about you. Do you think it matters in the end what anyone says? In Puerto Rico, they made fun of me for my hair color. I was an outcast at school and within my own family because I was the only one with red hair. But I always did what I was told. I never created grief for my parents. Everyone goes through the ridicule of others. I have spent my life under the assault of ridicule yet I have always managed to hold my head high. I am known in this town now as the husband of the crazy woman. It never makes me hide myself. I go out more, to show them I am not beaten. Once you begin to cower from the world, it only gets worse. I want you to be educated, have a good future."

"I don't care about the future."

"Why not?"

"Why do you care? You don't love me!"

He seized my arm and shook it. "Who told you that I didn't love you? Who told you that? You are my daughter; I have to love you! You are my blood; I have to look out for your welfare!" He turned once again to Peter. "They reserve a special place in hell for those who refuse to take a stand. You have driven my wife to the hospital and you have taken my daughter to see her many times; for that, I am thankful. You have driven my daughter to school; for that, I am thankful. But in this moment, you have shown your true colors!"

"I don't want to argue, Louie. I want Margaux to be educated just as much as you do. But I've listened to her stories of what she goes through in school. I know how she's suffering."

"Tell me something. Are you an instigator? Did you plan this together?"

"No, I just understand how she feels."

"I am going to make something clear right now. You are either out for her best interests or you are not. It is that simple. Perhaps if she remains stubborn, you will refuse to take her to the Big Mouth arcade. That is one of the places you go, right?"

"That's right."

"I know because I found a token in her pants pocket doing her laundry. I am her servant. She is fifteen and she lives like the Queen of Sheba. I wonder how she will like reform school. When I call the police and they take her to a home for juvenile delinquents—"

I stood up. "Call the police! I'm sure you want everyone to see them dragging me out of the house kicking and screaming! Because I don't care! I don't care how we look! I'm not like you! I couldn't give a shit about these neighbors!"

"You know what, I am going to work. I am done with you! I will leave the money on the kitchen counter and that is it! Stay out of my way from now on! I do not want to hear you at all! You tiptoe down these stairs from now on! If you talk to your mother, you whisper! If you are on the phone, you take it into the other room! I do not want to hear your voice anymore! I do not want to know that you exist! You are erased, as of now! You hear me: you are dead in my eyes!"

True to his word, Poppa wouldn't speak to me or assist in my arrangements to be homeschooled. My mother and Peter did all of that, making the necessary calls and finally getting me diagnosed as a "school phobic," which allowed me to be homeschooled for free by teachers from the high school. I was taught English and geometry by a married couple in their sixties. I found myself so looking forward to Mr. and Mrs. Bernstein's visits that instead of wearing my nightgown as I did the first two times, I started to don my nicer clothes whenever they came over, even applying a fresh coat to my nails. I also wore the gray, black, and red striped dress I'd sworn I'd never wear. Catching a glimpse of myself in that dress with my hair in a ponytail, I realized that I almost looked like a very young teacher myself. I flourished under all my teachers' individual attention, earning nearly straight As, which Mommy tried to point out to Poppa, but he only put up his hand to silence her.

Poppa still did my laundry, and if I left a dish lying on the kitchen table or bedroom floor overnight, the next morning it would be gone. If I left magazines or books on the kitchen table, he wouldn't touch them, but would complain to my mother about it, and she'd relay the message. I started to store miscellaneous things on the living room floor: old textbooks, graded tests, paperback books, spiral notebooks containing stories or short novels, and back issues of *Cosmopolitan*. Also, I began to leave clothes on a chair in the living room. When they ended up in the wash, he would take the opportunity to fold and enclose them within drawers; but, in time, they would end up back on the chair. And he never said a word.

Our only form of communication was through notes. I began a note system when I needed money for sneakers. He wouldn't leave the money, though, and when I asked my mother why, she said it was because I had left him a note with ragged edges, an action he considered disrespectful. So I rewrote the note on a carefully cut rectangle of notebook paper, and the next day, three crisp twenties sat on the kitchen counter. After that, he started to leave me leftovers from dinner in sealed Tupperware. There would be a note on the kitchen table for me in the morning that said, "Eat spaghetti" or "Stuffed peppers: right-hand side, behind milk." Occasionally, he would even leave slices of cantaloupe, avocado, water-melon, or mango on a plate in the refrigerator.

I turned sixteen with my virginity intact. Following my wishes, Peter had made ten perfectly good attempts, but each time I involuntarily tightened my vaginal muscles and his penis hadn't been able to go in. To relax, I took Lorazepam and Klonopin that Peter had gotten from the veterans' hospital, and we played romantic music, lit candles. I tried thinking of a park ranger at Tallman Park I found sexy. The boy I'd talked to by the ocean who'd run away from me was still a sore spot even though it happened months before. Peter later insisted he'd wanted me to get the boy's number; but why, then, did he keep walking toward us? He could have hidden under the boardwalk and waited the whole thing out. Well, it didn't matter now. We would somehow get this goal accomplished and I'd get pregnant. I'd escape Union City forever. I'd be a different person once I was gone. I hadn't even known how to talk to that boy; sometimes in my mind I repeated my stupid remark about the jellyfish's mouth and his parting words that I really was a princess. It was like he was implying there was something wrong with me; that I was fragile, out of touch, a doll without a soul. He was a reminder of why I had to flee. I remembered learning in school that some emancipated slaves in the South couldn't bring themselves to leave their owners. This proved to me that it was hard to leave what you were accustomed to, no matter how bad it was. But we couldn't stay in Union City, my mother and I. Yet even as my mind knew what I had to do, my body wouldn't cooperate.

After yet another failed try, Peter said, "I think we should just forget it. I don't think you can get turned on by me. Look at me."

The wrinkles in his face did seem deeper than a few years ago. In the past, they hadn't affected his good looks, but now deep frown lines had forced his face into a perpetually morose expression and, perhaps because his cheeks were baggier, his once-full lips now seemed as thin as rubber bands and his chin was dwarfed. His whole face finally seemed to be collapsing under the weight of his difficult life. I didn't dare tell him, but he looked older than most men of sixty.

"Peter, you're a very handsome man," I said.

"No, I'm not," he said. "Not anymore."

Around this time, someone called a social worker to investigate our relationship. "I won't go back to jail. I can't go back to jail. I'll kill my-self first," Peter said as we packed our things into large black Glad bags while Paws stood by the door to his room watching us. All our note-books were in one bag; our photo albums and the wooden box contain-ing loose pictures were in another. The clothes I stored in his room were tossed into yet another trash bag, and our novels and the tapes we had made of our novels into still another. Love letters, trinkets, our laminated hair, videotapes, Peter's porn movies, the wooden dollhouse, the gray felt mice, our young girl/older man fiction: anything and ev-erything that could be considered incriminating went into the bags.

"You were in jail, Peter? When?" I couldn't believe it. He was like a matryoshka doll, each secret clasped within the belly of an-other, an endless cornfield maze I'd been running through for seven years now.

"During those two years we were apart. It wasn't my fault." Peter angrily swiped his tears away. "Why can't people just leave us in peace? No one has a right to look at our belongings. They're private."

"Well, won't she need a warrant to search this place?"

"Well, yeah, to forcibly search. But she could ask nicely if she can look through my things."

"And you can say no nicely. That's your right."

"Then I look guilty," Peter said. "And it becomes a bigger case. It might even go to court. The town of Weehawken versus Peter Curran. The good, kind people versus the big, bad wolf. Because that's all I'll be to them. It doesn't matter if we're in love. That won't hold up in a court of law. It isn't admissible as evidence. The how and the why don't ever count."

"Why were you in jail, Peter?"

"Well, I had these two foster kids, Renee and Jenny. It was just for a couple of months. Remember I put Renee on the phone with you? Well, Jenny, the younger sister, walked in on me and saw me naked once. When she was returned to her family, she told them. I happened to have the door unlocked and she just walked right in. It teaches a person to keep their door locked, that's for sure."

"So that was why you never got foster kids again?"

"It wasn't my choice. Even though the charges were dropped, I wasn't allowed any more foster kids."

I couldn't help but remember him saying he wouldn't get more foster kids because it was too sad to see them go.

"Peter, you didn't do anything, then? With Jenny or Renee?"

"No! Margaux, I tell you everything! Why would I keep that one thing secret and tell you everything else! My whole life story; I gave it to you. I let you be my judge, my jury, even my executioner if you'd chosen it."

"What about Karen?" My heart was pounding and I felt like I couldn't breathe whenever I thought about Karen.

"No, Margaux! Come on! I'm not in the mood for this. I was found innocent. I was only in jail for a couple of nights, but during that time I saw this horrible thing happen. Some inmates beat up this guy real bad and he was lying on the floor, bleeding, and then they pissed on him. I got some death threats myself. I think if I were ever sent back, the inmates would rip me apart limb from limb."

That night, thoughts of Karen haunted me. Was she safe? Happy? I could only hope her life was turning out better than mine. If he'd taken me to the basement, why not her? So a couple of days later, I asked him again and he repeated that he'd never touched her. He kept saying he'd had me, his true love, so why would he need anybody else? Still, I couldn't deal with these questions now. I had to mentally prepare for the social worker's scheduled visit to my house. She would come armed with whatever tactics these people used in order to get confessions. Peter said that she would try to paint him as a villain: she would use words like "rape." Once she had the necessary information, she'd convict Peter and he'd probably be beaten to death in jail. Also, thinking about Poppa knowing made my heart race. Everyone would laugh behind Poppa's back that he was stupid for letting me hang around with an older man. I couldn't forget Poppa's words, that a raped woman was better off dead.

————

The social worker was a no-nonsense woman in her sixties. She came to our house at around eleven in the morning on a Thursday. My father was at work and my mother was in the hospital again. This social worker had a yellow legal pad and a newly sharpened pencil. She wore pumps and khaki dress pants, and her navy blouse was long-sleeved. Almost immediately, she began a nonstop stream of questions without answering my question about who had called her. Every time I answered a question, she briskly wrote down my response. She wanted to know if Peter had ever touched me; she asked that question several times in several different ways, and kept saying, "Are you sure?" after I kept saying no.

What exactly was the nature of the relationship? What did we talk about? What did we do each day? She stared into my eyes as she spoke. She started to say things like, "It's up to you to protect other girls," which was such a joke. I *already was* protecting other girls. I gave him what he wanted in fantasy. He didn't have to hurt real little girls. I was a big girl and I could handle it. When Peter was sick, I was his medicine.

"There's something you're not telling me," she said.

Who had betrayed us? A random gossip? Was it Richard? Or Jessenia, bitter because their rent had been raised six months ago? Or Linda, vengeful toward Inès, knowing she would go down with us? Or maybe my mother had called. Maybe during one of her crazy, deluded states she had called someone. Or was it my father? Or someone who had lived in the attic and moved out, but had always suspected something? Peter insisted it must be Ricky's girlfriend, Gretchen. He said she had once made a weird comment to him, but he couldn't remember what it was; he had blocked it out. He said if it was the wig witch, he wished her dead. He then wished he could kill her with his bare hands. But for all I knew, it could have been my own mother.

The more questions I was asked, the more evasions I offered, until the social worker was forced to give up.

She had already been to Peter's house and seen all the pictures of little girls on the walls and all the girl figurines that in his frenzy he'd not thought to remove. He told me what was said, and I kept reconstructing the conversation between him and her in my head:

Why are there no boys on the wall? No pictures of your stepsons or male figurines?

We are estranged. As you can see, I don't have pictures up of my daughters, either. It makes me too sad to look at their pictures and realize what I've lost.

I've talked to them. One of your daughters insinuated that you had sexually molested her. She wasn't very clear, but that was the insinuation.

They were angry about the divorce. That's not my fault.

I would like you to answer the question: Why are there no boys on the wall of your room?

Isn't it my constitutional right to decorate my room any way I want? Does the law acknowledge my individual freedom?

You're not answering the question. In this room you have countless pictures and figurines of little girls. Only little girls, no boys and no adults.

I have a right to decorate in any way I please. I'll answer other questions, but my decorating tastes are my own business. And I don't think it's relevant. Now, if I had a dungeon back here filled with whips and chains and a collection of little girls' panties, that would be another story.

Why do you have a Ouija board?

That's Margaux's.

Why does Margaux keep a personal belonging in your room?

Her father didn't want it in his house. He is very superstitious and has a fear of ghosts.

What does the sign hanging over your door mean: Slave Quarters? What does it refer to?

It's a joke. It refers to me. I'm a retiree but I do a lot around here. It's my second job.

And is your main job entertaining Margaux? What does she offer in return?

Companionship. We enjoy each other's company. We're best friends.

Most sixty-year-old men do not have a sixteen-year-old best friend.

I think you're confusing the unlikely with the criminal.

And I think you are sexually abusing that girl.

Margaux. Call her Margaux. Her name is Margaux.

I think Margaux is one of your victims. You're a smooth operator. You've been doing it for a long time. You've removed questionable items from this room.

According to Peter, the social worker had gotten downright bitchy at the end, knowing she had lost the battle. She asked him if he was at all familiar with the Patty Hearst case; if he had ever heard of the term "Stockholm syndrome." He said no. Then she had said, "Well, I feel sorry for you the day that girl wakes up."

That night, after I got out of the shower, I saw my father standing by the kitchen stove light, smoking a cigarette. He looked at me and then stubbed out the cigarette in his ashtray.

"Come over here," he said in a low voice. "I have to talk to you."

"I'm tired. Tomorrow . . ."

"I have to talk to you!"

"Okay. What is it? Is it about my mother? When is she coming home?"

"Listen to me. You know what this is about. That woman, that social worker, she was hounding me. She was trying to break me down with questions! She wanted to know about the relationship between you and that man. I protected your honor. I said you were innocent. I insisted you were a good girl. Now I want to know the truth. Did that old man ever lay a finger on you? Did that old man touch you?"

"I'm going to bed," I said, turning away, but he came at me quickly and seized my shoulders.

"I protected you!" he screamed. "I preserved your good name! Should I have done it? Are you worth anything? Tell me the truth!"

"Let go of me!"

"That ugly woman said she had talked to the daughter of that man. He raped his own daughter; that was the gist of it! His own daughter!"

"It's not true—"

"What is not true? The thing about his daughter or what was said about you? Because I will tell you something: I do not care what that man did to his daughter, do you hear me? I do not give a shit about his daughter! That is not my business! I do not care if he raped all his daughters, you hear me! I only care about what went on between you and him."

"Let go of me. Let go of my shoulders. You think you can push me around. You think I'm weak like my mother."

"Stop the double-talk!" He started shaking me. "Stop it, do you hear me! You can go to hell and take your bad attitude with you! See where it gets you there. You and that old man: what is the relationship? You and that old, pathetic, weak, wrinkled, toothless old man. Did you allow that man to touch you? You better answer straight because I am willing to stand here all night. You look me in my face, goddamn you! I want the truth! Even if it means you are no longer worthy of my money or the home I provide for you! Believe me, I can cut you out without an ounce of remorse. You can live with the old man then. Become a woman of the streets for all I care and support that sicko. Because if you are not a nice girl, I will forget the day you were born! I will black out your birth date from my calendar!"

"Nothing ever happened. There was never anything," I said, shocked that I felt so much sorrow. I now had to swallow what I'd suspected for years: that he'd never love me again, that what happened in the basement, what he didn't even know about but sensed, had made me dead to him.

"You are a robot! Listen to you! You talk without conviction! Are you trained to say that? Are you a puppet? Do you have blood inside your veins? Or are you stuffed full of lies? Like a little parrot that just repeats what it is told without a single brainwave passing through its head? You had better be more convincing than that! If you are lying it is on your conscience, not mine! You are the one who will suffer for it! It will eat you alive, you hear me! It will tear at your guts!"

"How can I say it? How can I say it and you'll believe me? I'm not guilty! I'm not guilty!" My body grew light. His grip on my shoulders had loosened and I sank to the floor. "I'm innocent! I'm innocent! I'm innocent! I'm innocent!"

He put his arms around me. "Don't cry, baby, don't cry."

"Poppa, I'm innocent, I'm innocent, Poppa. Can't you see? Can't you see?"

"I know it. I know you are. I was testing you. I knew you would tell me the right things. These people, these social workers, they do not work for the good of families; they try to destroy families! They want sensationalism! They are like the paparazzi! That woman was a beast. Ugly thing. That face. That hair. Uglier than ugly, my God. She looked like a toad! With that notebook, writing so fast! That look, always staring. How dare she accuse my daughter of wrong-doing? I should call up her agency and complain about the way she treated me. Like a second-class citizen!"

"She treated me the same way. As though I was a criminal."

He brought me a tissue. "Clean your face. Clean your nose. Look, perhaps now you will finally stop going to that house. Perhaps this is a lesson . . ."

I stood up, infuriated. Poppa had just spent all this time making it clear that there was no possible way for him to accept me for who I was and now he wanted to take from me the only person who could. "No, Poppa, I won't stop. You can't make me. You have no reason to stop me now."

26

THE WOMAN IN THE TREE

That fall, I started listening to bands like Hole and Veruca Salt, donning dark red lipstick like Courtney Love and Louise Post. I also became obsessed with the blond, hot, brooding, and eternally twenty-seven-year-old rock star Kurt Cobain, who had died the April before of a self-inflicted shotgun wound to the head. Peter had once remarked on how young Kurt was when he died, and I said with a smirk that I admired him for making it as far as twenty-seven in this crappy world. His self-esteem might've been even lower than mine—his lyrics were all about feeling worthless and shunned by society. As we drove farther and farther from Peter's house, my Nirvana albums played constantly, though Peter found some of the songs unsettling. During those twenty-five-mile car rides to Palisades Park with Peter and Paws, singing along to my new idols, I felt as high as I once had talking about the Story.

From the man who ran the Overlook Lodge, a refreshment stand that sold grilled hamburgers, overpriced chips, and biscuits for the many dogs that people brought to the park, Peter and I learned a bit of Pali-

sades Park's disturbing history. Suicides were not an uncommon occurrence because of the large cliffs that overlooked the Hudson River.
The most haunting story was of a small, skinny woman who had jumped
off one of the cliffs, expecting an immediate death on impact with the
large rocks that lined the river's hemline. Instead, the woman had gotten caught in the branches of a tree on the way down and had remained
stuck for hours, suffering the pain of broken bones until she finally died.
It was her small frame that had allowed the tree to catch her in the first
place, and her slight weight that had failed to break its branches.

Since it was now fall, we looked for broad-winged hawks as well
as the ospreys with their definitive M-shaped wings. In the summer,
I had picked wild raspberries amid the flickering tiger swallowtail
butterflies; I had carved "Peter and Margaux '95" into one of the
picnic benches with a key. We had found secret streams and collected
rocks for Wicca healing spells.

I liked it here. Here, I felt like I was on a ship drifting farther and
farther from the real world; I had barely any interaction now with
anyone besides Peter and Paws. I'd been doing so well with home-
schooling but, because I was sixteen now, old enough to officially
drop out, the school board had put an end to it. I studied for and
passed my GED that November, but had no idea what to do with the
diploma. I missed my teachers, especially Mr. and Mrs. Bernstein, but
I told myself I didn't care. Like a sailor in the middle of the ocean or
an astronaut treading the moon, I did my best to leave that isle of hor-
rors far in the distance—Poppa's house in Union City, those psychiatric wards, the fights with Peter, those terrible schools. Here at
Palisades Park I could be free of all that. I rarely saw other adolescents,
so I wasn't reminded of the parties, dates, and dances I was missing.

I knew my new obsession with Kurt Cobain made Peter jealous, so it
surprised me when he came out of Barnes & Noble bearing *Hit Parade*,
asking me to read him the Nirvana tribute. One day, he even pinned a
black-and-white poster of a beaming Kurt to his wall.

"Ta-da!" he exclaimed, pulling back his hand from my eyes. "Remember that social worker who said there were no boys on my walls? Well, there he is, sweetheart, all yours!"

Peter may have not noticed it, but that poster, so modern, brought out the antiquated look of everything else in the room. Even though it depicted someone who was technically gone from this world, it always made me feel hopeful because I was being reminded that there *were* guys besides Peter who could accept somebody like me, because they themselves were damaged. As for Peter, he didn't seem to mind its place on his wall. Occasionally, he even stared at it with an unreadable expression, once remarking that it seemed Kurt was like a little boy wowed by circus lights.

Nirvana's and Hole's choleric music drew my own feelings of wrath toward Peter right to the surface; the subtitles I'd been too afraid to read for so long I now heard sung over and over. Consequently, we fought more often and more violently than ever before. Once, in a fight in the car at night that began because he said I didn't want to try intercourse again, I screamed: "You promised, just like I promised you, and I paid up for *your* birthday, right? Even though I was only eight. Guess what that makes you: a *child molester*. Child molester, child molester, child molester!" Peter jammed his fingers in his ears, and when I tried to yank them out he punched me in the face, spattering blood all over the dashboard and my shirt.

Peter pulled into the Pathmark parking lot to get gauze and medical tape. He couldn't go in right away because he was too upset. I pressed several tissues against my face, unable to believe blood was actually on the dashboard. My nose felt like it had been stuffed with Novocain. I stared at my ruined T-shirt. We have to get rid of this shirt before someone sees it, I thought, and then I heard myself voice the concern. He said that before driving me to Poppa's house, he would stop to get one of the shirts I kept in his room as a change of clothes.

Resting his head on the steering wheel, he said, "You make me so crazy. Just don't call me that awful name again, please, I'm begging you, let the past stay past. My daughters can't forgive me, and you have so much hatred in you now. What about all the good times? That's what I told my daughter on the phone. I remember sneaking into the back of the church on her wedding day and leaving before she could see me. I loved you, I really did; I wasn't trying to harm you. Don't forget that."

Despite my pledge to stop bringing up the past, I couldn't. In another shouting match Peter gave me a big black eye, which I hid with repeated applications of makeup. Twice, he had to replace the Granada's windshield because he had punched it. One day I tried to steer the car into a tree. Another time he took a knife and scratched out the face of the big oval photo of me at eight that had hung on his wall all these years. Afterward he regretted it, so he taped the picture, frame and all, under his mattress, along with that memoir he hadn't wanted to get rid of and a framed picture of his daughters.

One December night in Peter's room, I took my basal temperature to make sure I was ovulating, as I'd learned to do from a book about fertility. My body's temperature was raised, indicating that my uterine lining had sufficiently thickened, my estrogen was high—spiked with the lush brandy of luteinizing hormone—and I was ready to conceive. Never mind that all the dreams I remembered now were nightmares: deserted fun houses and serial killers, train tracks and ocean floors. I dreamed now of strange men raping me in parks, homeless women with pairs of dice for eyes, my body covered head to toe in roaches, dried-out gorges, a sun blacked out by shutters. I wrote in my diary of a dream that I had, of tying a noose to one of the basement's wooden beams, scrawling "whore" and "slut" across my breasts in red lipstick, then hanging myself for all to see.

Yet tonight I was ready to be a mother and have somebody love me forever, unconditionally. To start in motion the beautiful plan that would complete Mommy and Aunt Bonnie's dreams, as well as my own. The twin sisters would be reunited; we would all create a loving, harmonious family out there in Ohio. Even Poppa would be happy because he could finally live as he'd always wanted, free of his two burdens. Blood and pain were not going to stand in my way; I was strong. I was a woman. I had just taken two of Peter's Loraze-pams, smoked a joint that he had gotten from Ricky's friend who lived down the street, and drunk a Zima while we watched two hours' worth of Nirvana videos.

Of course, Peter still had his serious doubts. If the plan worked, he would be alone. Alone to rearrange the statues on the stands, which he had started to do compulsively, searching for some kind of perfect order he hadn't found yet. After the social worker's visit he'd re-painted the walls and the color was now the bubble-gum pink of a new tricycle. To discourage the teenagers trespassing at night to drink and smoke cigarettes in the yard, leaving aluminum cans in the ham-mock and cigarette butts wedged in the bark of the ailanthus tree, Peter had started to build a drystone wall. But even when the wall seemed high enough he didn't stop building it. He widened it when he couldn't make it higher, even when Inès remarked that he was risking serious back injury for no good reason. The wall began to take on the look of something ancient. I imagined that if I left with my mother to live with Aunt Bonnie the wall would grow so long it would enclose the entire yard, replacing the rusty chicken-wire fence and draping itself with the grape ivy that Inès complained made the house look haunted.

That night, he put down the bed with the crank and I lay naked as a stone, my pubic hair properly shaved and my hair in two braids tied at their ends with hard balls so I would look girlish. As he ap-proached me, a terrible look of sadness on his face, his freckled body white and old, I felt every joint and nerve tense like a porcupine curl-ing its warm body inward as it pushed every quill out. The Nirvana album *In Utero* played in the background. I looked at my poster of Kurt. He was smiling, clutching the knees of his ripped jeans. Peter allowed only smiling faces in his room.

"Sweetheart, please relax," he said, as he began to insert his penis.

"I'm trying."

"Pretend you're a boy. Pretend you're making love to Kurt or that you are him."

"I can't. I know what's going to happen. I'm trying to be brave. I'm trying so hard."

"I know you are, sweetheart."

"Please, even if it hurts. Rape me, like Kurt says. Just do it to my body and don't think of me at all. Even though it hurts, it'll feel good."

"You sound just like Nina. You sound like you've gone hard. You haven't gone hard, right? You're not just some tough chick."

"It's a little hole. It's my baby-girl hole. It's so little. I'm only eight years old. Daddy, I want you to. You've got a magic wand, Daddy. I want your wand inside me. I want to have your baby." I was exactly twice the age now as when I first started saying those things.

Peter's penis, which had gone limp, began to harden.

"Tell me more. Keep talking."

I closed my eyes so I could not see his long old body, his tired face and ancient skin. "Sweetheart, you've got to relax. Whenever I feel you tense up, I go soft. If this keeps up, we should just give it up for tonight."

"We can't. I only ovulate once a month."

"Let's do something lighthearted tonight. We'll try again tomorrow. Let's have fun. We can play Scrabble or gin rummy. Something relaxing. This is hurting my back."

"No," I said, feeling the need for the circle that had started when I was eight to finally be complete. This time I was so determined that even the rigidity of my own muscles couldn't defy me. I was on top as he'd asked, due to his back. I was dry, but we used Vaseline. During the sex, I tried to pretend he was Kurt but it didn't work, his room was too real to me. I could see the figurines on the stands, the faces in his alabaster angel lamplit, and crickets leaping in his terrarium, food for the anoles. I heard the refrigerator door open outside Peter's room and someone cough, and I felt ashamed. It did hurt. I tried to focus on the warrior nature of facing down my fear, and I was eager now to move toward, not away from, pain's hot, red center. Later would come the noble agony of childbirth and a true woman would emerge from the rubble of a girl. Though I didn't feel aroused I was glad to have his penis inside me because this attempt at creating new life justified my many, many gifts to him over the years. It seemed like I was finally solving the problem of an eight-year-old becoming sexual way before her time by taking charge of what it meant now, and he came inside me, exactly as I'd asked him to do.

Today was December 30 and tomorrow was New Year's Eve, Poppa's favorite holiday, and a Sunday. Let Peter and Inès have their trip; I'd have my own. On a pier somewhere, out of time, my real ship was waiting. It had no sails. Others had boarded it before me. The weather was cold, and there was still white snow on the ground, but a rusty spot on my light cotton panties marked my period's arrival, telling me what I should have guessed, that my body was too corrupted; it couldn't contain new life. I wasn't like Little Mama, that cat from the basement. And that basement was death to life. That dark, dingy, cobwebbed basement had taken all my life from me. That place was where I gave myself up, destroyed my own will for him, and now it was gone. My will was dead, so I might as well be dead.

So I crafted my two-page suicide note, my assiduous print a final show of respect to Poppa. Would I regain my honor now? Poppa was at the bar and my mother was upstairs sleeping in the master bedroom. I had complained to her about the draft coming through the window and insisted that I sleep in her bed in the kitchen extension. I couldn't bear the thought that my death would occur in that master bedroom. I took out Poppa's large bottle of whiskey and all ten of my mother's medication bottles. After I finished taking all of the pills with several shots of whiskey, I went into the bathroom with the whiskey bottle and started swallowing Tylenol, Advil, Robitussin, fever medication, Imodium, Pepto-Bismol, vitamins, codeine, and every other household drug I could find. I left the empty pill bottles scattered on the table and the half-empty whiskey bottle on the bathroom sink. The tap was running and the toothpaste tube was empty because I'd swallowed all of its contents as well.

27

THE CONTRACT

The first thing I saw when I woke up was bright light blazing in rectangular shafts above my head. Then I was vomiting black liquid that looked like melted asphalt.

"Don't panic," a man in green said. "We gave you charcoal to make you throw up. You're a lucky girl. You'll be okay; you'll be just fine. Just keep throwing up, honey. You're doing well."

With a kind of fascination, I realized I wasn't human anymore. I was tubes and wires. I had an IV taped to my hand with thick clear tape. I had no underpants and a catheter had been inserted inside me. My hands were free but my legs were tied with some kind of cord. I wriggled them violently but the cord wouldn't budge.

"Untie me, please, untie me."

The white world blurred toward me. I closed my eyes for a second and the hospital people vanished. "Undo me," I muttered. "Please let me go." It was hard to keep my eyes from shutting. My ankles flapped weakly against their restraints and I had a thought that the doctor wanted to have sex with me: that's why he'd tied me up.

The next time I woke, it was to the sound of voices, Poppa's and Peter's. They were at the foot of my bed. They were talking about me, so I pretended I was still sleeping.

"No damage to her internal organs? Are you sure?" Peter asked.

"No damage. I thank God for that. The doctor told me she must have left everything a mess on purpose, for her mother to find. It was a cry for attention, apparently. She knows her mother wakes up in the middle of the night to go to the bathroom."

"She left a note, you said? Cassie found a suicide note? Did she say why she did it?"

"She overdid it. That is why she lived. Had she taken just a few pills she could have died. But, you see, it was all for attention. It was a show."

"Well, what did the note say? You said you read it on the way to the hospital. Did it mention her mother or you or me or Inès?"

"I gave the note to the doctor. He can give it to whatever psychologist they have on the adolescent ward. It made no sense at all. Kurt Cobain, Ouija boards. She referred to some conversation she had with him on the Ouija board. I did not know she had a Ouija board. That is dangerous to fool with. Why didn't you stop her from playing it?"

"She played it with Inès. I thought it was harmless at the time. Is that all the note mentioned: Kurt Cobain and the Ouija board?"

I thought, Why is he harping on that letter? I'm still alive. That's all that should matter to Peter.

"Kurt Cobain. The love of her life; a heroin addict. It was a sick note. You could tell a sick person wrote it."

"It's unhealthy, that obsession," said Peter, and I couldn't believe he and Poppa were ganging up on me like that. I didn't want to keep thinking about it. Due to whatever drugs I was on, sleep was right within reach.

In the adolescent ward, there was a really cute guy who'd cut out his own tattoos on his arms with a knife. I wore my red lipstick for the group therapy sessions I had with him; my mother had to bring it in with the rest of my clothes. Mommy couldn't cry on all that medication, of course. It was hard to tell what she was thinking, whether she was worried that I'd end up like her or my roommate, Shawna, who wore twin globs of face cream. If a staff worker told her to rub it in she'd snap, "Eat shit and die." Luckily, I wasn't anything like Shawna: I was depressed but my head was still clear.

During my two-week stay at the psych ward I was given the Inquisition about Peter, put through tricky questionnaires and ink blot tests, and made to sign a ridiculous contract promising I wouldn't ever attempt suicide again. The psychiatrist said the questionnaires revealed I had a lot more rage toward my mother than my father, more proof in my mind that they didn't know what they were doing. How could I be mad at poor Mommy? It was Poppa who'd ruined our family. According to the psychiatrist, I had to think the best of Mommy to avoid thinking the worst, and despite my anger at Poppa, deep down inside I still loved him. I'd never in my life heard more nonsense than what these so-called experts were saying about me.

I kept bleeding. I told my new friend Kim it was probably a miscarriage to look cool, even though I was always having these types of prolonged periods. Shawna was gone, shaving her legs in a special tub provided for that purpose under the watch of a female attendant who made sure that you didn't slit your wrists, so Kim and I took it as an opportunity to talk alone in my room. I annoyed Kim by bragging that I didn't care when the counselor Greg pushed me against the washing machine during laundry time and rubbed his hard-on against my crotch.

I told Kim, "If he'd had the balls to rape me, I'd be glad because then I'd get him fired. And on top of that, I'd sue him because he has no right to touch girls, here or anywhere. Especially people here; everyone already has it bad enough. I was molested starting from when I was eight. I've probably been molested longer than anyone in this place." My words, coming out so fast, sounded so arrogant that I wished I could take them back.

Kim's face was without pity and I was grateful; all I wanted was for her to think I was tough enough to endure any test. "Was it your dad?" she asked.

"No, a man from Weehawken. No relation." The bad Peter of course was just a stranger. As long as I didn't mention his name, it didn't seem like I was talking about the man I loved, the man who'd demanded the doctor remove the restraints from my legs and arms.

"Well, freakin' Shawna's own brother felt her up. Weren't you paying attention in group therapy the other day? Her own brother. And what about Tracy?"

I was embarrassed. Even while I was listening to Tracy's horror story about being gang-raped, the thought had crossed my mind, "But at least she wasn't eight." It was somewhat shocking to think my problems weren't the biggest or the worst.

Kim said, "I hate Greg. I hate every goddamn pervert in this world. If I were making the laws, they would all be tortured and then executed with the electric chair hooked up only to their dicks."

"Yeah, definitely," I said, feeling more alone than ever. It occurred to me again that Peter was a child molester and that everybody would hate him here. I loved him still and had protected him from jail. So what did that make me?

28

"THE TIGER'S SPRING"

A few months after my release from the psych ward, I threw out the pills they'd prescribed. Zoloft, at first, had seemed to give me energy, but slowly it had taken away my ability to feel any emotions at all. The worst part was that it made me lose interest in writing my novel. Peter and I had bought a paperback a week, and I usually read to him for four hours a night. That stupid drug had stolen even my ability to enjoy literature.

Peter was now talking about going on medication himself; his psychiatrist at the veterans' hospital said he was now bordering on major depression. He had gotten to the point where he couldn't tolerate any criticism at all, even playful teasing. For instance, if a waitress kidded him about all the sugar he put in coffee he'd get so upset that the next time I'd have to go into the diner to get the coffee for him.

Then, one day, he came over so distressed that he could barely talk. Mommy made him sit down and I rushed for Poppa's ashtray. "Paws, Paws, Paws," was all he could say.

———

Immediately after Paws's death, Peter got a prescription filled and his high dose of Prozac, combined with his increased dependence on the tranquilizer Lorazepam, obliterated what was left of his sex drive; he was also now under assault from the side effects of diarrhea and nausea (during our walks he'd now sometimes have to use the woods as a toilet). Despite this, we still drove about twenty-five miles each day; I was addicted to the routine and so was Peter. The Granada eventually broke down, so I gave Peter permission to use a few hundred from my savings, which I kept stored in his bank account, to buy a used Cadillac Cimarron. A few years before, Peter had convinced me to put my money in his account, saying this way it would gain interest; I'd been too young to open up my own.

That fall, now seventeen, I started the process of applying to Hudson County Community College after Poppa said that I needed to either get a job or go to school. I'd not only seen his point, but I was thrilled by the prospect of starting college; I knew it would be different from high school. Peter was busy lamenting over the loss of his blow jobs and massages, saying he no longer felt like a man. But as far as I was concerned, it was a call for celebration; the bad Peter, the one from the basement, was gone at last.

When I started HCCC, majoring in early childhood education, I'd assumed I was unlikable, but now I was making both casual girl and guy friends. I'd tell guys in the beginning that I wanted to keep it strictly platonic, and for a while they went along with this, taking me out on Sunday or meeting me for coffee before class. If a guy asked me to be his girlfriend, I'd always lie that I couldn't date because I was still recovering from the pain caused by my previous boyfriend. Or maybe it wasn't a total lie. I'd been with Peter all this time, though it was hard to use the word "boyfriend" in regard to him. "A father that had sex with me" was still the more accurate description.

I was too ashamed to confide in anybody about Peter or my past, but others opened up to me. Jennifer snorted coke before classes; Keisha, who'd been hospitalized for depression twice, still believed

Jesus was calling her on the phone; Natalie, like me, had tried to get pregnant as a teenager, only she'd succeeded, and now she worked as an exotic dancer to support her son, all the while finding time to work toward a nursing degree. Katie had had a lot of sex with different middle-aged men and now thought she should get an HIV test at the free clinic in Jersey City, but was too petrified to go. Girls my age talked unabashedly about a potpourri of sexual positions they'd tried, the toys they used to pleasure themselves, what lingerie their boyfriends liked, but nobody mentioned *anything* about a guy having fantasies like Peter's.

On Sundays now, I occasionally took mall or NYC trips with Rocco, who'd emigrated to the United States from Nigeria a year ago, or shopped on Bergenline with Tania, a Puerto Rican girl with blond-streaked hair and a tongue ring. Whenever I hung out with Rocco we took turns deciding what to do, but with Tania, I let her control everything: what movies we saw, what music we listened to, even what food we ordered. She liked this role, and I enjoyed my place as a mirror in which her sexuality and power were reflected back to her. She had a wide feline face with broad, sensual nostrils, large breasts, a shapely neck, thick hair, and a righteous anger at cops, atheists, and conceited guys who had nothing to be conceited about. Mostly, Tania liked to talk about herself, which worked out well, since I preferred the role of listener. I could learn more this way. When I was with her, I wanted her to vent and brood while I remained indistinct and slippery, like a shadow she boxed with alone in her room at night. What was ineffable in me, I saw expressed at last through Tania, so my instinct wasn't to compete with her but to study her, to know her completely. By giving her no cause for envy, I coaxed her to reveal the pearl of her true self to me. This was worth far more than the immediate gain of impressing her; it was serious in a way nothing else ever could be, for often I felt like I had been much depleted these last years, and my personality needed somehow to restore itself. Like an architect, I needed solid blueprints first. The hardworking, gentle pastels of Rocco and the brash primary colors of Tania were two shades of a palette I mixed every night in my dreams.

Yet this bright work of venturing, of learning and trying, wasn't easy; it was like the pain of stretching wasted limbs after a long coma. I just wasn't accustomed to socializing: after a good four hours with Tania or Rocco I felt overwhelmed, sometimes slightly nauseated. I longed for Peter's room, the car, and Paws, whose death plagued me with a recurrent dream: finding him by the train tracks, his gutted belly swarmed with white roaches. During these times, I felt like I would do anything to burrow under the torn blankets of Peter's hospital bed, in the low bluish plant lights, smelling stale smoke and baby oil, retreating like an evening bat to a deserted building, to hang unseen.

When Tania and her boyfriend broke up, she noticed that I hung out with her only on Sundays, a fact that she regarded as strange. She knew I didn't have a boyfriend. I'd told her that I spent the rest of the week reading to my legally blind grandfather. At her insistence, I gave her Peter's phone number, and one Friday night she called on a spur-of-the-moment whim to go clubbing in the city.

After hanging up, I told Peter, "I have to go home now, and get something to wear. I'm so excited. We were talking about the Tunnel or maybe the Bank, this Goth club where you only have to be eighteen to get in."

"You're going where?" Peter groped for his pack of his cigarettes. "You're just leaving, just like that?"

"Yes, it's last-minute. I'll see you tomorrow, though."

"What am I, nothing? Just someone to fill your time and then somebody else calls, you just drop me?" His wrinkled eyes were already filling with tears.

"It's a rare opportunity. To go out and have some fun with people my own age. You want me to be with people my own age, right?"

"I knew this would happen. It was a matter of time. Why would you want to be stuck in here with an old man when you could be out dancing, having a good time?"

"It's just that she'll get mad, I know her; she'll think it's weird if I say no—"

"Go. Go have fun. Go get drunk. Go get high. I'm no good any-more. I wish I could take you out. I wish my back wasn't so bad. If only I were a young man again, then I could make you happy . . . we could go to a disco . . . well, go, just go."

I heard myself say, flatly, "I'd rather stay with you. Really. I just thought she'd be mad, that's all. But I'm sure she'll understand. It's not like we planned it."

Tania didn't understand, though, and that was the end of the friendship.

Sitting by a mossy pond, watching tiny frogs leap, Peter said, "So what did you do yesterday with Rocco?"

I tossed a rock into the green pond, watched it ripple. "We went to Central Park again and got a rowboat. Then we had a shish kebab."

"I took Inès there and we got one once. Imagine me doing that kind of intense physical labor now. So who rowed: you or him?"

"I tried to take an oar, but he wouldn't let me."

He exhaled a huge plume of smoke. I was tired of smelling it on my clothes, my hands. He never took into account that I had a sinus condition, which was worse than ever since he'd punched me in the nose. "So he's got a macho streak, then. He's passive, but they say it's the quiet ones you've got to watch for."

Rocco was the opposite of macho: he wrote children's stories, sewed cloth African dolls, and was too much of a gentleman to do more than occasionally put his arm around my shoulder. Peter was like a hound following the wrong scent. I hadn't told him about my friend George, who was helping me study for basic math tests. My math skills were only at a fourth-grade level when I took the entrance exam for HCCC; it was like everything I used to know had been erased. Somehow we'd gotten into a conversation about sex and he'd told me that he sensed I was a dominant woman posing as a girl-next-door type: my choice of footwear said it all. That and some low note of power he knew to listen for. Peter knew nothing of my knee-high lace-up boots; I'd bought them with Tania. George and I began an e-mail correspondence, unbeknownst to Peter, where we exchanged fantasy scenarios; his e-mail always began with "Dear Mistress Margaux." In person, he continued to tutor me and that was all.

I thought Peter was done, but then he said, "Did he insist on paying again?"

"Yeah."

"You know, if a guy pays, he's going to want something in return."

"We're just friends. I always bring money. He's just too polite to take it."

He looked gloomy.

"What's wrong?" I finally said.

"I don't have any problem with you going out with guys your own age. That's what you're supposed to do. It's just so hard to be on the sidelines. Even if he's just a friend, it's coming. I know it. And it's all right, sweetheart. This is inevitable. I give you my blessing. I'm just, you know, a little jealous. But can you blame me? I was at the veterans' hospital the other day; they want me to prick my finger every day now to test my insulin. I won't do it; I'd rather die. Then I saw this old man in a wheelchair. Who would want to live like that? How can he stand it? I told Inès, and she said people get used to it. I could never get used to something like that." He rested his head on my shoulder and said, "Please, please, think of me sometimes while you're with them. No matter where you are or who you're with, think of me."

"Okay," I said, but I recalled how my loyalty to him had already ruined my friendship with Tania. On the phone with her that night she'd wanted to go clubbing, she'd implied that I was a weirdo, and I never wanted to feel that way again.

That spring, I transferred to a four-year university where learning became my drug along with brief romantic entanglements with painters and musicians from turbulent backgrounds like mine. Like Eve, I was exploring a gated garden, playing and learning, falling in love, one day out of every seven, my spirit still bound to those old marriage vows even as my heart and body defied them. Though he was terribly jealous of my initial suitors, Peter wasn't alarmed until at twenty I met twenty-six-year-old Anthony.

Shortly after we started dating, I told Peter I'd be seeing Anthony every Friday night in addition to the whole weekend. All those years he had tormented me with his Inès outings when I'd been too depressed to be by myself. A Byron line I'd written in my journal after it was read aloud by my professor in class kept coming back to me whenever I thought of Peter's sadness:

Revenge is as the tiger's spring,
Deadly, and quick, and crushing; yet, as real
Torture is theirs, what they inflict they feel.

Every Friday when he drove me back home, he did what he could to delay me from my date with Anthony when all I wanted to do was get inside my parents' house so I could start preparing my hair and makeup. In the parked car, he unfolded his longest letter of the week and slowly read it aloud while he chain-smoked; these pages contained his memories of me at thirteen, at twelve, at eleven, at eight, at seven.

Peter often mentioned suicide in these letters. I wasn't sure if he was doing that in order to try to win back his lost time; all I knew was that I wasn't too worried. He hadn't done it when his second wife divorced him, and I knew firsthand what it took to work up the nerve. Lately, he'd gotten very religious and was always asking if I thought hell was real. With Magic Markers he'd even made a drawing of a crown of thorns dripping with blood, interwoven with pink roses, and the words inscribed underneath: "He gave his blood to redeem our sins." My mother was in a similar God phase so she taped it on the wall by her bed, along with magazine cutouts of animals and babies, pictures of me as a child, and scribbled self-help slogans.

He said all day Saturday he would watch his home movies of me and begged, "Think of me while you're with him, every couple of hours at least, and I'll think of you. Send me telepathic messages." I recalled now that he'd wanted me to do that when I was a little girl, too. Sometimes he'd even whisper in my ear that he'd heard my thoughts. He kept nagging about wanting me to introduce him to Anthony, and when I tried to stall him, he asked if I was ashamed of the way he looked (he didn't own a single piece of clothing that wasn't stained, torn, or paint-stippled, and he'd lost his false teeth so he couldn't wear them anymore for special occasions). I didn't know why he was so desperate for this meeting, but I told myself he was just being fatherly.

"I used to hustle, but you're not bad yourself," Peter said, shaking Anthony's hand after their game of pool. Anthony told me later that my half-uncle was sweet, but "a little out of his tree." I asked what he meant and Anthony said, "Well, at one point he didn't even notice he had two cigarettes going at once."

On Monday, watching golfers whack ball after ball as we ate hamburgers from a small stand, Peter said, "So do you think Anthony suspects?"

"That we're not blood-related?"

"Not just that," Peter said. "I mean, about us."

"What about us?" I said, shredding a napkin. There was nothing even going on between us now.

"Why do you do rip apart napkins? You've done that for the past eight years now," he said, looking to the golfers.

"Of course he doesn't know."

"I think he suspects. I didn't say he *knows*."

"Why are you smiling like that?"

He stiffened. "What? I'm not allowed to smile? It's a beautiful day."

I had accounted for the time I spent with Peter by telling Anthony I babysat for a woman named Gretchen during the week. I took another napkin, started whittling it down.

"I noticed he had a hairbrush and hand lotion in the cup holder of his car; didn't your father keep a comb in his glove compartment? That flashy sports car of his even looked like something Louie would drive."

"My father had a gray Chevy, remember?"

"Yeah, but Louie was about what, forty-five when we met? I mean back when he was Anthony's age . . ."

"I don't think my father ever cared about cars. Anthony can identify an exact make and model in two seconds. He's a car *nut*, especially hot rods. Do you know he started driving when he was only eight years old in an empty field with his dad? He took me to the exact same field and now he's teaching me."

"He also wore a lot of cologne. Not as much as your dad, but . . . oh . . . and his silver chain reminds me of your father's cross."

It was almost like he wanted to be back in time, meeting Poppa again at Benihana. Poppa had washed his hands of me after that. Did he want Anthony gone now, too? Like Tania? The question had begun to haunt me. Why, if he loved me, was he trying to keep me from moving forward? All he did now was obsess about was the past. "Well, they're nothing alike. You saw how quiet Anthony is."

"Maybe he just didn't like me."

"Well, why wouldn't he?"

The smile came back as he stared at his intertwined fingers. "Because I'm his competition, that's why. Even if he doesn't know about us, people sense things."

I started to worry then myself. I had gone to the bathroom while they were playing pool. Had Peter planted a clue? But there was no reason for Peter to do that, nor was there a chance Anthony could guess on his own, considering Peter's appearance. His hair had gone completely white and instead of getting haircuts he'd drawn it into a ponytail, a look that wasn't very flattering, for it further accentuated his deep wrinkles. He'd also decided to grow a mustache, not realizing it looked like a swathe of milk he'd forgotten to wipe off. When Anthony looked at Peter, he saw a sixty-four-year-old man who looked seventy-four. Peter thought he'd won that game of pool, but Anthony confided to me later that he'd thrown it on purpose.

PART THREE

29

RIVALS

That winter, I got my driver's license and my own car, a Toyota, which we started using for our rides just as often as Peter's car. One day, I had to drive Peter to the veterans' hospital when he unexpectedly ran out of Lorazepam. His addiction had gotten so bad he'd begun popping them at the slightest provocation. Shaking and sweating, he'd gripped my hand as we waited three hours in the emergency room for refills.

Driving him home that night, I turned the stereo off so I could better concentrate on the road but was then distracted by a hollow whistling sound like someone blowing air into a plastic cup with a hole cut in the bottom. After closing the windows so no wind slipped in, I realized that the spooky sound was just Peter's emphysema.

One weeknight I was invited to Barnes & Noble by one of my creative writing professors to read my work. Peter decided to ride along with us in Anthony's Firebird, saying that he didn't want to miss my big moment. I didn't really want Peter there, nor did I want to hurt his feelings by asking him to stay home. The reading was uneventful, except for the fact that a guy from my class kept flirting with me. On the ride home, Anthony kept thanking Peter for helping him keep his cool.

The next day, as I was pulling out onto Tonnele Avenue, Peter said with a weird smile, "He was sending me a message."

"What? Who?"

"Your boyfriend. Anthony." He stared out the window. "If it's one thing I've learned, it's you can't predict people you don't know. Be honest. Did you tell him something about me? I don't want him banging on my door one night, scaring Inès—"

"For the millionth time: why would I tell him? So he'll break up with me?"

"You should mention one time while you're with him that I still know kung fu. Once you learn it, you never forget. Doesn't matter how old you are."

"Look, Anthony likes you so much he doesn't want to see you destroy your car. I told him how you've been flooring it lately and he said that's really bad for the transmission."

Peter threw his cigarette out the window; the first time I'd ever seen him litter. "He doesn't know what he's talking about. It clears out the fuel lines."

"Oh, come on, Peter. You don't know cars."

He was quiet for a minute, then said in a low voice, "Just because you're sleeping with this guy means he knows everything, right?"

I wanted to punch him right in his gut, but I was afraid he'd really break my nose this time. For now, I told him, "Look, you don't even know if we are, so why don't you shut up and mind your own god-damn business." Then I said, "He's my *boyfriend*. What do you think?"

His smile cracked, warping his face so he almost didn't look human. "So tell me, can he make you happy? The most impossible thing in the world!"

"Impossible when you're selfish."

"What do you mean?"

"Let's just put it this way, he's never in his life come across any *tap dancers*, not a one, and believe me, he's all the *better* for it."

It took him a moment to realize what I was saying, but when he did, he demanded I pull over and then got out on Kennedy Boulevard with his mouth as tight as a wooden soldier boy's. It would be many long blocks until home for him, and at the rate he was going it would probably take a good four hours. Head down, clutching his spine, he crossed the wide intersection. He was so slow the light changed and a souped-up Honda blasting salsa almost clipped him. I made a U-turn, double-parked, and called out, "Come on, just get back in the car. You can't make this walk."

"No. You go be with him. I've had it with your vindictiveness. All these years: what I've had to put up with, the cruel and callous words, the taunting, the way you've tried to control me, and for what? Fourteen years down the toilet, fourteen years, our love. I thought our bond could never break, but boy, I was wrong."

I drove slowly back to my parents' house, resisting the urge to call him when I got there. Perhaps it was time to end it. He had Inès. It was hard for me to sleep that night. I tossed and turned, thinking, "It feels bad now, but every day, it'll be better. I'll get used to it. He'll get used to it, too." The following day, I came home from class to discover he had brought my mother a white pillowcase containing all the notebooks of letters he'd written to me, some pictures, and some figurines. "I want Margaux to have these," he had said. When I looked inside, I sank to the living room floor, drawing my knees to my chin, barely able to move. "Fourteen years," was all I could think. "Fourteen years." Almost my whole lifetime. My mother didn't know what to do. Petting my face, she said, "You and Peter are always having little arguments. But you always make up again."

I went to Anthony's every night that week, telling him Gretchen had fired me. Anthony couldn't understand why I was so devastated over losing a babysitting job, but I told him it wasn't just that: Gretchen and I had been best friends since we were kids. I didn't return Peter's calls for four or five days, but then I finally called him from a telephone booth at the university. I sat on the floor hunched in the corner of the booth, hugging my legs. For about a minute, there was just breathing on the phone. I felt like I was nine years old again, calling him to talk about the Story. At twenty-one, I felt nine. I felt eight. I felt seven. I felt like a little girl. The next day, he was picking me up again, at the usual time, and we were heading out for our afternoon ride.

30

THE LOAN

For my twenty-second birthday that April we went to the Red Lobster in Wayne. It was karaoke night, and Peter got up and sang "Leroy Brown" as well as any lounge singer could have, inciting loud hoots and cheers from the crowd when it was done. After that, he sang "Nights in White Satin," dedicating it to me. When he came back to our table, he clutched my hand.

"Twenty-two," he whispered, squeezing it. "I'm so far from twenty-two, it's incredible. Can you believe how much time has passed?" He continued, "Our bond has lasted fourteen years. People tried, but they couldn't break it. It was too strong."

He started crying silently and the tears got stuck in the many jigsaw runnels of his face. "You're so beautiful, sweetheart, so beautiful and grown-up. All grown-up."

I bit into a now cold cheddar bay biscuit. Red Lobster's lighting was low and golden and there was nautical art everywhere, which soothed me. I was tipsy on two piña coladas, but not drunk enough to get up and sing karaoke. Peter was brave about things like that, and for the first time in years, I'd felt proud to be seen in public with him.

"I was singing 'Nights in White Satin' and I got to the line about truth," he continued. "Truth and how no one can ever be sure of the truth . . . Well, there's something I've been holding back, and we don't keep any secrets, but I was afraid you'd be angry. The Escort's clutch is going. I'm worried because that Escort is all I have to get me around now. That car's my legs . . ."

"I can't go to my father if that's what you're getting at." He had suggested it before, getting a loan from Poppa. "Why don't you ask Inès?"

"I can't . . . I've borrowed a lot from Inès in the past and haven't been able to pay her back everything yet." I hadn't known anything about him owing Inès money.

He looked away. "You know, it seems I'm so emotional lately, maybe it's my age . . . men get more sentimental as they get older . . . I could barely keep from crying while I was up there singing, because it seems that song is about us, our drives are like a carousel and we go around and around, never getting to the end. Anyway, I've been dishonest with you. I secretly withdrew funds from the account to pay for something I didn't want to tell you about. I was hoping I could sneak back the money over time, but then the clutch started to go and I knew I'd have to tell you . . . I'm a thief, I stole from you . . ."

"How much, Peter?" I crossed my arms. I should've listened to Anthony; I'd mentioned once that I kept money in Peter's account and he'd urged me to get it out, saying that it wasn't that he didn't trust my uncle; it was just better to have my own account. I'd just never gotten around to it. Like a complete idiot, I'd trusted Peter, and now he'd stolen from me.

He began to cry. "Four hundred dollars."

"Are you kidding me?"

"I was hoping I'd never have to tell you about this."

Peter took a biscuit, the last one, and started squeezing it like a stress ball. The karaoke was still going on, which was good, because it was loud enough to drown out our conversation. Still, Peter seemed to be keeping a vigilant watch to make sure that no one overheard. "It's Gretchen, that witch. God I hate her, she's out to destroy everyone. She'll take you down with me; she won't hesitate to ruin your life along with mine. She's evil. They're making these accusations; well, *she's* made an accusation . . . I really think it's all her, not him. Ricky is a good kid. I raised him. I've never done anything to hurt him. He knows that."

"Are they saying you . . . touched him?" I had almost used the word "molested" but caught myself in time.

"Yes, they told Inès that. I spent four hundred dollars on a polygraph test. I showed Inès the results. Now maybe this whole thing will blow over. I can only hope."

"You passed it?"

"I'm innocent. I never did anything with Ricky. I don't like boys, you know that."

"Oh, I thought maybe . . ." I thought back to his story about the man sodomizing him as a boy. He'd always referred to the incident as a rape even though he'd "consented" in order to buy the B.B. gun. He'd seemed so outraged that a grown man could do a thing like that to a little boy. It wasn't that he was homophobic. In Palisades Park, he'd admired the gay men who had the guts to hold hands in public and he'd always said that love between gay men meant no less.

As though he'd read my mind, Peter said, "I told you that when I was ten a man hurt me. I didn't enjoy what he did because I'm not gay. If I was gay, it would have been fine. Besides, what he did to me wasn't loving. He didn't care that he was hurting me. He picked me off the street . . . he was a predator. You and I were in love. Believe me, before you came along, there was no one. I tried to be normal."

"Why would Ricky accuse you, though? Why would he make this up?"

"I don't know. I'm still thinking about that. Maybe he really thinks something happened. For some reason, he wants to believe it's true. Maybe he was secretly jealous of you all these years. Or maybe Gretchen's just got him so wrapped around her little finger that he'll do anything to please her, even destroy our lives."

"But what would Gretchen have against us?"

"It's not personal. She's probably jealous of anybody who might stand in the way of her and Ricky. Remember she cut him?"

"That wasn't Gretchen; that was Audra," I said.

"Well, whatever. They're all nuts, if you ask me. You just take one look at that Gretchen and know instantly that she's not the least bit credible. She's got so many piercings that I'm surprised she doesn't sprout a leak. When she stopped by, she was wearing a lace corset with her cleavage hanging out, with a wig of purple dreadlocks, half-moons painted by her eyes, and black lipstick. Imagine if she walked into a courtroom looking like that . . . they'd laugh her out of there. You know what gets me? Inès still believed her. She asked me to leave without any proof at all. I have nowhere to go! My little room is all I have, that and my car. I got down on my knees and begged her to give me time to prove the accusations false. And even though I passed the lie detector test, I still have a feeling that she wants me gone. Miguel gave me the nastiest look the other day. Just stared and stared until I turned away. Can't blame him. He has to believe his own brother. If Inès throws me out, I don't know what to do. How am I going to afford an apartment on a six-hundred-dollar-a-month income?"

I did wonder: where would he go, old and sick and poor as he was? Then I thought of my money and I was angry again. I didn't want to think about Ricky and the possibility that Peter had done something. What a strange balancing act it was, this trying not to think of one thing, because to allow one thought was to let them all in.

"And, you know something, I've become so dependent on that veterans' hospital that I could never leave this area. I've thought of going to Florida or Vegas, someplace warm. It's gone through my mind that whenever you start working full-time and maybe move in with Anthony, we'll barely see each other. No more afternoon rides. So I thought maybe I should try to start over, but I can't move too far away from that damn veterans' hospital. I'm too old to be moving anyway. You get to be a certain age and you find you don't want change. It's too scary."

I was scared, too. Every once in a while, I'd found myself fantasizing that he'd die of a heart attack. I couldn't imagine starting a new life with him always in the background, getting older, even more dependent and desperate. If I ever had kids, I couldn't even bring them anywhere near him. Just like Gretchen couldn't bring her child around him even though he'd passed the lie detector test.

A few days after our dinner, the clutch finally died on the Escort. Peter begged me to ask Poppa to lend him five hundred dollars since he was too nervous to ask him directly. I said he'd better pay us both back and he promised he would, even if it meant quitting smoking in order to save money. At least he was saving me a few hundred a year by insuring my car; because of his advanced age and clean driving record he paid only six hundred a year, low for New Jersey. I decided to ask on a day when Poppa was in great spirits because he'd just gotten a hefty tax return. He was in the kitchen stirring rice, humming the Beatles' "Across the Universe."

I was surprised when Poppa agreed to the loan, saying, "Tell you what, I am in a good mood. I will lend him the money to get a decent car, he can sell that lemon he has now and pay me back in increments. But the deal is I will pick out the car. And it will definitely not be a Ford!"

Poppa took us to used-car lots, where he would talk to the salesmen in Spanish; he insisted that there was no way a person could possibly get a good car around here without speaking Spanish. But we got nowhere with Poppa and so Peter finally told me to ask my boyfriend, the car expert. Anthony had a friend who was selling a black Mazda for fourteen hundred dollars, but he ended up letting Peter have it for a thousand. Peter agreed to pay Poppa a hundred dollars a month. But for some reason, he could never get an entire hundred together by the end of the month.

So, as expected, Poppa finally blew up one Sunday morning, after a few months of saying nothing. "That man swindled me! He took advantage of my good nature! He has deceived me! And you were his coconspirator! The two of you deceived me! I should have known better! You people live in your own world, driving around aimlessly for what purpose I can never fathom. I saw the mileage on that Escort; it was off the charts! Anyone would assume you people had driven to the ends of the earth and back again! He has no sense of responsibility and neither do you. You two live in a fantasy! And, let me tell you something, for your own sake, listen up! That man does not look good! Every time I see him he looks worse! He can barely walk! You hear me? You get my drift? You had better open your eyes!"

Every Thursday, we drove fifty miles up to Bear Mountain to sit on the large rocks, staring down at what Peter termed "the eternity fields." Hair grass, pitch pine, cow wheat. Black cherry and witch hazel. Oaks and tulip trees. Occasionally, white-tailed deer appeared, standing as erect as goose bumps. Another summer had passed, uneasily for Peter, darkened by Gretchen's accusations. Another autumn was upon us.

"Inès confronted me again last night," Peter said, as we sat on a white rock with the earth spread out full below and the seven p.m. sky streaked with pink. "She said she finally met with Gretchen at a café and showed her the results of the polygraph test. Gretchen still insisted Ricky had told her he was molested. She said, 'What are you going to believe—some test or your own son?' I told Inès that the only way to get the truth was to ask Ricky."

"Will she?"

"Inès has this irrational fear of confrontations. She'd rather let things go unresolved than deal with anything head-on. I told her she'd have to just ask him face-to-face. It's Gretchen, not Ricky. I'm convinced of that."

"What if it is him, though? Why would he say that?"

"I've thought about it. I've racked my brain and I think I've come up with a theory. For years, everyone has known about you and me, at the very least on a subconscious level. They've seen us alone in the room together; they've overheard our fights. They know, of course they know."

I felt a burst of shame so strong it was like sickness. I was aware that they knew but I couldn't stand to think about it.

"They know, and they don't understand because nobody does. Inès might understand a little, because she's in love with a drug addict. For years they've seen you slipping in and out of my room, staying for hours. Then there was that social worker . . ."

"Everybody protected us, though. If they knew, wouldn't they have said something?"

"You know, I was thinking . . . Gretchen brought her little boy here a few times to play in the yard, remember, and Inès used to babysit sometimes. Maybe Ricky, having seen us together all these years, thought that I would do something to Gretchen's kid. But he didn't want to say he'd stood by and watched us for years without saying anything. Gretchen would think he was a coward. She might even wonder if he'd be safe around her kid. But if Ricky made himself look like a victim, it would have the effect of keeping her son away from me without him looking suspicious or guilty. Anyway, I don't think it's him. He wouldn't lie like this."

"But what if he said it? Do you think Inès will really put you out?"

"I don't know."

"I remember you said once she would never make you leave. No matter what the circumstance."

"This is about her son. Miguel, too, could be pushing for me to go, for all we know. One of the things Inès said was 'I trust my son.' You know, in the days when we were fighting a lot, I used to be so afraid of you. I knew you held the power to destroy me. But you never did, you never would. It's this stranger . . . she doesn't even know any of us . . ." He paused to light a cigarette; it took him three tries to get the lighter to work because his hands were so shaky.

He went on: "Even if Ricky did say those things, it's her who's keeping Inès out of their house. Do you know what she told Inès? She came banging on the door one night, must have been about ten—Inès told me she was there in that black costume of hers with a crazy wig on—and she told Inès, 'As long as you're with him, we want nothing to do with you.' Then she left. Anyway, it will take time, but eventually, Inès will confront Ricky. Inès will hide from things as long as she can but, in this case, they're pushing her into a corner. If Ricky says I did it, I'm out. I know it."

"Ricky—he always made a noise or gesture to say hi, but toward the end, right before he moved out, he looked uncomfortable whenever he saw me. I used to have such a crush on him, and what he probably thought of me . . ." I buried my face in my hands.

31

THE INHERITANCE

Only a few months after the September 11 attacks and the anthrax scare, when I was a semester away from graduating, Peter stuffed a large, thick envelope in my mailbox and left. I was at the college, taking a final exam in British Literature II. With the war driving up gas prices, many people were carpooling. This Wednesday, I was driving home my friend Manuel, a young gay man who wore black nail polish and who, after seeing the second plane hit from his bedroom window, kept having nightmares about being poisoned with anthrax. Anthrax paranoia was so common that some local diners had stopped putting powdered sugar on French toast and Belgian waffles.

Numerous shops on Bergenline were selling "Osama: Wanted Dead or Alive" buttons and T-shirts. Nearly everyone was posting American flags on the fronts of their houses and cars. A devout Muslim woman in my journalism class who had previously worn a hijab had taken to wearing jeans after three men in an SUV had tried to push her car into oncoming traffic at Jersey City's worst intersection. When I told Mommy about this, she scribbled it into her latest Fact

Book, which had about twenty pages devoted to September 11 alone. Poppa was disgusted by the way she insisted the kamikaze pilots were evil, without thinking about the events that led up to it. "They were brainwashed since children," Poppa said. "It is wrong, what they did, but they thought they were being noble." My mother then called hotlines to say that her husband supported the September 11 attacks.

When my mother heard our gate snap, she went to the window and saw Peter walking away briskly with his head down, hands in his pockets. She checked the time, because she knew I'd ask later; the only other time he had come over to the house that early was when he came to drop off all that memorabilia. I felt like my evil wish was at last coming true and wanted more than anything to take it back. For the past few months, Peter had been saying he would be ending his life any day now, so I was constantly on edge, feeling like I needed to watch him. But I'd had to take a final today, and I hadn't fathomed he would really do it. "Why didn't you stop him, Mommy?"

"I didn't have time. He seemed like he was in such a rush."

I looked at the envelope, fat, sealed at the back with hasty Scotch tape since Peter disliked licking envelopes. On the table by the envelope was a brown paper bag of Chinese food my mother had gotten for our lunch; before I went out with Peter for the afternoon ride we often ate together. I opened the bag and smelled wonton soup and lobster fried rice, delaying the inevitable. I cut the envelope open with a pair of scissors as Poppa had taught me to do long ago, viewing the ripping of envelopes as barbaric. I eased out the thick stack of folded loose-leaf pages. The first paper I opened contained a crude drawing of some sort; I realized it was a map of Palisades Park. He'd drawn a car in the middle of an empty parking lot with an arrow above it, circled three times. As soon as I unfolded the other loose-leaf pages a key dropped into my hand. I realized it was an ignition key.

I shook as I read all ten suicide letters. They were difficult to read, the handwriting was worse than usual, and there were very strange misspellings scattered throughout. He spelled "Jesus" *Jesis* and "years" yares; he forgot the "e" on the word "shame." He stated many times:

"For the record, I never did anything to Ricky. But whatever he has to believe is up to him, I guess." Every letter specifically instructed me not to contact the police or Inès.

I dialed Peter's prepaid cell phone; it was the first of a hundred times I would dial it. And I wouldn't stop dialing after the police found him on a foggy Friday, on his back. When Peter jumped from that cliff in Palisades Park, he had his cell phone in his pocket. Oddly enough, I found out later that it never stopped working. When I called that day it probably rang and rang 250 feet down at the bottom of the cliff.

"You have the title now," he wrote. "Go get the car before it's towed. I don't want you to have to pay towing and storage; it will cost over a hundred dollars if they impound it."

Later, when I checked the dates of the letters, I found that they were all dated differently, the earliest one almost a year ago. He must have been gradually building up his nerve to go through with it.

He was right; towing and storage charges did amount to a hundred and forty dollars when we went to get the car, my father and I. Poppa drove me to the impound lot, which was a good thirty miles away. It was a miserable rainy day and Poppa, not used to driving anymore, went at least fifteen miles under the speed limit. I stared at the Hudson River half drowned by fog and cried silently as we entered River Road and started to pass familiar sights from my car rides with Peter: the River View Diner, a plaza containing a Barnes & Noble and the Wall music store, where I would occasionally buy CDs, the movie theater we went to. Every red light was occasion for Poppa to tell me to blow my nose. I had his white handkerchief, which wasn't as comforting as tissues, but better than nothing.

Our first stop was the Palisades Parkway police station, located at the end of the scenic road. My father explained that Peter was his wife's half brother, and we got directions to the impound lot.

"You need to sell that car as soon as you get it. You tell me he left you everything he had, right? Everything from his room? Right?" I nodded faintly, knowing he wouldn't stop until I nodded. "Well, get rid of those things. Sell what is valuable, throw out the rest. You hear me?"

"No. He wants me to keep everything. That was his final wish."

Poppa turned up the wipers; the rain had gotten worse. Poppa was the only person I knew who preferred driving in the rain to driving in sunny weather, a fact that always baffled Peter. I looked at Poppa; his face was starting to show his age and, now that I was grown-up, any stranger could see our strong physical resemblance. I also noticed how much thinner he'd gotten over the years; his clothes seemed to hang on him now. It was probably because he did much more drinking than eating. I wondered how much he had drunk that day and how much more he would drink later that night.

"Let me tell you a story, Keesy. It is about me. Lately, I have been talking about moving. I have always disliked Union City and now I have begun to dislike my house as well. But the thought of moving . . . As a young man, I moved many times. In the army, there is no stability at all. I never minded that. Then, after I got out, I went here and there; I lived in Harlem for a while, Queens, I even moved back to Puerto Rico temporarily. When I was younger, I had nothing, so these moves were never a problem. But, as I got older, I started to collect things. I began to store items that were of no immediate use, yet they symbolized something. Exactly what each one means, I cannot always put into words. It is like that Beatles song about places and things. Anyway, when we moved from the apartment building, I tried to get rid of as many things as possible. But some things I found I just could not part with. Since my house contains a shed, I figured I could put all these things I do not want to part with inside it, where they will be no bother. Years go by and I go into the shed to take an inventory of what I have. I see novels I read when I was younger, some in English, some in Spanish, some in French; poetry by the greats that was beautiful at the time but that I will never again read and I know it . . . record albums, but I do not listen to Jefferson Airplane anymore . . . Some of these records are scratched anyway; I have no idea why I bothered keeping them. Old clothes; I even have a uniform from when I was in the army. Letters, so many letters and photos in shoeboxes, pretty girls whose faces I am sure I vowed never to forget but, looking at them now, sifting through these pictures, I have no choice but to laugh under my breath . . . There are several pictures of a young man, he must have been a good friend at the time, we stand arm in arm, but I see him now and my mind draws a blank. I must have been about your age . . . twenty-two . . . twenty-three?"

"Twenty-two," I said.

"This rain is so depressing. Look at how it has tapered off again. I like strong rain that comes with force, torrents that seem to wipe out everything. You know what, I think we are lost. Let me turn around."

We were on a suburban street somewhere; Poppa turned in a driveway to get back to the highway. He checked the paper I held for directions and said, "Oh, that's it, now I see. That cop's handwriting is like a doctor's . . . Anyway, so much junk in that shed, souvenirs from trips I have taken, gifts I did not particularly like from people I couldn't care less about. Even the birdcage that held my old parrot: what was I thinking, keeping that? At the time, about fifteen years ago when we moved, these things must have been important to me. I thought I needed them. But you know what, I moved into my house and put them in storage, and a few months later I had forgotten all about them. Each day, I got up in the morning, ate an avocado or a hard-boiled egg, brushed my teeth, put on my tie, went to work, then I came home, ate, usually some white rice and black beans by myself, brushed my teeth again . . . I never gave that junk a single thought, never!" But I knew this wasn't true. Poppa was obviously thinking of those things now, and he still hadn't thrown them away.

For the first two months after Peter died, my days were marathons of sleep, waking up, eating a little, and trying to sleep again. In the daytime, I slept on my mother's bed in the kitchen extension. Only at night would I go upstairs, forfeiting my mother's bed because she would never have been able to sleep in that big bed upstairs. I didn't mind the master bedroom at night. At night, nothing mattered.

During the day, as I wrote in my latest diary, I wondered if I'd *really* done my best to talk him out of it. I remembered him saying he'd jump off a cliff, and I'd warned him that if he did, he needed to find a spot where there were no trees. And why, despite my depression, had I just gotten my hair highlighted for the first time? I was also planning on getting a tattoo next week; if he'd seen one on me when he was alive he'd have sobbed. Had I been denying myself all these years? How much of what I'd assumed were my own tastes were actually his? Six months ago, I wouldn't have considered coloring my hair, nor would a tattoo have even crossed my mind. I felt scared. Where exactly did he end and I begin? This was the crazy question that caused me to go back and reread his suicide notes and comb through his notebooks of love letters, to remind myself that he was the one whose life had been a tribute to mine. Everything I'd inherited from him was proof that I was the one he'd held most dear. Yet a line from one of his suicide notes troubled me: "Margaux, I leave you my car because Inès can't drive it anyway." So was it a consolation prize? A thousand-dollar car that he'd bought with my and my father's money? I told myself he hadn't been thinking; his mind was all tangled.

One day my mother shut the blinds and then came back over to the bed. She sat down on it. "Margaux, I just hope you'll be okay with taking those exams. I checked the calendar. They're coming up soon, you know. You don't want those incompletes to turn into Fs."

"I know this is a selfish thought," I said. "But I wish he would have waited until after the exams. After I graduated. I don't know. Maybe he had to. Maybe there were reasons why he couldn't wait."

"He was suffering so much at the end. And everything happens for a reason. God works in mysterious ways. Believe me, nobody cared more about your college education than Peter. Peter was always your biggest cheerleader. Whenever your father put you down, he lifted you back up again."

"I just wish he were here now."

Mommy was stroking my hair. "Well, God always takes care of things. He did for me. God put loving people in my path. Like when you were little, I had trouble getting you to eat lunch. We went to Maria's and Maria fed you; she did the airplane for you, remember?"

"Yeah, she had that little boy. He was sweet."

"It was God's will that I lost those house keys. I firmly believe He made me misplace them that day so we could meet up with Peter again. I know you're hurting now, but you had years and years of joy and he took you to so many places and he taught you so many things."

"Where do you think Peter is now?"

"In heaven. Looking down on you, your very own guardian angel. Sometimes, you know, I still think it's possible he could have been the reincarnation of Jesus Christ. He was so wise and so pure of heart. I just wish he had gotten good psychiatric help. Maybe if he had just been on the right drugs, none of this would have happened."

"It would have happened anyway. Believe me."

"Well, you know him better than anyone. You two had a special friendship. It's a shame he was so old and had so many health problems. But it's like I always said, you can marry him in heaven."

"He died like a man," my father said a month later in the kitchen. "At least I can say that for him. It was not a coward's death. He did not go like a sissy. How he found the courage I do not know. You have to be crazy to do such a thing." Then softly, wrapping his lips around his Heineken, "I could not have done it." I was surprised because Poppa had always been so critical of suicide. Then I realized his voice had varied slightly in pitch, meaning that he'd said those words in a rare effort to comfort me, probably not really believing them. Or did he see something honorable in Peter's jump? Poppa cut up a papaya as he spoke; I watched the black seeds spill. I watched my father eat a little of the papaya, smacking his lips. He set it in front of me on a blue plate that was chipped with age and I started eating, if only for the chance to occupy my hands and mouth at the same time.

"That car, are you sure you want that thing?" I watched as he leaned into the kitchen cabinets, smoking energetically. He fanned the smoke away from his clothes, dragged, fanned, dragged again. "You should sell it, get my money back. That car is cursed now. I would not want to drive that car. I would walk ten miles before setting foot in that black car."

I told him I wanted the car. Again, the thought came back about Inès's not driving being the reason she didn't inherit the car. I tried to shut it out.

"You know what I did that night, the night the call came?" He ground the cigarette to ash. "I went to the bar. I drank. All the time I was drinking, I thought to myself: maybe this person has taken some pills, gone into the woods, maybe it is cold there. Or he has jumped from something and has a broken leg and is suffering. No one is there to help him. I wished him dead to God. I prayed: let this man be dead. I do not want to see people suffer. That is not my nature. Anyway, I find out he is dead, I am relieved."

He lit another cigarette. "You know, I always felt that there was something not right about him, something not normal. I couldn't place my finger on it. Anyway, I found him to be a considerate-enough person, helpful. He even lent me money once. You remember, the jewelry business was slow, I was out of work for a few months. He came to pick you up on a Saturday and I asked him to lend me twenty. So humiliating, to ask one who has nothing. Of course, I bought one of his cars, so I helped him ten times more." He paused. "Anyway, he always helped with your mother. But there was something strange about him, something distracted. He did not let go of his tragedy; he did not move on. Anything can happen in life, someone in your family can die, you can lose money, a job, anything can happen: still, you must survive. You cannot kill yourself. That is not the point of life. You must see it through, whatever it is."

"Even if you were old, let's say, and someone would have to change your diapers?"

"Whatever the case may be. Life is too precious. My oldest sister, Esmeralda, changed my father's diapers toward the very end of his life."

"Wasn't that humiliating, though? For both of them?"

"That is her duty! I changed your diapers, no? I can only hope you would care for me as I grow older. That is what life is about. Blood cares for blood. I thought about him, that he had helped me, lent me money even, though he was poor, that he had driven your mother to the hospital many times; I appreciated it, but he was not my blood. And he was not your blood. His death is sad, but everything is sad. We move on." He put his hand on my shoulder. "Listen to me, don't assume our lives mean anything more than the sun when it rises and sets. Don't assume it will do this forever; we can't know. I don't wake up expecting the sun to rise, and when it does, I take it as a gift." I thought of how he used to write poetry when he was my age and then gave it up. How he didn't really live life as though it was a gift; he repeated every day that he was a cursed man. But it was like his remark about Peter's suicide being a brave act; he said it not because he believed it, but because for whatever reason, he wanted me to.

"Despite everything that's happened to me, I keep going. I grieve but not too long. Life is too short to be always grieving. That is why, around here, they have a name for me, my friends call me the party man."

I smiled to myself; my back was turned so he couldn't see me. When I glanced at him, he, too, was smiling. "I am the party man. To Eduardo, Jose, Felix, Ricardo. To friends, bartenders, girls, whenever they see me they wave me over and we have fun. I am a good conversationalist. I know the right jokes. I walk into a place and it becomes alive. I can start a party anytime—in wartime, peacetime, during a recession, a natural disaster, a personal crisis; I may feel sad, but I keep drinking; I watch the horse race with my friends, the baseball game, I have a good time, I keep going. That is why I will never end up like your friend Peter."

Eleven months after Peter's death I took a job as head teacher at a Catholic preschool in Jersey City. Every time I made the commute back to the apartment I now shared with Anthony, I was exhausted.

One day, entering Route 7 from "The Circle," New Jersey's most treacherous intersection, in the pouring rain, I saw a couple of cars stuck in three feet of water; the owners hadn't injured themselves, but it was clear their attempts to drive through the flood had left them stranded. I started to slow down, meaning to park, and then on impulse I jammed the gas pedal to the floor. The Mazda couldn't go far. Surrounded on all sides by deep water, Peter's car lurched once, then shut down completely, water seeping into the cracks in the doors and floor. Firemen came with a boat to rescue me. I climbed in after saving what I could: my CDs and a few books I kept in the car. Everything else, from the upholstery to the engine, was destroyed, a whole grand flushed, Poppa would later yell. But when, with staunch pride, I told him now that I was working I'd reimburse him every cent of his five-hundred-dollar loan, he held up his hand, saying it wasn't up to me to pay someone else's debt.

Ever since Peter's death, it was like I'd been waking from a deep sleep to the sound of a dog or wolf howling in the wild somewhere. Like I was in the aftermath of some dream that was fading by the second. The air in the window was bluish black and the wind blowing the curtains made them look like eyes opening. It was two or three or some other time of nonentity. I could have been a newly hatched turtle plodding toward the sea's edge. I could have been an atom splitting or water changing to vapor. God could have been making my eyelashes out of ashes from a fire. I could have been an embryo growing bigger with eyes now forming in my soft skull. I could have died twenty times before, but that doesn't matter any more.

Coming back from Coney Island, in a sudden rain, Peter parks the Suzuki under a bridge and we French-kiss amid yellow crates, orange traffic cones, garbage flung out of windows. We're daring under the bridge where no one can see. Daring in Peter's room with the door locked. Daring on the deserted beach.

There's the Coney Island sky, pink and red. There we are in the subway going to the city. Look at us, at the top of the Empire State

Building, the wind practically scalping us. We're skating at the rink; it's risky because one fall might paralyze him. We're playing Super Mario Brothers 3; he's asking me to teach him how to make Mario jump. I'm reading him Mary Shelley's *Frankenstein*. There we are in church: he's reciting the Twenty-third Psalm. I am the only girl from my eighth-grade class who's married. There I am on the back of the motorcycle, my hair coming loose from its ponytail. We're lying on a grassy meadow in Bear Mountain, waiting for the stars to turn on their lasers. I am finally climbing that big hill by the entrance to the scenic road, gathering the red raspberries that grow at the top. So brave I stand at the top of the hill, with the raspberries in hand to show him I've conquered it. In the light, in the clear air, I smash the berries on a few sharp rocks and start down empty-handed, licking my hand dry.

Years after Peter's death, I'm sifting through all the pictures he took. Loose pictures, pictures in albums, pictures crammed into the wooden box I made in shop class. Me at seven trying a cartwheel, pink-and-white dress falling over my head, patent leather shoes sticking out like the star points of a jack. My panties, clearly visible, are My Little Pony. Eighth-grade graduation, I sit on a patio chair in the yard with a single red rose Peter had given me. His bangs are neat, and his face handsome. I'm fifteen, bending over the wooden dollhouse, holding a tiny felt mouse in a flannel shirt and suspenders.

Now I'm looking at a picture of my great rival, Jill. Unbeknownst to Peter, I had seen Jill as a grown woman during the summer of his last year; she was probably home from college. I was certain it was her. She had the same beauty mark under her eye that I remembered. Her fair hair was gathered into a low ponytail and she was wearing wedge sandals. She was tall, thin, pink-cheeked. Passing by her that day I was sure she had forgotten all about Peter. If he had given her any joy at all, it was as fleeting as a Mister Softee ice cream; her mother had always been present, and so their time together had been as ordinary as her Capri pants and ankle bracelet. No witching hours, no secret anything.

There I am sucking a grape Blow Pop at twenty, the sun on that secret trail so bright that it makes my face look as if it were under candlelight. There are other pictures: laughing into the sun, dipping my fingers into that hidden pond where I had once set a wood turtle free.

So many pictures of me with the rusted watering can, standing barefoot by the green gate in front of Peter's house, sitting on the motorcycle, my nose deep in a Max Graf rose. On the hammock, my head against his chest; he twirls my hair in one finger, my expression is lazy. In another, my head is against his arm, his face in profile looking at me, my eyes dazed with feeling, his eyes as sharp and clear as daybreak. In one I had never seen before Karen and I are in the bathtub and I'm washing her hair with baby shampoo. Winnie-the-Pooh bath toys are bobbing between us. The cameraman is unseen, of course. He's somewhere beyond our plane of vision, somewhere in the wasted hills, caught in the oval of a hand mirror. He flashes briefly in the mind of a dying grandmother, somewhere in the dark lake, the laughing woods. He makes up words and the music to go with them, he is a jack-of-all-trades, and handsome. He loves us very much.

AFTERWORD

ACKNOWLEDGMENTS

AFTERWORD

Today is October 6, 2010. I'm looking at a completely different set of pictures, which I just picked up from Walgreens. In one of the photos that my husband took of me and my daughter, we're sitting on a stone embankment surrounding a giant blue lake. I've donned square hippie sunglasses with purple psychedelic circles, and my daughter wears a hot-pink Hello Kitty fedora along with several sparkly plastic bangles. As usual, my daughter refuses to smile for the sake of the camera. I take this as a sign of her independence.

Last night, walking by the stairwell, I noticed the electric guitar missing from my seven-inch statuette of Kurt Cobain. Kurt stands on top of the CD rack on the left side of the lucky-8-ball candle I bought years ago in Binghamton. To the right of Kurt is a plastic red-eyed and fanged dark blue monster wearing a white T-shirt that boasts #1 HAIRSTYLIST.

"Did you take Kurt's guitar again?" I ask my daughter. "Yes," she admits. She's a music lover so the tiny instrument figures in many of her games. On the carpeted stairwell rest two taped-together rolls of brown butcher paper—"logs for my movie set," she's explained to me. She often makes her "sets" out of shoeboxes, empty water bottles, and discarded cardboard she finds in the recycling bin. I enjoy using everyday objects to create art with my daughter: green felt can be grass; flat creek stones can come alive with paint and googly eyes. We once made a wintry scene by spreading glue over a drawing on black construction paper and then sprinkling table salt all over it. It's something I got from an old notebook of craft ideas my mother put together when she had a job as a teacher's assistant—before her mental illness made it impossible for her to work.

By setting down my memories in this book, I've worked to break the old, deeply rooted patterns of suffering and abuse that have dogged my family through the generations. One thing I've learned through my writing is that because my grandparents didn't openly deal with the sexual assaults of my mom and aunt as children, the trauma was passed down unchecked. My mother had no idea how to recognize trouble, or to shield me from it. By insisting on silence and forgetting, my grandparents were probably trying to protect their daughters from more harm, but my own story is proof that they were tragically mistaken.

Secrets are what allowed Peter's world to flourish. Silence and denial are exactly the forces that all pedophiles rely on so their true motives can remain hidden. Going back over old papers and thinking carefully about my own experiences have exposed the many ways that Peter manipulated me and my family. As I was finishing this book, I read *Conversations with a Pedophile: In the Interest of Our Children* by Dr. Amy Hammel-Zabin, a prison therapist, and I became convinced of what I'd always suspected: that a sexual predator looks for children from troubled homes like mine but that he can also trick average families into thinking he's ordinary or even an upstanding member of the community. Pedophiles are masters at deception because they also excel at self-deception: they fool themselves into believing what they do isn't harmful.

Stored in my computer are the official 1989 court documents (which I saw last year for the first time) charging Peter with these four crimes against one of his foster children: sexual abuse, criminal sexual conduct, endangerment of the welfare of a child, and child abuse. The court deemed with certainty that Peter was "likely to respond favorably to probation." At that time, Peter and I, having been separated, were communicating by phone; a year later, when I was eleven, he would begin a second sexual initiation with me. Since I feel that the current justice system largely fails at both convicting and rehabilitating sex offenders, it is essential, if change is to take place, to see the problem of pedophilia through the eyes of those who have dedicated their lives to studying it. In *Time*, Dr. Fred Berlin, the founder of the National Institute for the Study, Prevention and Treatment of Sexual Trauma, confronts this issue pragmatically: "People want to see a monster when they say 'pedophile.' But the best public-safety approach on pedophilia is to provide these people with treatment. That will prevent further victimization." Berlin's website is a possible resource for anyone who is struggling with sexual feelings toward children: www.fredberlin.com/treatmentframe.html. Antidepressants were effective for Peter in his later years, and the subject of Hammel-Zabin's book was helped immensely by testosterone-inhibiting drugs. It's true that strict enforcement of current penalties such as prison time for sex offenders is a vital part of the solution. Unfortunately, most pedophiles would be hard-pressed to find treatment options before a conviction has occurred. Often by the time authorities have been brought in, a sexual predator has already abused numerous children and his troubled thought processes have become so ingrained that they're resistant to treatment. Help needs to be readily available to those who are *thinking* about offending; in this way, the problem can be addressed at its roots.

In a bedtime story that I've been telling my daughter recently, a witch halts the Earth's turning. Because time has stopped, there is no more night, just the sun's never-ending brightness. The sun is the only one who's happy about this because he's being stared at all the time; he no longer has to compete with the glory of the moon. Nocturnal animals are confused and can't come out of their burrows. Nobody can sleep until the spell is broken and the witch is locked up in an underground dungeon. "But it's not over," I assure my daughter, who loves the drama of cliffhangers: "The witch has text-messaged her sister to help her escape."

I make up stories for my daughter just as my father had done for me when I was her age. Some family traditions I keep; others must end with me.

ACKNOWLEDGMENTS

I cannot possibly thank everybody to whom I am grateful for showing me friendship, generosity, kindness, or tenderness this past decade. I don't want to chance an oversight in that regard. So I limit myself to those who have had a direct impact on my writing of *Tiger, Tiger*. I want to thank:

John Vernon of Binghamton University and Edvige Giunta at New Jersey City University, my mentors, for teaching me what I needed to know in order to tell my own story. To you I owe my deepest gratitude.

Terra Chalberg, for your immense precision, care, and energy; for your incredible first edits, unflagging confidence, and patient detective work in unearthing the 1989 court records; and most of all, for being a "tiger" of an agent.

Courtney Hodell, for your superb and tireless editorial work, your boundless intuition and deftness, and for digging deep to bring out what was hidden but had to be expressed. You are an editor par excellence.

Tom O'Connor, for editing my drafts over the years, and for giving me the courage to speak to "the unspeakable."

Mark Krotov, Marion Duvert, Sarita Varma, and every other supportive and caring voice at FSG and the Susan Golomb Literary Agency.

My overseas editors, for bringing my story to a global readership; I cannot thank you enough.

The teachers I'd worked closely with on this book at Binghamton University and at New Jersey City University and who offered outstanding critiques: Pamela Gay, Nancy Henry, Leslie Heywood, Maria Gillan, Jaimee Wriston Colbert, Ingeborg Bachman, Joshua Fausty, Emily Bernard, Connie Sica, and Chris Wessman. Thank you to NJCU's fine writing teachers Bob Hamburger, Bruce Chadwick, and Charles Lynch for helping me to develop as a burgeoning writer. Also, I'm greatly indebted to the members of creative writing workshops at both NJCU and Binghamton University who offered their valuable input on individual sections of *Tiger, Tiger*.

Louise DeSalvo, for her great advice and excellent write-a-life blog.

Steven McGowan, Kathi Difulvio, Aaryn Nardone, Quana Brock, and Sarah Jeffries, for reading the early full-length draft and offering important editorial contributions and/or wise insights.

Finally, I want to thank my daughter for continuing to teach me every day what really matters in life.